D1319753

That's Not Funny

That's Not Funny

HOW THE RIGHT MAKES COMEDY WORK FOR THEM

Matt Sienkiewicz and Nick Marx

UNIVERSITY OF CALIFORNIA PRESS

University of California Press
Oakland, California

© 2022 by Matt Sienkiewicz and Nick Marx

Library of Congress Cataloging-in-Publication Data

Names: Sienkiewicz, Matt, author. | Marx, Nick, author.
Title: That's not funny : how the right makes comedy work for them /
    Matt Sienkiewicz and Nick Marx.
Description: Oakland : University of California Press, 2022. | Includes
    bibliographical references and index.
Identifiers: LCCN 2021047030 (print) | LCCN 2021047031 (ebook) |
    ISBN 9780520382138 (cloth) | ISBN 9780520382145 (epub)
Subjects: LCSH: Comedy—Political aspects—United States. | Right-wing
    extremists—United States. | Political satire, American—United States. |
    Political culture—United States.
Classification: LCC PN1929.P65 S54 2022 (print) | LCC PN1929.P65
    (ebook) | DDC 817/.609—dc23/eng/20211206
LC record available at https://lccn.loc.gov/2021047030
LC ebook record available at https://lccn.loc.gov/2021047031

Manufactured in the United States of America

30 29 28 27 26 25 24 23 22
10 9 8 7 6 5 4 3 2 1

Contents

Acknowledgments

We wish to express sincere gratitude to our families, colleagues, and to everyone who supported this book: Raina Polivka and Madison Wetzell at University of California Press; developmental editor Christopher Lura; indexer Cynthia Savage; research assistants Josh Moss, Maya Rao, Kiah Bennett, Jaren Zinn, and Kelly Chapple; and peer reviewers Viveca Greene and Amber Day.

Introduction

"That's not funny" is a powerful, complicated thing to say. It can be an opinion stated as a fact. It can be a motion to dismiss. It can be, and often is, a moral judgment aimed at others or even at one's self: a tsk tsk for laughing when you shouldn't. When liberals discuss right-wing comedy, "that's not funny" is always lurking around the corner, ready to deploy one or all of its potential meanings in conversational combat.

Often, liberals use "that's not funny" to express a bored disinterest in conservative attempts at humor. This book will introduce a number of new, odd, and sometimes terrifying right-wing comedians doing reactionary jokes. Nonetheless, a lot of mainstream, high-profile right-wing humor is simply stuff from the past dragged into the present, a beat-up old Cadillac trying to turn heads with a new coat of paint. Think of Tim Allen, star of the 1990s sitcom *Home Improvement*, resurrecting his macho dad schtick with the MAGA-fied, Trump-friendly sitcom *Last Man Standing*. Politics aside, the retread nature of much right-wing comedy just isn't funny to people with less paleolithic tastes in humor.

There is also, however, a blithe, dismissive way in which "that's not funny" frames right-wing comedy. If something does not or, even better, cannot exist, then surely no one needs to worry about it being funny. The

1

prevalence of this approach to right-wing comedy became apparent as soon as we dared admit to our fellow liberals that we were working on this book. The mere mention of right-wing comedy provoked raised eyebrows and dropped jaws during our countless Zoom calls throughout the pandemic. We were, it seemed to many, playing with an obvious oxymoron, a phantasm. Instead of wasting our time with an impossible combination of humor and politics, perhaps we should instead take a close look at unicorn mating rituals or investigate the finer points of plumbing infrastructure in the underwater city of Atlantis. Such topics, we were told, are no less absurd than right-wing comedy. Better yet, they can be studied without suffering through a single Ben Shapiro video, let alone the hundreds we had to endure. In other words, for some, there is simply a definitional contradiction between conservatism and comedy.

And then there is, of course, the moral approach to "that's not funny"-ing away right-wing comedy. This book delves into the depths of right-wing humor, taking readers into comedy crevices that make traditional dirty jokes look like kindergarten curriculum. And it's not much better at the surface-level of the right-wing comedy world. Even Tim Allen's banal brand of broadcast television humor trades in jokes based in racial stereotypes, smug sexism, and barely disguised homophobia. If something is morally abhorrent, why should liberals allow the possibility that it is also, for conservatives, funny?

But closing our eyes doesn't make the monster go away. Dismissing right-wing comedy with any species of "that's not funny" means overlooking the growing influence of conservative comedians, and it encourages a fundamental misunderstanding about the nature of contemporary politics and entertainment. Take Fox News's Greg Gutfeld, for example. For years, he hosted *The Greg Gutfeld Show*, a weekly conservative *Daily Show* knock-off featuring cheaply produced satirical sketches, strained right-wing monologues, and celebrity guests unknown to most readers of this, or really any, book. It sounds, we admit, dismissible. The show's ratings, however, tell a different story. By the time he transitioned to the nightly *Gutfeld!* in 2021, he was consistently outperforming liberal late-night luminaries like Trevor Noah and Stephen Colbert. Clearly, Gutfeld's comedy appeals to a considerable audience, expanding Fox News's content and offering new ways for people to understand their identity as a conservative in America. Furthermore, as we show throughout this book, Gutfeld is ensconced in a constellation of right-wing comedy that goes well beyond the confines of Fox News and wields considerable cultural and economic power. For people who disagree with Gutfeld politically, his jokes are not funny at all. In fact, they should be taken quite seriously.

Outside of this book, serious analyses of Allen and Gutfeld are extremely rare. Even humor scholars fall into this blind spot. Academics tend to write about the many successful comedians who fit their liberal sensibilities: Jon Stewart, Trevor Noah, Stephen Colbert, and Samantha Bee, for example. When scholars do cite right-wing comedy, it is almost always to point out its failures. For example, in 2007 Fox News ran an ill-conceived, poorly rated news satire called *The ½ Hour News Hour* for a few months. For many on the left, this failure is still an exemplar of right-wing comedy, despite its fleeting, forgettable place in TV history.

The comedy institutions we examine in this book are not forgettable footnotes, regardless of their moral or aesthetic failings. They are established, viable elements of the world of contemporary comedy as well as, in some cases at least, innovation hubs for truly pernicious right-wing ideologies. Greg Gutfeld dismisses racism and dabbles in sexism. He celebrates the most egregious actions and uncouth sentiments uttered by the likes of Donald Trump. And Gutfeld is one of the more innocuous ones. It gets worse, so much worse. The ways in which people discover new comedy today—algorithmic suggestions on YouTube, retweets on Twitter, cross-promotion on podcasts—provide a set of pathways that connect more banal right-wing humor to the truly evil stuff, up to and including actual neo-Nazi comedy spaces. In a few clicks, one can move from Gutfeld on Fox News laughing at a story about immigrants, to a libertarian comedy podcaster interviewing a race scientist, to a song parody on YouTube of Oasis's "Wonderwall" featuring the line "Today is gonna be the day / that we're gonna fucking gas the Jews."

To be clear, this book considers a wide range of right-wing comedy, some of which will feature mild, clever, comedic insights. Other elements will be utterly revolting. It is not our goal to convince you that any of it is funny. We do, however, offer a forceful argument that none of it should be ignored. For years, the limited options of the American mediasphere left little room for right-wing comedy to become a significant economic and political force. Mainstream media tended to use comedy either to appease the moderate middle through sitcoms or to court somewhat younger, leftier viewers during late night. Outlets such as HBO and Comedy Central in particular aimed for more urban, educated audiences by offering countercultural fare. There was little room for anything else, instilling a sense that commercial comedy is perpetually and exclusively liberal.

It's not.

This book maps the robust, financially lucrative, and politically impactful world of right-wing comedy in the United States. Certainly, much of this humor fails the tests of comedic quality and moral probity that many (ourselves included!) wish to apply. And, just as certainly, the cultural pervasiveness of right-wing comedy pales in comparison to that of long-standing center-left institutions such as *Saturday Night Live*. In the fractured world of contemporary media and culture, however, right-wing comedy need not dominate or even cross into the mainstream in order to shape American society and politics profoundly. In fact, it may be all the more effective because it goes nearly unnoticed by the liberal world. Right-wing comedy has reached a point of economic sustainability and significant influence. The future of liberal politics, we argue, depends in part on facing right-wing comedy, recognizing its economic success, and acknowledging its aesthetic appeal for conservative viewers. "That's not funny" is a perfectly fine way to express one's tastes and moral principles. It's just not a very good political strategy.

This book warns readers not to bury their heads in the sand. We confront right-wing comedy with two specific goals in mind. The first goal is to avoid taking for granted the left's significant recent advantage in the comedy arms race. For years, left-leaning comedians have had serious impacts by pushing boundaries and attacking norms, shaping conversations around racial justice, LGBTQ rights, and other liberal political objectives. Such comedic efforts also inevitably, occasionally, invite criticism for being too incendiary or edgy. If liberals believe that only they possess the power of comedy, it is tempting to over-police humorists in order to reduce the risk of insensitivity. Our second goal, then, is to urge liberals to foster the freest possible space for the best comedic talents to work in. Understanding the potential appeal of conservative comedy should motivate the liberal world to be excited for, and forgiving of, good faith comedic experimentation, even if it pushes against the mores of the moment. The left must overcome the impulse to respond to conservative comedy by saying, "That's not funny." Instead liberals must understand how right-wing comedy has expanded its reach and embrace the need to combat it with new, progressive comedic weaponry.

A TALE OF TWO COMPLEXES

Right-wing comedy is a complex: a networked structure of conservative, comedic TV shows, podcasts, streaming media, and websites that work together, directing viewers to each other and circulating them throughout intertwined ideological spaces. It is robust, growing, and profitable. Acknowledging this fact reveals a different kind of complex—one of the psychological variety—that leaves the collective liberal world defensive and eager to repress the increasing influence of right-wing comedy today. The growth of this type of complex among liberals is also robust—and profitable, but more for our therapists—as liberals move further into a defensive state of denial about the growing popularity of right-wing comedy. Many of today's young liberals, whose comedic tastes matured in a post-9/11 era when celebrated satirists such as Jon Stewart defined so much of left-wing identity, understand comedy to be central to their own political and ethical selves. Consequently, within liberal discourse there is an instinct to deny, obscure, or ignore any political comedy coming from right-wing people and media institutions.

These two types of "complexes"—one of which is a metaphor for the contemporary media industry, the other for a liberal psychology—have jointly allowed for right-wing comedy to emerge in recent years, engage large portions of the American public, and go mostly unnoticed by the left. This denial of right-wing comedy among liberals, we argue, is not only comforting, but also a mark of good taste, allowing everyone from pundits to professors to gain cultural capital by assuring fellow liberals that they are the only ones who know their way around a joke. But ignoring the prevalence of right-wing comedy means more than just missing the conservative joke. It also means overlooking the tools that conservatives use to reshape the cultural and political landscape in America.

*There Goes the Neighborhood: Building the Right-Wing
Comedy Complex*

Imagine entering a representation of the contemporary mediascape of the
United States. Envision it not like the boxy virtual reality of a 1990s erotic
thriller, but as a city or community like the one in which you live. Hundreds of buildings dot the landscape, representing all of your favorite content on a given night. As evening approaches, you walk by an office park
of familiar sitcoms, and Dunder Mifflin's Jim Halpert gives you a knowing
look out the window. You navigate toward several towering skyscrapers,
each marked with the iconic logos for Marvel movies, *Sunday Night Football*, or Netflix. As night falls, you retreat toward a cluster of modest bun-
galows, the voice of Rachel Maddow or Anderson Cooper beckoning you
home. Of course, this serene scene also contains hundreds of back-alleys
bustling with social media chatter, variously distracting you from or driving you toward more established neighborhoods.

For much of the twentieth century, the mediascape was less densely
developed and chaotic than it is today. There weren't as many destinations
then, and they were all on the same few major thoroughfares. The map
was not yet organized around specific demographics, identity groups, or
political affiliations. Studios, networks, and advertisers—the construction
outfits that produce and sell media—provided broadly appealing attrac-
tions that were only marginally different from those of their competitors.
For instance, the Hollywood system of the 1920s–50s played it safe, with
powerful studios producing formulaic films that, given meager competition, beckoned large, undifferentiated audiences. The classic network
era of American television from the 1950s to the '80s took a similar tack.
During this stretch, the three broadcast networks of NBC, ABC, and CBS
controlled what viewers watched and when. Sure, they competed with one
another, but they did so by producing similar programs aimed at similarly
widespread audiences. Even a famously contentious sitcom like *All in
the Family* (1971–79) enticed people from across the political spectrum,
resolving disputes between the conservative Archie Bunker and his liberal son-in-law Meathead, through humanizing, non-partisan dialogue.
For the most part, then, twentieth-century audiences wandered the mediascape along well-worn paths, with each storefront taking a "come one,
come all" approach to potential customers.[1]

As the twenty-first century approached, the media map got messy. Two trends, media convergence and audience siloing, motivated a whole new approach to developing media real estate. With convergence, both creators and consumers stopped emphasizing traditional media content categories. Once-distinct media forms such as film, TV, and radio began to blur as the internet brought all sorts of digital content onto single devices. In the past, *The Daily Show*'s Trevor Noah would have been just a TV star. Today he is a multimedia presence, moving viewers from place to place, bringing them from his cable program to streaming social media clips to podcasts and so on.

Media convergence coincided, perhaps ironically, with increasing divisions—or siloing—among media audiences. The advent of digital media radically reduced the cost of construction for new media spaces. Creators produced new content at an unprecedented rate. For example in 2019, American television produced a record 532 scripted shows, more than double that of just ten years prior, to say nothing of the countless options available on YouTube and beyond.[2] The inevitable consequence of this construction boom is that each unit must be built for a smaller, more tightly defined target audience. Nowhere has this effect been more profound, and perhaps more alarming, than in the realm of news and political media. Since the collapse of network news broadcasts, audiences have increasingly taken up residence in ideologically divided cable news outlets like Fox News and MSNBC. From there, even more interest-specific division awaits on social media, where news from professional journalists struggles to stay afloat in a morass of disinformation and distraction. Podcasts and YouTube channels further slice up audiences into razor thin segments.

Whereas once both Republicans and Democrats got their news from Walter Cronkite, today's consumer can pick a precise point on the political spectrum and find something that seems made just for them. This politically motivated audience siloing is both economically useful and democratically problematic. Smaller audiences, in order to be attractive targets for advertisers, simply must become more ideologically and culturally homogeneous. At the same time, this dynamic contributes to an increasing possibility that your real-life next-door neighbor spends their time in a media zone full of opinions and facts you barely recognize. Audience siloing can also, we argue, create a world in which entire subgenres, such as right-wing comedy, are invisible, or at least ignored, by those who are not targeted by them.

As media both come together and pull apart, the fundamental order of the modern media landscape can be difficult to recognize. The metaphorical "complex" discussed earlier in this introduction provides a start: right-wing comedy is an integrated structure of TV shows, podcasts, streaming media, and websites that work together, developing a shared audience and keeping them contained as a relatively homogenous, easy-to-advertise-to grouping. As a means of comparison, think of the sort of modern mixed-use real estate complex found in many of today's American suburbs. Built just off the highway on an old industrial site or vacant lot, these complexes try to do it all without actually doing very much. Centered around an ample parking structure, you'll find condominium housing, retail shopping, a few entertainment venues, a Chili's, a more expensive place that's basically a Chili's, and so on. The logic of the space is to provide a sense of convenient familiarity and, most importantly, to keep the residents/shoppers on-site. Sure, there's probably a more interesting restaurant to visit somewhere downtown, but who needs the traffic, and what's wrong with Chili's anyway? Today's mediasphere operates in a similar fashion, creating comfortable, interconnected systems of content that allow audiences to flow among related, if disparately owned, programming, while ensuring they remain in the complex as much as possible.

Liberal comedy's version of this media structure has been going strong for decades. Viewers have shuttled between broadcast network fare like *Saturday Night Live* to slightly edgier cable programming such as *The Daily Show*, to blue light HBO specials and back again. For example, you might become a fan of Chris Rock on *SNL*, come to appreciate echoes of his comedy on *The Daily Show*, anticipate his HBO specials, and return to watch him host *SNL*, all the while enjoying similar programming along the way. Like the stores in the mixed-use complex, these shows are not owned by a single entity. Nonetheless, they work together, in this case sharing talent, program formatting, and comedic sensibilities in order to keep their consumers in the complex and foster greater predictability in an unstable media market.

For years, right-wing comedy struggled to put together a coherent, profitable complex. As noted above, the aesthetic subtleties of comedy and entertainment have proved challenging for the right. Perhaps most importantly, there simply was not as much real estate for developing a right-wing comedy complex in the past. The dominant comedy structure was of a more center-left orientation, and the right-wing media world focused on the purer political spaces of news and talk radio. However, over the last several years, the media industry has moved toward providing more options, with each geared to more narrowly defined groups of viewers. When traditional media boundaries were just beginning to fall toward the end of the twentieth century, attracting a wide range of conservative viewers with comedy may have been difficult. Today, however, as media producers have grown adept at targeting very specific audiences, and as production costs have fallen, focusing on a smaller, politically engaged cadre of right-leaning consumers with comedy has proven to be a viable business strategy.

The right-wing comedy complex, perhaps surprisingly, consists of a range of media properties that embrace a number of ideological positions. This reality sits uneasily with liberals' received political wisdom, which, until recently, tended to emphasize conservative Republicans as uniformly ideological, in contrast to the more flexible, coalitional nature of the liberal Democratic Party. The rise of Donald Trump, however, has shown that today's American right can succeed in coalescing despite significant internal disagreement and even utter logical inconsistency. A club inclusive of both strict Christian moralists and a man who brags about infidelitous sexual assault is certainly diverse, if only in the worst possible way. And so, perhaps, are the media we discuss throughout this book. Ranging from cold-hearted libertarianism to red-hot regressive nationalism, the television shows and podcasts we consider are united not by a single set of beliefs, but by a series of connections to a common enemy: liberalism.

In this book, we define "right-wing media" as that which participates in the conservative fusionism most influentially articulated by the political philosopher Frank Meyer. Traditionally, fusionism has meant combining individualistic free-market fiscal policy with traditional, often religious, value systems.[3] Full of tension to begin with, this uneasy conceptual marriage has become all the more complicated since Trump's rise in the Republican Party. The latest evolution of American right-wing politics has added an additional fusionistic element, whereby crass populism somehow coexists with individualistic economics and an ostensible dedication to cultural conservatism. The Trump era has also forced us to consider the growing connection between the mainstream conservative coalition and more intensely reactionary politics steeped in extreme nationalism and overt prejudice against minority groups. Of course, not all forms of conservatism are the same in either political or moral terms, and we are careful to distinguish the different ideologies—mainstream Republicanism, libertarianism, fascist white supremacy—that make up the contemporary American right. However, we contend that comedy serves as a lubricant that helps audiences slide among these disparate aspects of right-wing ideology, with a certain gravity pulling them down into the lower, dirtier depths of the complex.

This book is a tour of the right-wing comedy complex. Like any good trip to a shopping center, it starts with a well-known big box store. In today's right-wing comedy complex, that's Fox News. For years, right-wing media outlets failed to create a mainstream comedy around which other conservatives could gather. The aforementioned ½ *Hour News Hour* failed, as did a half dozen other lesser-known efforts. But, just when no one was looking, Fox News built a quiet hit in Greg Gutfeld's *Gutfeld!*, a late-night political comedy program that, as we discuss in more detail in chapter 1, represents the complex's Walmart or Target. Though old fashioned and offline, Gutfeld nonetheless provides a consistent, legitimizing presence in the complex and lets customers know there is plenty of ideologically similar content to explore elsewhere. In chapter 2, we visit the gathering place for dads who were cool in the '90s—let's call it the complex's cigar shop—where a style we dub "paleocomedy" flourishes. This type of right-wing comedy centers mostly on aging white men like Tim Allen and Dennis Miller who, once upon a time, may have been considered edgy. Today, though, their reactionary jokes are designed to take down woke culture and provide a template for a new generation of old voices such as Bill Burr. In chapter 3, we stop by the right-wing comedy complex's religious bookstore, where Ben Shapiro and Steven Crowder punch up their pseudo-intellectual arguments with jokes that punch down on liberal and particularly minority voices. It is also where *The Babylon Bee* does the apparently impossible, producing a profitable, conservative, religious(!) version of the news satire website *The Onion*. Though not quite reaching the popularity of that liberal satirical publication, some of the *Bee*'s stories receive millions of social media shares and attention from the likes of Elon Musk, stuffing mailboxes with circulars advertising the broader right-wing comedy complex. Then, in chapter 4, we visit libertarian comedy podcasts like *The Joe Rogan Experience*, the complex's extremely popular, dusky bar that, although inclusive of a range of political perspectives, uses comedy to introduce listeners to right-wing personalities ranging from alt-right trolls to elected Republican politicians. We even sneak you into the bar's backroom, where the hedonistic, libertarian *Legion of Skanks* overindulge in racist epithets and retrograde sexism under the guise of comic freedom and free expression. Finally, we give you fair warning before descending to the ugliest of places in chapter 5: the hidden basement of the right-wing comedy complex, where white supremacist figures like Proud Boys founder Gavin McInnes and neo-Nazi programs such as *The Daily Shoah* and *Murdoch Murdoch* beckon consumers not satisfied with the reactionary jokes of Gutfeld or the messy libertarianism of Rogan. Perhaps most importantly, we'll show you how all of these forms of right-wing comedy connect through a complex series of algorithms, recommendations, and appearances by notable right-wing personalities across media platforms.

Nothing to See Here: The Origins of Liberals' Psychological Complex

So, how is it that so many liberals fail to see this large right-wing comedy complex lurking only a few clicks away? Importantly, when we write about liberals, liberal audiences, liberal psychological complexes, and so on, we by no means suggest a uniformity of thought among the millions of Americans—and perhaps billions of people worldwide—who identify with the left side of the political spectrum. We use the term *liberal* in the broad *demographic* sense drawn from the world of contemporary culture industries. We point not to specific liberal people but instead to how entertainment media, journalism, and academic scholarship address liberal audiences and mediate ideas about contemporary comedy. Of course, some liberal readers will already be aware of, and take quite seriously, the popular right-wing comedy players that we discuss throughout this book: Greg Gutfeld, Dennis Miller, Luis Gomez, Jay Oakerson, Dave Smith, Ethan Nicolle, Michael Malice, the creators of *Murdoch Murdoch*, and so on. And, just as certainly, some liberal writers, both scholarly and popular, are familiar with these people and their work. Liberal discourse, however, features these right-wing comedians with a frequency that pales in comparison to their true cultural impact, and it tends to dismiss them when they do make an appearance. You, as a liberal individual, may have a wide-ranging understanding of comedy across the political spectrum, including on the right. We collectively, as liberals, do not.

Of course, everyone knows that some humor is mean and regressive. Bullies get laughs. Jeff Dunham, the massively popular, cartoonishly racist ventriloquist who voices Ahmed the dead terrorist, gets laughs. Even Donald Trump, whose schtick isn't so different from Dunham's, gets laughs. Once, theorists of comedy went as far as to define the entire genre as an exercise in pathetic self-aggrandizement. As far back as 1651, the philosopher Thomas Hobbes explained laughter primarily as a mechanism for asserting one's superiority, describing it (with delightfully old-timey spelling and capitalization) as a "signe of Pusillanimity."[4]

Scholars writing more recently, however, have tended to take a rather different approach to defining comedy, identifying it as a powerful and progressive tool. Today, comedy is understood as having political import and as a serious form of engagement in ethical debates. Some philosophers have taken great pains to assure their literate, largely liberal audiences that *real* humor is, in fact, ideologically monogamous and only has eyes for them.[5] Alenka Zupančič, an influential if rather abstract theorist of humor, describes "subversive" comedies—those that tend to articulate a left-leaning worldview—as "true" ones and "reactionary" comedies—those that tend to articulate a conservative worldview—as "false."[6] Zupančič offers a sophisticated explanation for these terminologies, but ultimately, her true/false binary is a choice steeped in a political project. There are many ways to distinguish the comedy of Jeff Dunham from, say, radical anti-capitalist satirists such as The Yes Men. Zupančič's choice serves not only to distinguish, but also to safely remove Dunham from the picture. It also ends up reinforcing the liberal viewpoint that there is no such thing as "true" right-wing comedy.

Zupančič is not alone in arguing that comedy must be defined in a fashion that excludes access to it for the reactionary. The cultural critic Umberto Eco, for example, argues that true "humor" must expose the oppressive structures of society. Jokes that excuse or reinforce conservative world-views may make people laugh, but they are mere examples of "carnival."[7] His point is likely heartening to liberals but, ultimately, semantic in the same manner as that of Zupančič. Simon Critchley, perhaps the most celebrated contemporary philosopher of comedy, describes conservative, reactionary jokes as the humor of "untruth."[8] They are, he argues, funda-mentally different from progressive jokes, to be studied as a species apart and used only as a lens into what's wrong with those who employ them.

It is through this lens that some important comedy scholars have acknowledged the role of comedy on the right. Historian Kobena Mercer, for example, analyzes the persistence of minstrelsy in comedy, arguing that racist, blackface performers evoke a carnivalesque tone to express "ugly, comically distorted, ludicrous, and bizarre" images of African Americans.[9] Throughout this book, we cite contemporary examples of this phenom-enon. Sociologist Raúl Pérez looks broadly at the intersection of racism and comedy, showing that "racist humor and ridicule has long been used as a mechanism for fostering social cohesion among whites at the expense of nonwhites in the United States."[10] Our project in this book is, in signifi-cant part, to show how these nefarious aspects of right-wing humor have integrated themselves into the comedy industry while still going mostly unnoticed by liberal observers.

A direct contributor to this obfuscation of commercial right-wing com-edy is media commentators and scholars' celebration of liberal political satire throughout the first two decades of the 2000s.[11] During this period Jon Stewart, Stephen Colbert, Samantha Bee, Trevor Noah, John Oliver, and others of their ilk forged a tight cultural bond between political satire and the critique of conservative institutions ranging from the George W. Bush administration to Fox News. Undoubtedly, their brand of political comedy was well suited to the task, using knowing irony and selective anger to poke at the logical inconsistencies that abounded in post-9/11 America. Polls during the period confirmed that, for many young, lib-eral viewers, *The Daily Show* became a major source of both news and comedy. Liberal academic discourse established a binary coupling conser-vatism with Fox News's right-wing outrage and liberalism with *The Daily Show*'s ironic humor.[12] As one study put it in pegging a politics to satire, "The nature of conservatism does not meet the conditions necessary for political satire to flourish. . . . [Conservatism] originates from a place that repudiates humor."[13] This certainly seemed compelling at the time. Television networks were building out new brands, using countercultural edge to court younger, leftier audiences. Liberals were on the attack, with satirists leading the charge. Conservatives, in power and having made a series of obvious post-9/11 blunders, were cranky about being called out on them. And, on top of all of that, the discipline of academic media studies was rapidly expanding during this period, leading to fantastic analyses about how it was all going down. For this shining moment, laughing was, understandably, seen to be in blissful marriage with left-wing oppositionality. As comedy scholar Amber Day notes, however, this fact should not suggest the eternal, exclusive nature of that union.[14]

Recent political communication research has further encouraged liberals' denial of the existence of right-wing comedy by arguing that there are fundamental differences in the ways that liberals and conservatives process humor. This research often generates breathless news headlines such as "Why Aren't Conservatives Funny?"; "Liberals Love to Laugh—Conservatives, Not So Much"; and "Can Conservatives Be Funny?"[15] The left's need for reassurance from cold, hard data has been understandable since the start of the Trump age—after all, how could anyone who shares a worldview with Trump have a good sense of humor? And yet, even the empirical facts generated by laboratory studies require contextualization—especially when they reaffirm an existing worldview.

Social scientists' concern with the media's effects on consumer behavior and voting patterns often precludes a full consideration of the history, economics, and aesthetics of actual television shows, movies, and podcasts. In one study, for instance, researchers sought to construct a politically neutral format for evaluating subjects' responses to political humor by showing them "videos of jokes delivered by a professional male comic in the style of Weekend Update's 'desk jokes' from *Saturday Night Live*."[16] However, television comedy is not the same testable input as a doctor injecting lab rats with antibiotics. In striving for neutrality, the researchers' "desk jokes" reproduce a media text with a clear history and political connotation for many viewers. *Saturday Night Live* was born of a countercultural impulse in 1975 and aimed at a young, liberal audience. Since the start of the Trump presidency, it has avowedly (if mawkishly) taken to task the policies and idiosyncrasies of right-wing political leaders. A parade of *SNL*-inspired voices across American media, ones intentionally targeting young liberal viewers, have emphasized the association of this format with a specific political vantage point. In other words, *Saturday Night Live* and its "desk jokes" are always enmeshed in a broader cultural discourse that very likely predisposes liberals and conservatives in different ways.

In the influential 2020 book, *Irony and Outrage: The Polarized Landscape of Rage, Fear, and Laughter in the United States*, scholar Dannagal Goldthwaite Young argues that liberals naturally prefer to engage politically through ironic humor, and conservatives through outrage, because of key differences in the political psychologies of the two groups. This argument bolsters the liberal psychological complex, using social science methods—quantitative experiments and surveys—to show how audiences react under certain conditions. The book does not, however, consider the reality of the contemporary media industry, overlooking the many examples of right-wing comedy that are actively shaping the cultural conversation in America through humor—albeit a humor that liberals generally don't find funny. As we show in this book, in order to understand right-wing comedy, we must closely consider what the actual, wide range of right-wing comedy looks like, who makes it, and the cultural and economic conditions under which they do so.

In one revealing example of the way social science research can reinforce liberals' belief that comedy only exists for liberal audiences, *Irony and Outrage* looks at two short-lived media experiments from the George W. Bush era: the liberal radio network Air America (2004–10)—whose shows used liberal outrage to reach its audiences—and the Fox News comedy news satire *The ½ Hour News Hour* (2007). *Irony and Outrage* points to the fact that both of these products were short-lived in order to indicate that they were failures. It then goes on to explain those failures by suggesting that although liberals can sometimes do the conservative thing by expressing outrage in their humor, and conservatives can sometimes do the liberal thing by trying to be funny in their outrage, in the end these efforts are doomed to fail. Liberals and conservatives are simply hardwired to understand political humor differently. From this perspective, the shows were unsuccessful because they failed to cater to their intended audiences' inherent psychological proclivities. *The ½ Hour News Hour* failed particularly badly because "Fox viewers are conservative and are thus endowed with all the psychological traits that make people less comfortable with and less appreciative of political satire as a mode of political expression and argumentation."[17]

Although it is impossible to know what led to Air America's and ½ Hour's demise, it is also true that these cases both involve media producers trying something new and offering it to an unprepared audience. They are akin to watching a nineteenth-century mustachioed gentleman struggle with an old-timey bicycle and then drawing conclusions about the present-day Tour de France. It may, in other words, take more than a single attempt for liberal media makers to get outrage right or for conservative audiences to appreciate political satire. Slight technological innovations— say the growth of digital media or the realization that you don't have to make the front wheel of a bike five feet tall—can also radically change what is possible. Indeed, as we discuss throughout this book, right-wing political comedy today has exploded across contemporary media, suggesting that it was not merely the psychological profile of the audience of The ½ Hour News Hour that led to its low ratings or short duration. Similarly, although Air America also did not last, Marc Maron, one of its key voices, has gone on to wild success hosting the podcast WTF with Marc Maron (2009–present). As its title suggests, Maron has stuck with outrage, blending it with a liberal comedic sensibility to great effect. Dozens of other podcasts do the same. In a similar vein, as we discuss in chapter 1, over the last decade Fox News has produced several shows that use ironic modes of address, comedically critiquing powerful political figures, and maybe—just maybe—actually being funny sometimes. Today, both humor and outrage are hallmarks of the right's political and comedic discourse. So, in this book we invite fellow comedy fans, political pundits, and academics to open their minds and explore the right-wing comedy complex with us.

THE STAKES OF SEEING
THE RIGHT-WING COMEDY COMPLEX

Our tour through the right-wing comedy complex will be, at times, disturbing. Many of the figures we discuss in this book create comedy steeped in and celebratory of racism, misogyny, homophobia, anti-Semitism, and other forms of hate. Right-wing comedians normalize these virulent ideologies. What first breaks through as a joke may well show up later as part of a political platform or a rallying cry among violent extremists. No, we do not think that listening to Joe Rogan or chuckling at *The Babylon Bee* is likely to turn a listener into a fascist. We do, however, argue that the centrality of fascist humor to the increasingly influential world of right-wing comedy provides cover and succor to those inclined toward the ugliest of ideologies. You don't necessarily need to recognize this type of humor as funny, just acknowledge and stand guard for its potential to support true evil. Doing so, we believe, is a crucial step in freeing ourselves from comforting, but ultimately incomplete, understandings of what comedy is and how it relates to politics.

The goal of this book is not to convince you that right-wing comedy is funny. And even though early on we warned against ignoring it with the "that's not funny" dismissal, we don't want to deny you that visceral reaction to it, either. Instead, our hope is to contextualize the "that's not funny" reaction in order to understand why it is common among so many likeminded on the left (including ourselves), and to show how it is bound up in bigger cultural and political factors beyond personal taste. Comedy—right or left, edgy or tame, punching up or down—is always contextual, urging viewers to connect what they see on-screen to the historical moments that both produce and situate particular jokes. In the case of right-wing comedy, scholars and critics have failed to fully account for what's out there and why it lands with right-wing audiences. For both intellectual honesty and political strategy, *That's Not Funny: How the Right Makes Comedy Work for Them* takes up this important project.

1 Fox News and Mainstream Right-Wing Comedy

Imagine you've had a long day at work. Your cubicle mate was at it again, audibly chortling to himself about the "libs" as he scrolled his Facebook feed. Your cousin wouldn't stop texting you about new research discovering a link between vaccines and halitosis. All you want is to pour a drink, plop onto the couch, and watch a show that takes aim at the absurdity of the current political climate. For old time's sake, you decide to turn on your television and flip channels, stopping on someone in the general shape of a late-night host—an unthreatening white man with a telegenic, smirking smile—making fun of Trump's speech that day. The burned-out pixels on the lower right corner of your TV make it so you can't actually see the name of the show or network. But you figure this'll do.

In his speech, Trump reminisces about partying with celebrities so past their sell-by dates that you can't help but laugh. The host of the show knows and notes how silly it all is. Trump jeers at Nancy Pelosi, then says a bunch of things no one could possibly believe to be true. The host raises his eyebrows and shakes his head in disbelief. At some point, the faux newsman just starts incredulously repeating Trump's most outlandish non sequiturs, rendering the speech into randomized refrigerator magnet poetry. He giggles, gleefully quoting one bonkers soundbite after another. Trump's speech is now a surrealist audio montage, and the effect is surprisingly amusing. Yes, it's weird. But it's also fun, topical, and gets at exactly what makes the conservative world so infuriating. But oddly, it pulls the punch. You know what the point must be—Trump is an unfit leader—but the host doesn't say it. You start to get suspicious, coming to realize that you can't quite tell if the host is laughing at Trump, with him, or something in between.

The next segment on the show clarifies things in just the way you weren't expecting. It's about the Trump campaign selling "Trump 2020"-branded straws, exactly the kind of inanity you'd expect to be the target of a bit on *The Daily Show* or *Saturday Night Live*. But the host likes the straws. Loves them, in fact. They are, in his telling, the perfect, ironic response to the self-serious, symbolically excessive liberal crusade to ban plastic straws for environmental purposes. This time, the host makes his political perspective fully clear: "The Republican party can harness the power of mockery, long the turf solely owned by the smirking left. Now the libs are the cranky old farts shaking their rakes at those teens on skateboards and the right are laughing their asses off drinking whiskey from plastic straws."[1] The show goes on to a recorded comedy sketch about other potential Trump-branded products aimed at tweaking liberal sensitivities. You don't like it, but now you've got to wonder where your sense of humor ends and your sense of politics begins.

Suddenly, you realize that you've been watching Fox News's late-night comedy/talk show host, Greg Gutfeld. You're not sure if he's funny, but you suspect some people think he is. He's certainly more ideologically complicated than you would expect from Fox News, mixing jokes directed at Trump with ones on behalf of him. Flummoxed, you quickly Google Gutfeld. You are more than a little shocked to discover that his show routinely doubles the audience of cable comedy competitors like *The Daily Show* and *Full Frontal with Samantha Bee*. He has even beaten bigger broadcast shows like *The Tonight Show Starring Jimmy Fallon*, *Jimmy Kimmel Live!*, and *The Late Show with Stephen Colbert*.[2] How does a right-wing comedy show get so popular, going mostly unnoticed amid so much successful liberal political humor?

The answer lies in this book's central metaphor, the complex. For the right, Gutfeld represents the most successful face of a rapidly developing, wide-ranging comedy business structure. At the same time, liberals' psychological complex occludes the right's comedy complex from view. Liberals simply cannot, will not, see it. Even those who would seem most attuned to this emerging threat—practicing political comedians—have developed a remarkable blind spot to the right-wing comedy complex. In a 2017 interview, the cast of *The Daily Show* were asked "Could a conservative equivalent to your show ever work?"[3] The result was confused bemusement, as if they were a group of mathematicians asked to calculate the area of a two-sided triangle. Eventually, one of the show's star correspondents, Hasan Minhaj, adjusted the question for greater liberal comfort: "Why do you think, as liberals, we're just funnier?" The consensus among the group was that right-wing political comedy was inherently oxymoronic, safely precluded by the comedy equivalent of a geometric proof. To be fair, Roy Wood Jr. did acknowledge Greg Gutfeld's strange talent and his potential as a comedian, but referred only to his then defunct Fox News show, *Red Eye*. The cast was unaware that *Gutfeld!* was challenging them (and winning by at least one metric) on a weekly basis.[4]

It has taken some time, but over the last decade or so, the right-wing comedy complex has tried, failed, and finally succeeded in disproving the headline (and its many variations): "Why Does Every Conservative *Daily Show* Fail?"[5] In *Gutfeld!*, the right has a topical news satire that serves as a reliable, genre-defining big box store for a broader structure of ideologically adjacent right-wing comedy products. Like *The Daily Show*, *Gutfeld!* provides an institutional center that combines irony with politics, serving as an entry point for consumers interested in exploring the overlap. Before discussing Gutfeld in detail, however, we must first consider: How did *The Daily Show* come to define both liberal political satire success, and conservative comedy failure?

The answer lies, in part, in the immense, genre-defining influence of *The Daily Show* and its importance for Comedy Central and the television industry. Indeed, for the first two decades of the twenty-first century, *The Daily Show* has been at the heart of the liberal news satire universe. One of Comedy Central's earliest hits (alongside the crude animated sitcom *South Park*), the show thrived with Jon Stewart as host, routinely providing liberals' core comedic critiques of the Bush administration after 9/11. Equal parts news media deconstruction and political satire, *The Daily Show* spawned a brand of liberal humor that lives on today through alumni of the show such as Steve Carell, Olivia Munn, Stephen Colbert, John Oliver, Jessica Williams, Ed Helms, Michelle Wolf, Rob Riggle, Hasan Minhaj, Josh Gad, and Samantha Bee.

One often overlooked aspect of *The Daily Show*'s legacy is its influence on television industry economics. For years, it was at the forefront of Comedy Central's efforts to court a small, dedicated audience, a strategy that would become increasingly important across the cable landscape in the first decade of the twenty-first century. A 2006 *Variety* report notes, for instance, that *The Daily Show* and its lead-out, *The Colbert Report* had become "key to courting 'the irony demo': the coastal, college-educated cadre of young viewers who get much of their political analysis in the form of satire."[6] As we discussed in this book's introduction, the success of *Daily* and *Colbert* in the climate of opposition to the George W. Bush administration inspired dozens of studies examining the link between those shows, voting patterns, and the political attitudes of young people. The studies range in tone from expressing concern about the "increased cynicism" of those in the irony demo to optimism about how liberal satire television mitigates "disaffection" for and inspires excitement in the voting process among young viewers.[7]

These studies about Comedy Central's stable of satirical news shows and their "irony demo," however, are tied to a specific moment in American television history, and we suggest that it is dangerous to apply the perspective of one time and place as a universal, everlasting truth. Indeed, not all Comedy Central programming has courted young, irony-literate viewers in the service of political liberalism, as evidenced by the sexist humor of hits like *The Man Show* and *Tosh.o*. As Raúl Pérez and Viveca Greene argue, for instance, viewers often excused Tosh's ironic rape jokes and thus supported a broader "dominant patriarchal framing" of comedy.[8] In other words, Comedy Central has long sought to pair viewers and shows in profitable, though not necessarily politically liberal, combinations. In the case of its news satire, Comedy Central successfully targeted young, educated viewers by making liberal politics and comedy seem like a natural fit in the 2000s. During this peak of *The Daily Show*'s influence, George W. Bush provided a steady stream of mockable malapropisms, and cable audiences after 9/11 were big enough to make Jon Stewart a household name. If we start the story today, however, the seemingly natural connection between liberals and irony is much more tenuous. Certainly, current *Daily Show* host Trevor Noah aims for a liberal viewership. It just happens to be much smaller than Stewart's. Today, both young viewers and comedy consumers have scattered throughout the mediascape, across ever-multiplying entertainment options.

The Daily Show's sense of humor, then, isn't determined exclusively by its political ideology. It's also shaped by commercial mandates to program for an audience—young adults—attractive to advertisers. The practice of audience siloing discussed in this book's introduction has allowed liberals to nest in their own televisual enclaves while ignoring—or at least discounting—the possibility that comedy might be flourishing financially just down the dial and coming from the conservative viewpoint. Overall, the dual dynamic of television's profit imperative on the one hand and liberal viewer siloing on the other has helped create the (false) impression of a seemingly natural relationship between liberal politics and comedy among liberals. But, as we'll see with the case of Fox News, there is nothing natural about this relationship.

There is, to be fair, another reason for the assumption that only liberals can do political comedy well: a *lot* of right-wing *Daily Show* attempts have been really, sometimes famously, bad. Today, the right-wing comedy complex has its big box store in Gutfeld, who attracts *Tonight Show*-size audiences and refers customers to other nearby conservative comedy storefronts. However, liberal discourse tends to focus on the curious, failed right-wing comedy development project across the way, a ghost town full of clunky, ill-conceived, and ultimately unsuccessful efforts to appropriate *Daily Show*-style comedy toward right-wing ends. Think of it as the abandoned mall next door, the names of the stores faintly visible via the rust marks left by their long-removed signs. Despite their short lives, these failed right-wing *Daily Shows* garner outsized attention from the left, in large part because they reaffirm deeply held assumptions about comedy's liberal politics. When the liberal world thinks about right-wing comedy, it tends to zoom right by the real thing and instead spend time kicking around the tumbleweeds of failure across the way. And who can blame them? What's more fun than watching the other team lose? Join us for a quick tour of all that can, and has, gone wrong, when the right tried to do the *Daily Show* before *Gutfeld!*

THE CONSERVATIVE COMEDY GHOST TOWN

Live from Jacksonville, It's . . . Headlines Tonight

The economy of Jacksonville, Florida, is fairly strong. Unemployment is relatively low, and certain sectors are thriving: retail, insurance, waste management. Jacksonville is not, however, a boom town for either comedy or media production. Yet the most recent failed effort to build a conservative political satire show, *Headlines Tonight with Drew Berquist* (2019), is live, or at least live to tape, from Jacksonville. To spoil this story's ending, no, Berquist will not claim the title of the right-wing Jon Stewart. His budget is too small, his audience is too news focused, and, frankly, the show's circumstances are just too odd.

Also, Berquist is not a comedian. He is a military special operations veteran for whom killing has not been a metaphor for getting laughs. His media company, OpsLens, provides security analysis for other right-wing news outlets and produces talk shows about military affairs from, yes, Jacksonville. The show's production circumstances are far removed from the New York cosmopolitanism of *The Daily Show*. These production limitations have not, however, stopped the *Daily Beast* and *Esquire* from using the presumed failure of the ultra-niche program on the ultra-right-wing One America News Network (OAN) as the latest evidence of the failure of conservative comedy. As *Esquire* puts it, "*'Headlines Tonight with Drew Berquist'* Is What Happens When Conservatives Learn the Word 'Skit.'"[9]

It is easy enough to see where liberal outlets like *Esquire* are coming from. *Headlines Tonight's* opening episode has more than its share of rough, uncomfortable, and crude moments. Staged like *The Daily Show* but burdened by a stationary, single camera, the majority of the show features Berquist looking intensely into the lens, offering sarcastic news commentary, and listening into an earpiece for an artificial laugh track, added later for home viewers in postproduction. The targets are predictable—Democratic congresswomen, Joe Biden, Kamala Harris. Written by Berquist and a tiny production team, the jokes are simple, and often very amateur. They also drift with frequency into the thoughtless and superficial, fraught with derisive stereotypes. A remote call-in to Berquist from "Bernie Sanders" features the latter rambling about "Shapiro's deli," in what is hard to read as anything other than a means of needlessly signposting and making

Daily Show knockoff *Headlines Tonight with Drew Berquist* clumsily lampooned left-wing politicians like Alexandria Ocasio-Cortez and Bernie Sanders. (OAN)

suspicious Sanders's Jewish heritage. A taped person-on-the-street segment features interviews in which mostly Black respondents offer uninformed political opinions. An exercise in cheap mockery, the show's racism becomes apparent as Berquist refers to one of the respondents as "Dreads McGee" due to his hair style. The humor is overwhelmingly forged by the mocking of liberals and racial minorities in cruel ways, a strained attempt to make prejudice funny.

The failure of *Headlines Tonight* comes not only from its lazy racism and wildly uneven joke writing, but also from the demands placed on it by the hyper-partisan One America News Network. As Berquist puts it, the outlet aims to differentiate itself from Fox News by being "more straight news" and "very patriotic, very Pro-America," which, reading between the lines, means more Pro-Trump than even the pro-Trumpiest pundits on Fox News.[10] Unlike *The Daily Show*, which humorously critiques the news for an audience already primed to laugh, Berquist has no such advantage. This tension is most apparent in Berquist's strained attempts to occasionally push the show away from the news. Episode six, for example, features the segment "Morning Thoughts with Drew Berquist," in which the host offers inane observations about politics and everyday minutiae while his beefy, naked physique stands under a running shower for nearly three minutes. Imagine *Saturday Night Live*'s "Deep Thought by Jack Handey" meets a softcore, late-night Cinemax special. Smooth, erotic jazz fills the soundtrack as Berquist muses about Pete Buttigieg's sexuality and the difference between a driveway and a parkway. It is very strange and, as Berquist admits, it did not seem to resonate with the far-right news junkies watching OAN.

Ultimately, Berquist determined that the show needed to reverse course and embrace more actual news coverage so as to be less jarring to OAN viewers. The final episodes of the show feature long-form interviews with affable but serious guests discussing conservative policy perspectives. Whereas Jon Stewart had comedy shows like *South Park* for a lead-in to *The Daily Show*, an ample budget, and the best comedy talent New York could offer, Berquist did fake news to a real news audience and wrote jokes with a team best versed in counterinsurgent military strategy. And all from the discomfort of a cramped Jacksonville studio. The show failed, and for many very good reasons. It did not, however, provide evidence about the broader potential of right-wing comedy, especially when seen alongside other efforts to more clearly reproduce *The Daily Show*'s success.

Delusions of Grandeur: The Flipside with Michael Loftus

First-run syndicated TV shows—ones whose new episodes air outside of national network affiliations—are nearly as old as television itself. Some syndicated shows become very famous—think of *The Oprah Winfrey Show* or *Ellen*. Most syndicated TV shows, however, go unnoticed. You can't think of them because you've forgotten their names, if you ever knew them. *The Flipside with Michael Loftus* (2014–17) belongs firmly in the latter class. *The Flipside*, at its height, aired sporadically at odd hours of the night, sandwiched between infomercials for George Foreman Grills and Body by Jake. According to creator and star Loftus, the budget was "super low," and the stations that played it were "really bizarre."[11] If a show has a miniscule budget, a writing staff of one, and gets stuck in the 11 p.m. slot on a rural Oregon UHF station, it probably doesn't deserve to be called a failed conservative *Daily Show*. And, yet, *The Flipside* received all sorts of media attention for supposedly being just that.

Announcing the effort in 2014, the veteran sitcom writer Loftus gave interviews wherever he could, announcing that Jon Stewart now had a cross-aisle rival. Liberals took the bait. *The Atlantic* positioned *The Flipside* as "the right's *Daily Show*."[12] *Crooks and Liars* pounced on it, assuring its left-wing readership that conservative voices can never "make us laugh."[13] Liberal commentator Frank Rich gave the obscure show serious consideration in *New York Magazine*.[14] The Canadian Broadcasting Company devoted an astounding eighteen-minutes to the show before it ever aired, framing the effort as a test of the ideological limits of comedy.[15]

The Flipside's comedy is light, competent, and only occasionally based in cruelty. Many of the bits mimic the styles of more successful shows, but never those of *The Daily Show*. In a typical episode, Loftus stands on a comedy club stage with decor reminiscent of a midlife man cave or a late '90s TGI Fridays. He calmly channels Bill Maher's "New Rules" schtick in a segment titled "Michaeltopia," which would often start with simplistic patriotism: "in Michaeltopia there are no V.A. hospitals, there are regular hospitals and veterans get to go to the front of the line." It would then turn slightly hotter and bit a more offensive, suggesting, for example, that veterans move to El Salvador, sneak back across the border, and claim the health care benefits that liberals want to bestow upon undocumented immigrants. Airing largely on Christian-owned family stations, Loftus intentionally kept the comedy tame, racially inflected scapegoating notwithstanding. In the end, *The Flipside* went the way of most first-run syndicated television, airing erratically for three seasons and ending abruptly when Loftus accepted a writing and producing role on the Kevin James sitcom, *Kevin Can Wait*.

The Flipside is most notable for its smallness in comparison to how much hype it garnered among liberal commentators. Despite Loftus's grand ambitions, *The Flipside* both started and ended as a humble, low-budget effort. For those on the left convinced that conservatives simply can't make or appreciate comedy, the reason for Loftus's failure is self-evident—his comedy simply wasn't very good. *The Flipside*'s story, however, does not automatically support this conclusion. So few people had a chance to see the show that it is impossible to make claims about why certain viewers did or did not enjoy it. Despite the show's extremely small audience, the liberal commentariat artificially inflated Loftus's importance, if only to dismiss him as a failure. In actuality, three seasons of TV is a relative success. In fact, it lasted three times longer than the most notorious, and well-funded, right-wing comedy failure, Fox News's *The ½ Hour News Hour*.

"How Would That Work?": The ½ Hour News Hour

Most know Fox News today as the mouthpiece for right-wing political ideology. It's a retirement home for former Trump administration officials and a safe-haven for conservative pseudo-intellectuals to craft bad-faith arguments, create radical liberal strawmen, and frighten its aging viewership. Don't forget, though, that Fox News has also been a den of sexual iniquity. For years, powerful men at the network like Bill O'Reilly and Roger Ailes harassed, abused, and blackmailed their women colleagues for sexual favors. So it's either a historical curiosity or another example of conservatives telling on themselves that sexual indiscretion prominently figures in two memorable segments from Fox News's 2007 effort at political satire in the style of *The Daily Show*, *The ½ Hour News Hour*, a show that liberals love to hate as yet another example of the failure of right-wing comedy.

In one example, the show's co-anchors—characters named Kurt and Jennifer—sit backstage before a show. Kurt, concerned that he's being cut out of the show, leeringly says to Jennifer, "Is there something I should know about? I keep hearing these things about somebody sleeping with the writers." In another bit, Kurt and Jennifer welcome a sexual harassment expert to the show to report on workplace instances of men accusing women of sexual harassment. It is, you see, a comedic reversal of most sexual harassment claims. The expert, dressed in the Fox News house style for women (glasses, blonde hair, revealing top), proceeds to demonstrate how woman-on-man sexual harassment in the workplace might look on Kurt, who grudgingly, hilariously plays along. When the expert suggests that woman-on-woman sexual misconduct "happens all the time," Kurt removes himself from between Jennifer and her and smugly asks, "How would that work?"

The ½ Hour News Hour lasted for just seventeen episodes at the tail end of the George W. Bush administration. The show was the brainchild of producer Joel Surnow who, after the success of his neoconservative war fantasy 24, pitched the right-wing news satire to friend and Fox News chair Roger Ailes. Riding a wave of popular acclaim for left-friendly satire like *The Daily Show* and *The Colbert Report*, ½ *Hour* mimicked those programs' form and function from the right. It featured fake news anchors joking about recent events, correspondents doing field pieces, and special appearances from conservative personalities like Rush Limbaugh, who opens the first episode pretending to be president. Even the show's promotional slogan, "A *Daily Show* for the rest of us," asked Fox News viewers both to think about ½ *Hour* in the same televisual context as *The Daily Show* and to place themselves on the opposite end of the political spectrum from the Comedy Central show's liberal worldview.

However, as is at least partially evident from the two segments centered on sexual indiscretion, ½ *Hour* often "failed to offer meaningful engagement with the actual world of politics and current events."[16] Unlike *The Daily Show*, ½ *Hour* was not daily, but weekly, making its satiric attacks diffuse and strangely atemporal. In other more explicitly political examples, it went after leading Democratic figures of the time like Barack Obama and Hillary Clinton. In one segment, Kurt mockingly urges admirers of Obama to follow the then senator in "B.O." magazine, and he later claims Clinton would staff her White House with "a diverse, multiethnic group of angry lesbians." To be sure, these jokes play to the racism and misogyny of so much conservative comedy—Black men have body odor, you see, and ambitious women must be lesbians. But they do not display a contemporaneous engagement with events and ideas of the day in the same way that *The Daily Show* does.

Even though ½ *Hour* struggled to adequately reproduce *The Daily Show*'s comedic appeals, its failure must also be attributed to industrial factors. Simply put, the Fox News brand was not yet expansive enough to incorporate comedy. If you watch clips of ½ *Hour* today, you'll first see artistic reasons—it's lazy and toothless—why it didn't work. But if you watch Fox News today, you'll see why another version of ½ *Hour*, one whose jokes are crafted around a more informed understanding of its audience, could work. There is perhaps no clearer indication that Fox News didn't trust its audience to understand ½ *Hour* in 2007 than this disclaimer, which it ran before one early episode: "*The ½ Hour News Hour* is next. It contains satire and comedy."

In 2007, neither Fox News nor the broader conservative media universe had suitably prepared viewers for their own version of political satire. By the time of Trump's rise in the mid-2010s, though, Fox News had baked comedy into conservatives' expectations, priming viewers for a right-wing comedy show they could truly call their own. The first sustainable success came with Jesse Watters (whom we discuss in the next section), the former protégé of Bill O'Reilly, whose *Watters' World* (2017–present) approximates the form and tone of *The Daily Show*. Further cuing viewer expectations for comedy, Fox News has packaged both *Watters* and *Gutfeld!* (much like Comedy Central packaged *Daily* and *Colbert*) into the same programming block on Saturday nights, a timeslot synonymous with political satire thanks to *Saturday Night Live*. In other words, ½ *Hour* failed, but it did provide a point of departure for future comedic success on Fox News in the Trump era.

Today's commonsense perspective on mainstream right-wing comedy derives from a handful of forgettable efforts that were unable to give the right-wing comedy complex its big box store. Moreover, popular coverage of these shows reinforces narratives and psychological presumptions among liberals about the necessary failure of conservative comedy. This sentiment is outdated and shortsighted. *The ½ Hour News Hour* ended during the second George W. Bush administration, while *The Flipside* and *Headlines Tonight* lacked the economic support that franchises like *The Daily Show* enjoy. However, focusing on these failed comedic attempts obscures the much more recently successful development of political comedy in Fox News's programming strategy. It also prevents liberal critiques from understanding the size, scope, and strength of today's right-wing comedy complex.

FOX NEWS GOES IRONIC WITH JESSE WATTERS AND *WATTERS' WORLD*

Fox News pundit Jesse Watters is perhaps best known to conservative viewers from the roundtable talk show *The Five* (2011–present), *Watters' World*, and the bygone *O'Reilly Factor* (1996–2017). To liberals, however, he is most infamous for an *O'Reilly* segment in 2016 about New York City's

Chinatown. Bill O'Reilly introduces the report with a self-conscious smirk, claiming Watters has visited the neighborhood to gather political opinions on the upcoming presidential election. In reality, Watters does little more than mock his Chinese and Chinese American interlocutors. In a series of rapidly cut interviews punctuated by movie clips, Watters asks Chinatown residents about Hillary Clinton and Donald Trump but consistently finds more amusing distractions. He goes on to reinforce ugly, Orientalizing stereotypes of China as a land of mystical healing powers. He sophomorically sexualizes Chinese medicine, asking if herbal supplements are "for performance." He practices cartoonish tae kwon do in a karate studio, heedlessly conflating Japanese, Korean, and Chinese martial arts traditions. The bit was, quite rightly, identified by commentators such as the Asian American Journalists Association as "rude, offensive, mocking, derogatory and damaging."[17] For all of this ugliness, however, one must acknowledge that it is meant to be funny. Furthermore, given Watters's success, this bit and others like it earn laughs from their intended audience of knowing Fox News viewers. It may be racist, it may punch down, but it is also clearly an early attempt to employ Watters as a comedic voice aimed at earning Fox News its slice of *The Daily Show*'s vaunted irony demo.

For Fox News, Jesse Watters embodies many of the comedic appeals of Jon Stewart. A charismatic, handsome, white man who simultaneously personifies both the essence of a television news anchor and a parody thereof, Watters offers reactionary defenses of the policies and politicians that *The Daily Show* has spent decades skewering. He smirks and chuckles to punctuate his commentary, signaling to the audience that the objects of his derision are both serious political threats and risible jokes at the same time. Watters's rise on Fox News, then, demonstrates how the network has learned to successfully adapt and redeploy central elements of *The Daily Show*'s playbook. Most importantly, *Watters' World* provides a key precursor to *Gutfeld!*, which would see Fox News realize the full potential of political satire.

Watters began his career as a production assistant on *The O'Reilly Factor*, becoming a producer and, eventually, an on-air ironist devoted to exposing the supposed hypocrisy of liberal America. His weekly "Watters' World" segments (like the Chinatown bit) on *O'Reilly* centered on

Fox News personality Jesse Watters is the right-wing Jon
Stewart—a charming, smug parody of a news anchor. (Fox News;
Comedy Central)

jauntily edited vox pop interviews of the sort made famous in Jay Leno's
"Jay Walking" segments on *The Tonight Show*. They are also extremely
similar in form to a number of *Daily Show* bits, perhaps most strikingly
Jordan Klepper's "Jordan Fingers the Pulse." Both Klepper's and Watters's
segments use the format to force interview subjects into absurd positions
designed to evoke counter-interpretations on the part of the viewer, an
ironic twist on the conventional news remote piece.

The 2016 presidential election usefully underscored the formal and
generic similarities of Klepper's and Watters's shared sensibilities, their
respective comedic skills notwithstanding. During this cycle, Klepper
established himself as a rising star in the world of liberal satire television

through his confrontations with supporters of Donald Trump. In one popular segment, *The Daily Show*'s Klepper visits a rally in Wisconsin, asking Trump voters if they believe in the candidate's professed values of religious freedom, gay rights, and gender equality. The producers of the piece then edit down interviewees' responses in order to highlight the hypocrisy, Islamophobia, homophobia, and misogyny of many Trump supporters in answering Klepper's prompts. For example, one interviewee bemoans the lack of respect for women in the Muslim world while wearing a shirt reading "Hillary sucks, but not like Monica." A laugh track punctuates the shirt's reveal.

A month earlier, Watters aired a strikingly similar segment while on location at the Democratic National Convention, asking attendees to say something positive about Donald Trump and finding enough absurd responses to fill a five-minute segment. The joke, of course, is that the DNC crowd has nothing nice to say about Trump, with the overdubbing of cricket sounds used for individuals who enter a shuddered silence when approached. Others, however, assert outlandish, hypocritical positions, including one man who attests that while he does not want to know about Trump's stances on key issues, he would be willing to hear what the Islamic terrorist group ISIS has to say about global warming. Instead of a laugh track, *Watters' World* leans on the vast 20th Century Fox movie archive to cue a sarcastic interpretation of the man's statement, inserting a clip of a confused Igor in *Young Frankenstein* (1974). It is, essentially, Klepper's bit in reverse.

After this taped segment plays, O'Reilly and Watters, back in their New York studio, note with disbelief that the man is "serious" about trusting ISIS over Donald Trump, thus emphasizing a *Daily Show*–style, ironic relationship to the material. These post-tape interviews offer an important insight into the subtler ways that comedic satire on Fox News has evolved after *The ½ Hour News Hour* and increasingly emulated the spirit of *The Daily Show*. During these conversations, Watters, roughly thirty years O'Reilly's junior, plays an educational role, bridging the gap between O'Reilly and the younger demographics Fox News seeks to add. In one bit, Watters translates the phrase "Oh, snap!" to O'Reilly, explaining that it is "a thing from the 90s" and, in the process, positioning himself as a younger person adept in irony-laden popular culture. Together, these snippets highly resemble Demetri Martin's "Trendspotting" *Daily Show* segments, after which he would briefly discuss some element of youth culture with the older Jon Stewart.

Having introduced these comedic elements in the established news space of *The O'Reilly Factor*, Fox News has quickly spread both Watters and *Daily Show*–style satiric bits throughout their schedule in recent years. Watters himself now plays two roles, hosting the daily program *The Five* alongside four cohosts and anchoring an hourlong *Watters' World* political comedy show on Saturday nights. The latter draws heavily on *The Daily Show*, mixing together media criticism, hyperbolic correspondents, comedic field reports and relatively straightforward interviews into a genre-defying pastiche. In doing so, the program offers a targeted conservative response to the ironic comedy that drove young liberal viewers to *The Daily Show* during the 2000s.

Perhaps *Watters' World*'s closest aping of a *Daily Show* convention is its use of what might be called a "media hypocrisy montage," in which clips from other news outlets are juxtaposed so that Watters can offer an ironic commentary. For example, in the opening of the March 25, 2017 episode, Watters employs headlines from *Time* magazine, *Meet the Press*, *This Week*, and *The Lead with Jake Tapper* in order to establish that each outlet uncritically repeated the fact that Donald Trump had falsely accused the Obama administration of tapping his phone. He then excerpts clips from Republican Congressman Devin Nunes, Trump, and others proving that (to Watters's mind) the tapping had in fact occurred, thus vindicating the president. As a punchline, he says, "On the same day that this bombshell wiretapping information came to light, this is what CNN had on the screen," presenting viewers with a CNN screen image of Trump with the text "Is the President afraid of stairs?" Though one may disagree with the facts at hand or the comedic value of the segment, there is little doubt that Watters's satirical strategy of painting other media as thoughtless and inclined toward the trivial resonates with, and was very likely inspired by, the humor of *The Daily Show*, particularly during the George W. Bush years.

Watters' World incorporates actual news of the day, a *Daily Show* practice that ½ *Hour* failed to replicate but that *Watters' World* seamlessly mixes with Fox News's conservative media brand. *Watters'* borrows liberally (or is it conservatively?) from liberal satire conventions in order to lampoon a range of issues from the right. Like *The Daily Show, Watters' World* features a diverse cast of fake experts and correspondents who talk about real news stories via fictionalized personae. *The Daily Show,* of course, has featured now-famous-in-their-own-right correspondents such as Stephen Colbert, Steve Carell, and Samantha Bee. *Watters* has far less star power, but is up to something similar. For example, the program regularly features guest interviews with The Party Bros, a comedy duo made semi-famous through their passionate advocacy on behalf of Los Angeles–area house parties.[18] In their recurring bit, Watters asks the actors for a liberal perspective on cultural issues, with the result always being a garbled mix of stoner talk and millennial clichés. They are *Watters' * fun house version of Stephen Colbert's far-right pundit character, who, via cartoonish arguments for right-wing positions, offered succor and laughter to the left.

Watters' World demonstrates how right-wing comedy has successfully incorporated the commercial and political appeal of liberal comedy successes like *The Daily Show.* Furthermore, the fact that liberal pundits are more likely to focus on the obscure failure of Michael Loftus and Drew Berquist than the ongoing, *Daily Show*–inspired satirical aspects of *Watters' World* is stark evidence of the liberal psychological complex that makes right-wing comedy invisible. *Watters' World* and *The Daily Show* have even aired virtually identical bits. In one *Watters* episode, he interviews Colin Waugh, the self-styled creator of Liberal Preppers, a nominal (they have no apparent real-world presence) group of American liberals stockpiling supplies for the potential doomsday. During the interview, Watters pushes the amiable Waugh into increasingly tenuous explanations of his position, asking him what a "Trump-related disaster" would look like and wondering if perhaps he is taking his politics to "a little bit of an extreme." Waugh plays along, happy for screen time, providing an ironic point of entry for viewers inclined to read his fear as partisan paranoia expressed in overwrought apocalyptic terms. At one point Watters and Waugh briefly break character, describing one another as "entertaining."

Months after Watters's interview with Waugh, correspondent Desi Lydic of *The Daily Show* did her own segment featuring him. Though he is unnamed and partially masked throughout the bit, his glasses and physique are clearly visible for the half dozen people other than us who watch both *Daily* and *Watters'*. In her version of the bit, Lydic contrasts Waugh's obvious survival incompetence with that of an ultra-skilled conservative prepper. Whereas the conservative expertly deploys weapons and crafts makeshift shelters, Waugh moronically spins around with a sword. In this instance, the ironic interests of the more conservative *Watters' World* viewers and the more liberal *Daily Show* audience coalesce around a single character. Whereas a conservative might view Waugh's fears about Trump as a hysterical inversion of reality, the left-leaning viewer sees his earnest incompetence as evidence that neurotic prepping and cool-headed liberalism do not mix.

It is quite understandable that liberals blanch at the idea of associating, let alone equating, anything on Fox News with *The Daily Show*. There is a substantial difference between Watters and Stewart (or current host Trevor Noah), one that means a lot at the level of moral judgment. It does not, however, change the reality that *Watters* embodies the same aesthetic strategy that much liberal comedy does, addressing the news comedically in order to edge Fox News's aging audience a step in the direction of youth. Watters almost never strays from the realm of politics, using comedy as a tool but not a raison d'être. If there is a choice between a funnier, less political joke or a dryer, more forceful attack on a liberal, Watters will always choose to own the libs. He is not, in other words, a true right-of-the-aisle correlate for Stewart, Noah, or *The Daily Show*. His popularity across the Fox News schedule, however, illustrates the growing importance of levity and satire in right-wing news coverage and, perhaps most importantly, motivates Fox to expand its commitment to conservative comedy. It is Greg Gutfeld, however, who completes Fox News's journey to a fully realized conservative comedy show, providing a big box store in the right-wing comedy complex.

GREG GUTFELD AND FOX NEWS FIND
RIGHT-WING COMEDY SUCCESS

Greg Gutfeld has been in the Fox News universe for over a decade, consistently representing the network's hope to compete for younger viewers and expand its brand identity away from pure, partisan, news commentary.

A libertarian with a background as a men's magazine editor, Gutfeld made his name as a comedic provocateur, first gaining national attention in 2003 by hiring three dwarves to loudly eat potato chips in a successful, if appalling, effort to disrupt a publishers' panel discussing buzz creation. *The New York Times* described him as a "pest" who would "annoy, harass, mock, and traumatize," his rivals.[19] At its most charitable, the *Times* noted that Gutfeld possesses a "bizarro" sense of humor that most people, or at least most *Times* readers, probably would not understand.

He did, however, demonstrate an obvious knack for garnering attention through what would now be described as trolling, a practice we examine more closely in chapter 5. Developing a highly performative, occasionally over-the-top style of comedic presentation, he became the host of the panel talk show *Red Eye* in 2007. The show was an experiment for Fox News and highly unusual by any standard of television. Airing at 3 a.m. Eastern time, the program combined political commentary with occasional comedy sketches, a variety of recurring segments, and a general sense of disjuncture and improvisation. Although loosely resembling liberal satire shows in its reliance on news commentary, *Red Eye* was in many ways more akin to Adult Swim's absurdist, experimental comedies *Tim and Eric's Awesome Show, Great Job!* and *The Eric Andre Show*. Very low budget and mostly unconcerned with ideological coherence, *Red Eye* often unfolded as a live deconstruction of the news, talk show, and late-night genres all at once, all with an absurdist bent. Gutfeld's relentless intensity and insistence on laughing a little too much at every joke evoked a funhouse version of Jay Leno, Jimmy Fallon, or Stephen Colbert.

Inside jokes erupted and expanded on *Red Eye* across episodes. For example, the show's "halftime report," an errors and omissions bit that was weird enough on its own, went through weeklong phases in which Gutfeld would disrupt his editor by pummeling him with cat puns and attributing to him a variety of improbable feline interests. Panel discussions would swell to sixteen pundits, none of whom had time to do anything more than introduce themselves. Yes, the politics were mostly right-wing and the show's language pushed against discursive norms. However, in a rare instance of the left acknowledging conservative comedy, *The New Yorker* described *Red Eye* as "mindlessly sarcastic, sneakily smart, patently absurd, and generally refreshing."[20]

Most importantly, people watched. *Red Eye* regularly beat its overnight competition of infomercials and sitcom reruns, garnering Gutfeld a shot at prime—or at least primer—time every Saturday evening. His promotion resulted from a number of converging factors. For one, he had provided evidence that at least some Fox News viewers would tolerate both political comedy and, on occasion, pure nonsense. Just as importantly, there was a major shift in right-wing culture, and particularly right-wing comedy, over the course of Gutfeld's *Red Eye* tenure. His stunt with the chip eating little people, so odd in 2003, foreshadowed a contemporary moment in which ostensibly comedic 4chan memes and Twitter trolling play tangible roles in electoral politics. Indeed, it's no coincidence that right-wing troll Gavin McInnes, whom we discuss in chapter 5, broke through to mainstream success as a regular panelist on *Red Eye* during this period. Whereas before conservative viewers may have scoffed at Gutfeld's bombast, irreverence, and utter disregard for intellectual or ideological consistency, Donald Trump has primed viewers to accept these, as well as a number of far uglier, traits. The rise of Trump and Trumpism in the 2010s offered a transitional moment for existing Fox News viewers to reconsider Gutfeld's style. Embracing Trump's eccentricity, while deemphasizing much of the brazen racism and misogyny of *Watters' World*, Gutfeld promised Fox News leadership a chance to appeal to a younger audience hungry for comedic content.

As *Gutfeld!* thrived in the Trump era, it became clear that *The Daily Show's* irony demo, and the comedic aesthetics that appeal to these young viewers, were not the exclusive domain of the political left. In 2019 Gutfeld regularly drew a larger average viewership (1.73 million total viewers) than any other late-night show, except for the broadcast stalwarts *The Late Show with Stephen Colbert* on CBS and *The Tonight Show Starring Jimmy Fallon* on NBC. By late 2021, *Gutfeld!* (2.12 million viewers) was even beating *Colbert* (1.896 million viewers).[21] Gutfeld's success came on the heels of Fox News's attempts that summer to broaden its appeal to advertisers, reminding them "that its audience is wide and can be found across the nation, not just in so-called 'red states.'"[22] Fox News's expansion of its brand is a curious reversal of the industrial logics driving broadcast and cable television, respectively. Broadcasters like CBS have traditionally been home to a big tent of viewers across the demographic spectrum, yet its late-night host (Colbert) has been among the loudest voices doing anti-Trump comedy. Fox News, by contrast, has focused with laser-like precision on older, whiter, almost exclusively conservative viewers. Yet the cable network is now clearly deploying Gutfeld to siphon off younger viewers who perceive late-night as a much more politicized space than it was before Trump.

Many *Gutfeld!* segments are drawn more or less directly from preexisting, liberal comedy shows like *The Daily Show* and *Real Time with Bill Maher.* The show opens with a monologue and media montage either pointing to the hypocrisy of other cable news outlets or underscoring the foibles of Democrats. The July 27, 2019, episode, for example, begins with a montage of clips from Robert Mueller's congressional testimony, stitching together the multiple instances in which he demurred during the hearing, stating that questions were beyond his "purview." The bit uses editing to build comedic momentum through excessive repetition, evoking the classic comedy theory that humor readily emerges from human agents acting like automated machines.[23] It also makes a right-wing political point: the Democrats, the clips suggest, held a hearing with no purpose. The next moment in the segment emphasizes Gutfeld as a *Daily Show* competitor, capable of combining the political with the truly silly. Having completed the Mueller "purview" montage, a graphic advertising "The PurrView," a daytime talk show hosted by cats, appears on screen. Such jokes, which semi-logically combine news stories with popular culture through wordplay, have long been a staple of liberal satire television.

In addition to displaying a knack for purely silly comedy bits, *Gutfeld!* also routinely engages political sketch comedy à la *Saturday Night Live.* In a sketch from the August 17, 2019, episode, for example, two men sit across from each other in a nondescript office setting, one of them snacking. "What are you eating?" his coworker asks, to which the other blithely offers, "Macadamia nuts—want some?" This reply sends the first coworker into a tailspin of feigned indignation—no, he will not have any macadamia nuts because they're from Hawaii, where there's also a Trump international hotel. The sketch escalates the joke by singling out harmless cultural artifacts, sports affiliations, clothing choices, and pop culture preferences for their increasingly tangential relationship to Trump. Everything from Hallmark Channel movies to bandanas are declared symbols of white supremacy until eventually the first coworker—now nearly naked after his kilt is revealed to have a troubling connection to Trump's Scottish heritage—turns to the camera and stammers, "Thanks, Trump!"

The sketch mimics the satiric project of innumerable bits on *The Daily Show* and *Saturday Night Live*, taking to an (il)logical extreme some of the core ethical values of political liberalism. It clearly lampoons the left's "cancel culture," in which social justice–oriented progressives call out the problematic racial, gendered, or otherwise biased nature of a cultural artifact. What separates the *Gutfeld!* segment from other bits of conservative comedy, though, is its broad range of referents, one that doesn't stay confined to purely political targets like the humor of Watters. Moreover, it (and many others on *Gutfeld!*) demonstrates an awareness by the show that political comedy need not—indeed, cannot—be purely political. The thrust of the sketch's humor is equal parts Trump boosterism and scattershot pop culture references, offering a touchpoint of engagement for viewers who might not be as securely anchored in red-state politics as the rest of Fox News's viewership. In other words, it's a comedy sketch on a comedy show on a right-wing news network—clear evidence that the political right does comedy.

Gutfeld! creates other comedic bits that embrace political ambiguity in the process of crafting funny performances. This irony and ambiguity are most apparent in the show's regular deployment of an unusual double-act segment, a vaudevillian performance style in which two comedians rapidly bounce jokes off of one another—think Abbott and Costello's famous "Who's on First?" routine—in the creation of a single bit. The segments cut back and forth between clips of Trump giving one of his trademark, rambling bizarro speeches and Gutfeld commenting from the studio in the role of straight man. The resulting product has a sense of surreality, presenting Trump as funny, yes, but also strange. One such segment begins with Gutfeld talking to the camera, commenting on the then outrageous, now somewhat quaint, controversy about Donald Trump's interest in purchasing Greenland from Denmark:

GREG GUTFELD: He [Trump] now wants to buy Greenland. That is awesome. And it's no surprise, he's a real estate guy, he probably wants to buy it so he can flip it. Add some granite countertops, a subzero fridge, some nice bathroom amenities, done. It leads me to wonder, do you love cranes or trucks?

This last phrase is, of course, a comically nonsensical transition, and purposefully so. Gutfeld uses it to slide into a double act in which he interacts with a series of clips taken from a single, actual Trump speech that moves through a dizzying, profoundly silly array of topics:

DONALD TRUMP: I love cranes, I love trucks of all types. Even when I was a little boy at four years old, my mother would say, "You love trucks." I do. I've always loved trucks. I still do. Nothing changes. Sometimes, you know, you might become president but nothing changes. I still love trucks.

GG: Nothing changes. But what about the rain?

TRUMP: I said "Don't worry about the rain. Do we have umbrellas? Don't worry about the rain, umbrellas work very well."

GG: It's so true! He speaks the truth about the umbrella. And what do we send them, wheat?

TRUMP: We send them wheat. Wheat. That's not a good deal. And they don't even want our wheat. They do it because they want us to at least feel that we're OK, you know, they do it to make us feel good.

The bit goes on and on in this fashion, with Gutfeld playfully providing the connective tissue for Trump's incoherent effort at political messaging. These double-act segments are unusual both in terms of their comedic strategy and their ideological ambivalence. Framed in the general context of Gutfeld's wild exuberance and obvious admiration for Trump, it is fair to say that the segments are friendly to the former president. They are, however, much more complicated than simple cheerleading. Much of the humor comes from the seemingly unintelligible connections and juxtapositions, as the bit takes political speech and twists it into a kind of avant-garde spoken-word performance. The content of Trump's original speech is rendered not merely hard to follow; it is impossible to even guess what the president actually said in the fuller version of what Gutfeld excerpts. To try to follow along is to engage in serious literary interpretation, as Gutfeld molds Trump into a Joycean hero whose stream of consciousness somehow includes loving trucks, admiring the effectiveness of umbrellas, and feeling OK about selling wheat. All of which creates a mountain of incongruity that is fun and funny to the extent that you believe that

Trump's popularity on the right and political power resolves, or at least nullifies, all contradictions.

Trump gave the original speech to advance his political agenda. But the above-quoted edited version, complete with Gutfeld's emphasis on its most bizarre phrases and inscrutable transitions, is something entirely distinct. Reminiscent of *Saturday Night Live*'s "Fun with Real Audio" sketches, which created non-sequitur animations to illustrate often banal political speech, the double-act both uplifts and mocks Trump's words. It is engaging and funny insofar as it lays bare the artifice of linguistic convention that underpins all communication. Taking only complete sentences uttered in a single monologue, it seems comically improbable that an adult human, let alone a president, could be edited to sound so unmoored.

This unmooring, of course, is where the politics of the piece become both powerful and prone to varied interpretation. Gutfeld's double act does not, as so much of *Watters' World* does, embrace the humor of punching downward at those in lower positions of cultural power. If anyone is being mocked in the bit, it is Trump. However, people are not the main target of this high-concept humor. Gutfeld's likely intention is to praise Trump's disregard for norms and his zeal for destabilizing hierarchies, linguistic or otherwise. Gutfeld here avoids the uglier, hateful elements of Trump's rhetoric and much right-wing humor. He is, however, quite visibly enthused by the damage Trump does to institutions and traditions. For Gutfeld, his double-act with Trump emphasizes what reactionaries can gain when they lose the pretense of seriousness. Gutfeld portrays Trump as a fool, yes. However, he also signals to conservative viewers that they can express their politics through the process of ironic distanciation so often associated with the postmodern left. Whereas most Fox News programming is fueled by anger and fearmongering, Gutfeld's comedic double act celebrates the right's self-realization that unseriousness can be wielded by and attractive to a wide array of demographic groups within its ideological coalition.

At the same time, Gutfeld's double-act bit runs the risk of making Trump look incoherent or making Gutfeld appear anti-Trump. It is a near certainty that some conservative viewers won't get the joke. Media scholar Linda Hutcheon describes the dangers of irony, noting that any good bit of ironic joking fundamentally requires that some portion of the audience be confused or even hurt by the joke.[24] Ambiguity is a central feature of any comedy that plays with satire and irony. Pop culture commentators and political communication scholars have argued at great length that liberals tend to tolerate humorous, intentional ambiguity while conservatives do not.[25] Gutfeld's success, we argue, proves that, given an accommodating industrial and cultural context, right-wing viewers are in fact open to political comedy, ambiguous and otherwise.

HERE TO STAY: *GUTFELD!* AND FOX NEWS ANCHOR THE RIGHT-WING COMEDY COMPLEX

When Greg Gutfeld scaled up the success of his weekly show to the nightly *Gutfeld!* in 2021, the liberal commentariat took the opportunity to perform disbelief at the possibility of right-wing comedy. *The New Republic*, for example, asked if *Gutfeld!* was "the worst show on television," and declared it to be "the latest evidence that conservatives have no sense of humor."[26] And, depending on your vantage point, *Gutfeld!* may well be both. *Gutfeld!* is not, however, *new* evidence of anything whatsoever. *Red Eye* did well for years. Jesse Watters has been using irony to enhance the Fox News brand since 2014. And *The Greg Gutfeld Show* was already beating cable competitors before transitioning to the higher-profile *Gutfeld!* Once more, Greg Gutfeld is making a comedy show that conservatives like and that liberals would rather wave away with "that's not funny." The liberal psychological complex dismisses right-wing comedy as it plods along growing in stature and influence. It is understandable to be upset at how expensive the heating bill is every February, but at a certain point it shouldn't be hard to remember that winters are cold.

And winter is something that ought to be taken seriously. For years, the right couldn't keep a sustainable tenant in the big-box spot of its comedy complex. Liberal tastemakers, understandably, came to see the failing occupants of the conservative comedy ghost town—*The ½ Hour News Hour, The Flipside, Headlines Tonight*—described above as defining all right-wing comedy. Fox News since the Trump era, however, proves that the business of right-wing comedy can and does thrive. The rise of mainstream right-wing comedy described in this chapter is hegemonic, gradually shifting popular conceptions of what is possible comedically, what is proper, and most importantly, what is profitable. While scholars and critics have for decades focused on the left side of this dynamic, Fox News now provides a framework for imagining it from the right. Gutfeld and Watters, in particular, reimagine commonsense conceptions of the relationship between political ideology and comedy aesthetics. From liberals' perspective, this evolution has helped to mask a fundamental change in their political opposition. Fox News's incremental approach to adding comedy content while maintaining its brand-defining outrage programming served it quite well during the Trump years. Of course, many conservatives may have simply nodded along to whatever Trump tweeted, enjoying the spin that star Fox News anchors such as Sean Hannity or Laura Ingraham put on it. For other right-wing viewers, however, Trump was *simultaneously* appealing and ridiculous. For such viewers, the development of Watters and Gutfeld became crucial resources, able to bridge the Trump Show back toward the heartland of American conservatism.

Fox News's success with comedy also bridges together the range of right-wing perspectives that must congeal in order for conservative politics to succeed in the United States. Gutfeld and Watters serve as one nexus point, introducing established conservatives to newer, more nefarious forms of right-wing ideology, using ridicule of the left as a means of papering over the many intellectual inconsistencies in Republican fusionism. As we show in chapter 5 of this book, Gutfeld is quite happy to play along with right-wing trolls like Michael Malice and Gavin McInness who, in turn, gleefully introduce the Fox News viewership to online comedy based in fascist ideologies and employed by extremist groups such as the Proud Boys. If, as scholar Viveca Greene argues, it is a "deadly serious" matter to study such online trolls, it is also, we argue, necessary to understand the various pathways that lead people into these spaces.[27]

Together, Gutfeld and Watters represent a central force in right-wing comedy, with *Gutfeld!* now serving as a focal point around which other purveyors are able to position themselves. And like any good commercial complex, the world of right-wing comedy is replete with specialty boutiques. One of those is the right-wing comedy complex's cigar shop, a business that calls out to Fox News's aging audience and welcomes it in with conservative humor that is comfortable and familiar when the news of the day becomes too much to bear. In the next chapter, we consider "paleocomedy," right-wing humor that nostalgically, perhaps romantically, recalls previous eras of humor and connects them to a contemporary conservative project.

2 Making Comedy Great Again

PALEOCOMEDY

Mike Huckabee is a conservative media pundit, a former Republican governor of Arkansas, and a teller of truly terrible jokes on Twitter. The jokes are so bad, in fact, that the progressive comedian Patton Oswalt has created a recurring bit on *Jimmy Kimmel Live!* entitled "Yuck Yuckabees!" just to mock them. During these segments, Oswalt recites a series of jokes culled from Huckabee's social media feeds. Reading Huckabee's tweets verbatim, Oswalt gives the viewer a tour through the dusty dinosaur exhibit that is Huckabee's comedy repertoire. There's a fart joke: "CNN usually breaks wind—not news." There's a barely intelligible pun about Hillary Clinton entering the Oscar Mayer Weinermobile: "To be frank, she's in trouble!" And there's one about breakfast that meanders through just about all 280 of the tweet's allotted characters, somehow landing on the absolute daddest-of-dad-joke punchlines: "#CEREALKILLER." Oswalt's send up of Huckabee is hip, innovative, and fully legible as real comedy to liberals. Huckabee's own material, of course, is none of the above—and purposely so. The former governor is enacting what we term "paleocomedy," backward-facing humor that creates pleasure, and conservative political meaning, by knowingly indulging in hackneyed old jokes and comedic formats. When he tweets, Huckabee uses comedy in order to harken back to a good ol' days in which people like him (and his voters) understood all the jokes and felt represented by the joke makers.

A closer look at Oswalt's satiric "Yuck Yuckabees!" illustrates both Huckabee's comedic aims and paleocomedy as a concept. Most standup performances on *Kimmel* take place in front of a sleek, contemporary, late-night television studio backdrop. For Oswalt's "Yuck Yuckabees!," however, *Kimmel* brings in a bright red brick wall in order to make an overt visual citation to a popular form of 1980s standup comedy. First made famous on the A&E Network's standup showcase program *An Evening at the Improv*, the red brick backdrop was a familiar, genre-defining sight for comedy fans in the 1980s. Since then, however, red bricks have become a quick way of denoting the most formulaic, outmoded elements of hacky, old-school standup comedy. By the 1990s, cutting-edge comedies like *The Simpsons* began using the red brick wall in order to parody the already retrograde aspects of 1980s standup. Today, the red brick backdrop instantaneously signals to viewers, even those who may not remember the '80s, that the Huckabee jokes recited by Oswalt are not simply poorly constructed; they're also archaic and regressive.

Despite liberal comedians like Oswalt making fun of this kind of comedy, for someone like Huckabee, the archaicness is the point. He knows full well that the homophonic knee-slapper "cereal killer" is something short of groundbreaking material. His message is thus not necessarily humorous, but instead one *about* humor. Like all comedy, even bad jokes can serve to craft a community out of those who appreciate them. The red bricks from the *Kimmel* parody are a zing of a touch on Oswalt's part. But one man's zing may be another's dog whistle. The red brick era was one in which the vast majority of standup comedy—especially that which broke through to higher-profile film and television exposure— was performed by white men telling jokes to audiences presumed to be unmarked by racial or gendered power imbalances. Huckabee's paleocomedy is every bit as outmoded as the world implied by a red brick backdrop, and he's just fine with that.

Paleocomedy, as we discuss in this chapter, intentionally uses outdated forms of comedic address—the multi-camera sitcom, AM-style talk radio, clichéd standup routines, dads making dad jokes—in order to craft simple humor imbued with subtle layers of additional communal meaning for conservative audiences. It revels in its unhipness and often

Adam Sandler performs against the infamous red brick backdrop of *An Evening at the Improv*, a stand-up comedy convention that *The Simpsons* has satirized. Comedian Patton Oswalt uses it while ironically performing jokes from Mike Huckabee's Twitter feed. (*An Evening at the Improv*; *The Simpsons*; *Jimmy Kimmel Live!*)

prompts enjoyment less by evoking laughter in the present tense than by nostalgically, perhaps romantically, recalling previous eras of humor. Paleocomedy ranges in its engagement with the political. Huckabee's puns intersperse harmless wordplay with partisan sniping—they're both things dad just gets to impose on you at the dinner table. Dennis Miller, whom we discuss below, dipped in and out of politics, surfacing sometimes on Fox News to use the network's central position in the right-wing comedy complex to find new customers for his podcast, a paleocomedic show that largely consisted of rehashing his old standup routines. Tim Allen, long-time television star and paleocomedy's iron horse, whom we also discuss in this chapter, used the tried-and-true conventions of the multi-camera sitcom to offer long-dead solutions to today's most pressing social concerns. Currency, however, isn't an ambition for comedians like Miller and Allen. Paleocomedy comforts the discomfited, referencing back to an era in which the comedy world was smaller, simpler, and far less inclusive. Huckabee's dad jokes are, of course, not mom jokes. Paleocomedy is the red brick wall that keeps innovation, progressivism, and diversity out of the comedy club.

In naming the phenomenon of "paleocomedy," we draw directly upon the right-wing ideology of paleoconservatism, a philosophy present in aspects of Trumpism and perhaps most notably exemplified by pundit and former Republican presidential candidate Pat Buchanan. Standing in stark contrast to the globalizing worldview of neo-conservatism that reigned on the right in the early part of the twenty-first century, paleo-conservatism aims at a "fundamental revision of the conservative project" centered on the "revitalization of ethnicity, class, gender, race, and nation."[1] In the words of one founding paleoconservative thinker, "authentic" conservatism is one aimed at the preservation of the "institutionalized cultural expressions" of a "particular people."[2] Unconcerned with free-market ideals and particularly dismissive of globalization and racial or ethnic diversity, paleoconservative philosophy argues that human flourishing occurs best when like-minded people are able to engage in long-established ways of life. While avoiding directly racist language, there is, quite clearly, a deeply exclusionary element to the paleoconservative project. There is also a disturbing "know-nothing" aspect in paleoconservative thinking, whereby one's near-exclusive concern with one's own community results in raced, gendered, and otherwise prejudicial social structures.[3] In other words, by inventing a homogenous past to celebrate, paleoconservatism excludes and vilifies all manner of differences. Paleocomedy takes this political philosophy, wraps it up in humor, and puts it up for sale in the right-wing comedy complex.

The main figures we discuss in this chapter, Dennis Miller and Tim Allen, use their comedy to look back to a time when white male comedians could much more easily avoid engaging with questions of diversity, gender equality, and systematic racism. Certainly, such issues have always been present in American humor. However, the most economically viable forms of American comedy—the sitcom and standup set—have long been tethered to conservative norms in both style and substance due to the commercial nature of American mass media across the twentieth century. The television sitcom, for example, may occasionally take up a controversial issue, but it nevertheless remains rooted in traditional social structures and maintenance of the status quo. Much standup comedy pushes boundaries as an artform, but TV airtime and late-night hosting gigs tend to go to the most conventional of (white male) performers. Paleocomedians thus aim to recreate a world of pre-problematic comedy, in which social issues either do not exist or can be neatly resolved by a bumbling dad doing his best over twenty-three minutes plus commercials.

In the right-wing comedy complex, paleocomedy is the cigar shop, tucked between the Men's Wearhouse and the Nevada Bob's golf outlet. A little retro, a little retrograde, not explicitly exclusionary, but clearly aimed at the polo and khakis dad demo. For many who catch a whiff, the place simply stinks. The average young person is likely to be confused and repulsed both by Huckabee's #cerealkiller joke and by the idea of lighting a bunch of non-psychoactive carcinogenic dirty leaves on fire in a damp room ringing with the sound of slightly misquoted *Caddyshack* lines. It's a place where politics comes up quite a lot, but mostly in the form of off-color jokes about Alexandria Ocasio-Cortez and complaints about college kids these days majoring in "Native American Gender Studies or Something." For those who feel welcome in the shop, the aroma is one of comfort, generational wealth, and nostalgia. And the fact that the wife and kids won't set foot inside is nothing but a bonus. A comfort to some, an utter anathema to others, paleocomedy is the place where people who think Archie Bunker had it right all along hang out while the rest of the family tries out more interesting shopping options.

For most liberals, by contrast, and as Patton Oswalt's bit on *Kimmel* suggests, paleocomedy is one more example of the left dismissing right-wing comedy with "that's not funny." But this perspective is also built around an attempt to mock conservative comedy out of having any relevance for contemporary culture. Most liberals find the kinds of paleocomedy that Miller and Allen represent to be, at best, passé, and rightfully so. But this dismissal of paleocomedy overlooks a popular subgenre of conservative comedy that, no matter how hard it is for liberals to believe, reaches millions of viewers. Consequently, by serving a key demographic in the right-wing comedy complex, paleocomedy also shapes today's political and cultural discourse, even as liberals cling to the idea that this could not possibly be the case.

DENNIS MILLER: FROM *SATURDAY NIGHT LIVE* TO FOX NEWS

In the years leading up to 2020, Dennis Miller was heading toward retirement. As he told his listeners twice a week on his podcast, *The Dennis Miller Option*, he had a great run. After working for years as a standup comic, he'd become famous behind the *Saturday Night Live* "Weekend Update" desk in the late '80s. He developed a signature style that mixed acerbic wit and obscurely intellectual references while drawing a premium cable audience on HBO's *Dennis Miller Live* in the '90s. However improbably, he did color commentary on *Monday Night Football* for a few years. He even costarred in *The Net*, the Sandra Bullock cyber-thriller that, while dated before the credits ran at its premiere, remains a pretty fun watch. Since those high-flying days, Miller has comparatively coasted, appearing on cable news shows, going on tour with Fox News's Bill O'Reilly, hosting an AM radio talk show, and rolling out a few episodes of his podcast *The Dennis Miller Option* each week. Yet, in the spring of 2020, as COVID-19, Black Lives Matter, and the coming Trump-Biden election dominated the news cycle, Miller emerged from his semiretirement and found himself back on top for a minute. Overnight, the *Option* shot to number nine on the iTunes comedy charts, beating out literally thousands of younger, hipper podcasters.

Miller's brief rise from back-burner podcast host to conservative comedy star is a perfect example of the right-wing comedy complex at work. In the spring of 2020, as news and social media began to be consumed with the spiraling national pandemic crisis and the emerging protests around police brutality and racial justice, Fox News's Sean Hannity scheduled Miller for a recurring weekly segment on his eponymous show. In each appearance Miller opens with a joke aimed squarely at Fox News's hard right audience. "I know he lost his fastball," Miller says in reference to Joe Biden, "I think he's lost his curve, he's lost his slider, and he's wearing his cup as an N95 mask." He mocks Congresswoman Alexandria Ocasio-Cortez for what seems to be a minor tax miscalculation. He skewers liberal San Francisco and its Democratic congresswoman, Nancy Pelosi, with a potty joke about the city's sanitation crisis. It's a red-meat performance aimed at red states. And it works. A quick hit on *Hannity* translates to thousands of politically rabid listeners for Miller.

But, perhaps surprisingly, Miller's podcast approach is not particularly pitched to capture all of the ideologically intense viewers that *Hannity* introduces to him. Instead, it aims to be a sort of retirement home for conservatives who want to feel comfortable, avoid progressive ideas, and stay at arm's length from the culture wars. On his *Hannity* appearances, Miller is aggressive and topical, jamming in trending references even when they don't quite fit into the joke. *The Dennis Miller Option* podcast, however, is something else entirely. It is an old-sounding show with old-sounding jokes, peppered with old references, made by an increasingly old man. The show revels in the once was, while grudgingly taking the occasional trudge through the headlines. On Fox News, Miller tries to match the topicality of Gutfeld. On *The Dennis Miller Option*, he turns the dial to paleo, losing the edge of Trump-era rage and replacing it with *Wonder Years* nostalgia. Though this inevitably leads to a smaller, aging audience, Miller's paleocomedy helps tie a certain, more relaxed set of conservatives into the broader right-wing comedy complex, connecting them to the comedians old and new that he brings onto the show. Whereas liberals understandably focus on the more offensive, angry aspects of right-wing performance, Miller's comedy facilitates Republican fusionism, bridging together disparate conservative sensibilities.

On *Option*, Miller is just as likely to spend fifteen minutes dishing about Ali McGraw's casting in *Love Story* as he is to break down the latest political controversy. Even as his audience ballooned from the Hannity appearance, Miller calmly refused to take on the same hot-button issues that brought in the new listeners, declaring "I'm staying out of everything [political] from here on in." Given the nature of the contemporary media industry, Miller's best chance to develop a viable audience is by tapping into the more partisan aspects of the right-wing news and comedy complexes. To do so, he'll play pundit on *Hannity*, join *The Ben Shapiro Show* as a guest, and bring onto his podcast a steady stream of conservative voices, ranging from the Hoover Institute historian Victor Davis Hanson to the comedian Adam Carolla. Miller is Trump sympathetic and derides left-wing talking points when the issue is forced. However, even his more topical podcast jokes have a softer, older feel to them. For example, in sending up the "therapy animal" phenomenon that right-wing talking heads associate with liberal weakness and eccentricity, Miller suggests dressing up a friend like Sigmund Freud and demanding an extra seat for his "therapy therapist" on his next flight. He then falls into his 1990s show-off comedian persona, quickly comparing Freud to Carl Jung on a superficial but accurately name-dropped level. It's the sort of modest bit that comprises his latter-day career approach to humor; funny but comfortable, aimed squarely at the sort of suburban HBO audience that has been aging and perhaps growing more conservative with him for thirty years.

Media accounts of Miller tend to evoke a supposed political transformation in him from liberal *SNL* icon to conservative Fox News reactionary. There is some truth to this story, but a lot less than the liberals who loved him in the '80s and '90s would like to admit.[4] True, for decades he made jokes that liberals liked, but that's not the same as being liberal. Looking back at Miller's breakout performance behind *Saturday Night Live*'s vaunted "Weekend Update" news desk from 1985 to 1991, one finds a charming anchor full of loud, funny opinions but without a clear ideology. Working during the *SNL* renaissance of the late 1980s, the show's long-standing counter-cultural branding forged Miller's liberal reputation.[5] However, Miller was always a heterodox political voice during his *SNL* tenure.[6] While there are liberal moments to cherry pick from his time at Studio 8H, any left-wing designation of him derived more from the transitive property than anything else. Liberals like *SNL*, and people who liked *SNL* like Miller, but not necessarily for his politics.

It wasn't until near the end of Miller's HBO talk show *Dennis Miller Live* (1994–2002) that he embraced right-wing comedy and began his trajectory toward paleocomedy. Again, however, what is remembered as his early liberalism is really more a set of things that liberals happen to like. *DML* was a stripped-down talk show best known for Miller's weekly monological rants. These were glorified standup bits, lightly political but way overdressed with strings of literary, historical, and cultural referents that mostly, but not always, made sense. In a bit on air travel, perhaps the most mundane and clichéd of standup topics, Miller name checks the Bataan death march, Elsa Lanchester's hair in *Bride of Frankenstein*, Yul Brynner, *Marcus Welby, M.D.*, Captain Pike from *Star Trek*, Vasco de Gama, Boo Radley, and Queequeg from *Moby Dick*. The references, deployed as comical analogies to things on airplanes (jamming your bag into the overhead is like fitting "Pavarotti into a wetsuit" etc.), marked Miller as a unique, if occasionally insufferable, comedic voice. But, more than anything, the references flattered the high-income, highly educated 1990s HBO premium cable audience. On a network that self-branded as "not TV," *Dennis Miller Live* was a can of televisual Zima, the 1990s "not beer" beverage of choice. Although marketed as the sophisticated alternative to the everyday, it was really just a slightly more expensive way to spend a buzzed suburban Friday night.

Miller's overt move into the right-wing comedy complex began in the late 1990s, when the foibles and misdeeds of the Clintons became the most reliable wholesaler of raw comedic materials for many on the right. Although Miller evinced a certain creepy respect for Bill, he turned a decidedly sexist eye toward Hillary. In a 1999 rant devoted to her New York Senate campaign, Miller acknowledges the misogynistic tendency to demean ambitious women before doing exactly that. The punchline, arrived at via a zigzag of references and off-color remarks, is that if Hillary got more sex, she wouldn't feel the need to seek political office. It's a monologue dripping with misogynistic contempt and undoubtedly informed by right-wing talking points from outlets such as Fox News and *The Rush Limbaugh Show*. Well before people noticed Miller's turn to the right, he was, it seems, sensing the coming polarization of political comedy in the 2000s and pitching his tent in the vacant lot that would soon become the right-wing comedy complex.

It was only after the attacks of September 11, 2001, that media critics began to recognize that Miller was not the liberal satirist long assumed by those devoted to equating comedy with liberal politics. In the aforementioned, pre-9/11 Clinton monologue, Miller describes George W. Bush as a nitwit. A few years later, he said of Bush, "I like him. I'm going to give him a pass. I take care of my friends."[7] In the meantime, his rants became increasingly jingoist and Islamophobic. In one of his final HBO *Dennis Miller Live* episodes, he engages in the sort of "revenge and humiliation" fantasies that erupted in the world of regressive comedy in reaction to the terror attacks perpetrated by al-Qaeda.[8] In an ostensible defense of free speech, he praises American anti-war protestors because they give him "someone to hate whose name [he] can pronounce." Discussing Arab protestors, he suggests that they "drape their head" in the American flag and "desecrate it with a large caliber bullet." These moments served as a change of address card, telling his dwindling HBO audience that he was moving out of comedy's mainstream capital district and into the cozier confines of the emerging right-wing comedy complex.

Miller, who was also serving as a color commentator on *Monday Night Football* at the time of 9/11, quickly exited the centrist media space and became a fixture on cable news and AM radio. He reemerged in 2003 on Fox News's *Hannity & Colmes*, slotted in as an Andy Rooney–style essayist whose main job was to affect a light sense of erudition while attacking liberal politicians. For example, in describing the 2004 Democratic presidential candidates, he alludes to their empty-headed debate as a "Pez dispenser seance," a reference that succeeds in the Millerian criteria of cruelty and abstraction, but does not quite congeal as a metaphor. Despite his awkward transition into more purely partisan comedy, Miller was then given a talk show on CNBC, on which he doubled down on his new, overtly right-wing persona, frequently evoking Abu Ghraib torture photos in pursuit of laughs.[9] Criticized repeatedly by media watchdogs, Miller returned to Fox News, appearing on *The O'Reilly Factor* and *The ½ Hour News Hour* and waiting for the right-wing comedy complex to develop itself into a more fully self-sustaining ecosystem. In the meantime, he turned to AM radio where his syndicated talk show ran from 2007 to 2015, consistently garnering millions of live listeners on conservative-branded stations.[10] Although drawing some right-wing fire for his socially liberal stances on gay marriage and abortion, he stuck to the party line on partisan matters, weaving his standup style into a conservative talk format to considerable success.

A MORE COMFORTABLE *OPTION*

When the radio show ended in 2015, Miller found himself in an entirely new, increasingly fragmented media environment. His days of large, mainstream audiences were behind him. However, the world of right-wing comedy had grown with the siloing of media audiences, giving Miller an opportunity to maintain a scaled-down presence by embracing paleo-comedy to establish a new, softer personal brand. Although still occasionally popping up on Fox News, Miller's contemporary persona is one that embraces the old and even the out of touch. His social media material, which is tellingly more successful on older-skewing Facebook than on Twitter, often swerves directly into Mike Huckabee territory. "Fittingly, lots of guys are going to see *Solo* alone," he posted in 2018, giving *Star Wars* nerds the full dad joke treatment. In May of 2020 he posted to Facebook demanding "Sanctuary Cities for American Citizens who want to go outside without a mask."[11] Indulging right-wing preoccupation with liberal immigration policy and combining it with Trumpian self-destructive anti-mask machismo, Miller offers a contemporary joke straight out of a 1980s red brick standup set. The paleocomedic branding is still conservative, but it is an intentionally duller brand of humor aimed at inviting older, less feisty shoppers to relax inside the cigar shop at the right-wing comedy complex.

His most recent project, *The Dennis Miller Option (DMO)* podcast, went even further in this toned-down, nostalgic effort, crafting a paleo-comedic tour de force that harkens to previous eras of comedy in both form and content. *DMO* was a blend of AM radio and old-style standup comedy that, while laced with soft jabs aimed at the left and gentle puffery pointed at the right, found its real political valence by simply pretending the past twenty years never happened. The show's approach to production was entirely anachronistic, eschewing the technological advancements that make podcasting what it is.

A June 2020 episode featuring Jay Leno illustrates the extent to which *DMO* turns what might seem like a bug of outdatedness into a paleocomedic feature. Miller begins the show by embracing a sense of liveness that is, of course, entirely untrue. The show could not be heard live and was, despite its improvisational tone, always edited before release. As opposed to conducting the Leno interview and going back to record an introduction, Miller and his cast talk while they wait for Leno to call in, presumably from a brick-sized cellphone he's been using for twenty years, crafting a distinct drive-time AM radio feel right from the start. Miller chats with his producer and sidekick, reenacting the host-centric content model that dominates talk radio. As Leno calls in, Miller steadfastly maintains the codes of terrestrial broadcasting. Every five minutes he reminds listeners, "We're talking to Jay Leno," in case they've just gotten in the car after a long day at the office. Of course, this being a podcast, literally no one has just tuned in ten minutes into the program. During the show Miller takes "callers," by playing a series of mostly flattering voicemails and discussing them with his crew. These choices are, no doubt, forces of habit. They are also, however, matters of "habitus," as the theorist Pierre Bourdieu might put it. They are markers of the "culturally and historically constituted values of the artistic field" of broadcast radio that create shortcuts to understanding for seasoned listeners.[12] There's nothing inherently conservative about taking callers, but doing so on a podcast quickly situates a listener in a comfortable place directly adjacent to America's most notably right-wing medium of AM radio. It turns an iPhone into a time machine.

The Leno episode's content is also straightforward in its backward gaze, even as the two old pros discuss current events. The pleasure comes from remembering the good old days when they ruled the stage and screen. Somehow, Miller and Leno agree that even tech superstar and Tesla founder Elon Musk, the very embodiment of twenty-first-century ambition, represents a rare vestige of a time gone by when people were still willing to "think big." They bemoan the technological successes of India and China, and Miller sighs that "it's unbelievable the way the world's gotten" in response to Jimmy Fallon apologizing for having once performed in blackface. Miller tells Leno that the two comedians "bail[ed] out" of the limelight just in time, as though their fading from the center of the comedy world was both recent and entirely of their own volition.

And, then, the real comedy begins, with Leno producing a rapid fire set of punchlines that goes back in time, bursts through the red bricks of 1980s comedy clubs, and lands squarely in the Catskills circa 1960. Evoking Rodney Dangerfield's Borscht Belt ratatat but without the Semitic sensibility, Leno offers what seems like dozens of one-liners about the

COVID-19 crisis. Much of the humor derives from stressing certain syllables (italicized here to indicate Leno's emphasis):

> "The whole world is upside down these days: I went to the bank and they called the cops on me [because] I *wasn't* wearing a mask."

> "I went to the doctor, he said turn your head and *don't* cough!"

Injecting some "take my wife, please" old school soft touch misogyny, he goes on:

> "This coronavirus can live up to three days on plastic, so if you're in Beverly Hills, don't touch the women!"

How bad is the economy?

> "It's so bad women in Beverly Hills are marrying for love."

> "There are polygamists with one wife."

> "Women in Beverly Hills are suntanning . . . in the sun!"

Some of the jokes are pretty good: Things are so dire

> "a funeral director committed suicide. He didn't want to, he just needed the business."

Others, unless you're a fan of Mike Huckabeean humor, are decidedly not good:

> "People say we have to control cow flatulence. I can't even control my own flatulence."

Throughout the riff session, Miller laughs and eggs Leno on, occasionally dipping into his HBO bag of tricks, noting that Joe Biden "is in the basement more than that chick in *The Silence of the Lambs*," a macabre joke that slams the Democratic then-nominee for his fear of dying in a pandemic and makes a movie reference that resonates with his aging baby boomer audience. When the mirth dies down, they transition to car talk, a favorite topic of Leno and the broader paleocomedy community.

Miller waxes nostalgic about his high school car, a 383 Roadrunner, and then smoothly transitions into an ad-read for the eye-bag tightening product Plexiderm. He notes the boomer-scourge of "Zoom meeting eyes" and attests that, after putting it on "I look just like me, only ten years younger."

He also sounds like himself, only ten years younger. And probably ten years older too, if we're being honest. On *DMO*, Miller fell into a comfortable pattern, keeping himself tied into but not tied down by the right-wing comedy complex through the use of a nostalgic, self-citational style of humor. When hot button issues came up, listeners could be confident that Miller would nod toward conservative opinion, excusing Donald Trump while mocking liberals, particularly women. The listener, however, could mostly just relax, reclining into the sounds of AM radio and the rhythms of old-school standup comedy.

It's those very rhythms of old-school standup that Miller invoked in the closing weeks of 2020, which would be the last of *The Dennis Miller Option*. In one of the *Option*'s final episodes, Miller takes a call from standup comic Bill Burr, perhaps the greatest prospect for the future of paleocomedy. Like Miller, Leno, and the soon-to-be-discussed Tim Allen, Burr is known for backwards-looking comedy and for thinking that things used to be a bit better than they are now. Burr's biggest success outside of standup has been the paleocomedic Netflix show *F Is for Family*, an animated sitcom about a working-class New England family set in the 1970s, with Burr voicing the Archie Bunker-esque patriarch.

Burr's appearance on *DMO* allows Miller to welcome the new guy into the shop, pass him a freshly cut cigar, and ask how his short game is these days. Their conversation begins with Burr describing his week hosting *Saturday Night Live*, during which he stirred up a mini-controversy by bemoaning "cancel culture" and suggested that white women had "hijacked the woke movement." He riffs with Miller about playing to socially distanced audiences in parked cars during the COVID-19 crisis and being able to tell how fun the show will be according to how many Priuses versus pickup trucks are there. Miller lavishes Burr with effusive laughs in the same manner he did with Leno, positioning the younger, Generation-X Burr as one of the inheritors of the paleocomedy tradition, now that boomers like Miller and Leno are driving off into the sunset.

As we'll see later in this chapter in examining the work of Tim Allen and his sitcom *Last Man Standing*, paleocomedy consistently expresses political contention through nostalgic longing for a time of falsely remembered consensus. It does so by positioning white patriarchal authority, be it Burr's cartoon dad or Miller's AM talk show host, as America's default political setting—a dynamic made abundantly clear by four years of the right longing to make America great again. To hear this perspective—jokingly!—expressed in the monologic form of podcasting to a small cluster of dedicated listeners is one thing. But when paleocomedy gently melds conservative positions and old-school standup into more traditional, mass appeal media forms, it creates an even more powerful invitation to aging conservatives to come in, escape the political chaos, and light a victory cigar. Sure, your kids might be bugging you about their pronouns or something called social justice, but your home's value increased 15 percent during the pandemic, so let's see what's on TV other than the news. Of course, there is no genre more prone to nostalgic comfort and conservative narrative than the television situation comedy. In the next section we consider how the domestic-set sitcom, or "domesticom," became the natural home for Tim Allen, star of FOX's *Last Man Standing*, and perhaps the most prolific purveyor of paleocomedy.

THE PALEO-POLITICS OF THE SITCOM

Not unlike the career of Dennis Miller, the sitcom itself began as a plucky stage performer willing to push a few boundaries. Whereas Miller grew up in front of the red bricks of The Improv in the 1980s, the sitcom got its start framed by the red velvet curtain of urban burlesque theaters in the early twentieth century. It was known at that point as vaudeville and, in parallel to Miller's more risqué HBO days, its appeal included some edge. In vaudeville, dancing girls, wild animal acts, and sexual innuendo played alongside character sketches and, it must be noted, a lot of racism and ethnic stereotyping. At first glance, this hardly seems a likely origin story for the domestic sitcom and all of its current, staid, overtones. However, the evolution of much commercial comedy involves the taming of vulgar performers and ideas in order to reach a stable audience. To move from

the anarchic vaudeville stage to the orderly confines of a network television schedule, comedy legends such as Jack Benny, George Burns, and
Gracie Allen honed and toned down their characters and recurring bits
from the stage, creating hit television shows in the process.[13] Eventually,
all sorts of outrageous comedians learned to listen to their accountants
and shape their humor to fit the basic parameters of the sitcom, including
predictable plots that always end where they begin. The sitcom's recurring scenarios provide comedians with stable settings to create familiar,
repeatable, and often sanitized stories that broadcast networks believe
ensure viewership. Over the decades, the genre has thus become a bedrock
for both conservative stories and television industry practices.

Scores of scholars have examined how the domestic settings of many
popular early sitcoms reflected the country's postwar suburbanization.
Often, the televisual representation of home life in domesticoms bolstered conservative worldviews on subjects like race, class, and gender.[14]
Shows like *Father Knows Best* presented an all-white world in which the
family patriarch settled the children's squabbles while his wife cheerfully
attended to cooking and cleaning. Popular domesticoms of the 1960s
and '70s like *I Dream of Jeannie* and *The Brady Bunch* blithely operated
with a sense of know-nothing-ness to the social upheaval around them.
Decades of such insular, formulaic programming created a popular consensus that the genre is "fundamentally a conservative form."[15] However,
as Jane Feuer argues, the idea of sitcoms as somehow inherently conservative relies on the genre's common depiction of the nuclear family, an "ideologically conservative social unit that supports the status quo of 'family
values.'"[16] It is not that sitcoms are incapable of representing progressive
values; some certainly do. However the genre's most frequent creative
choices—middle-class domestic settings, deference to white patriarchal
authority, subservient women characters—have repeatedly sought to keep
things just the way they are. Sitcoms needn't be conservative, but over
half a century of mostly conservative deployment of the form provides an
ideological baseline for paleocomedians like Tim Allen to evoke in shows
such as the '90s megahit *Home Improvement* and *Last Man Standing*.
Allen is another key player in the right-wing comedy complex that liberals
consider irrelevant in their bubble, but whose work has reached millions
of viewers and amplified important trends in the right-wing mediasphere.

Of course, liberal fans of the sitcom point to the "socially relevant" shows of Norman Lear and Mary Tyler Moore in the 1970s as evidence of the sitcom's progressive possibilities. The most notable of these was undoubtedly Lear's domesticom *All in the Family*, which frequently pit Archie Bunker's bigoted family patriarch character against the hippie liberalism of his son-in-law Michael, a.k.a. Meathead. Over the course of nine ratings-topping seasons, the two squared off over hot-button issues of the day like the Vietnam War, civil rights, and gender roles. Although it served as a televisual forum for then-young baby boomers to voice their countercultural critiques of the country, the conservative Archie proved to be just as popular with viewers. As television historian Aniko Bodrogh-kozy puts it, "Both hard hats and longhairs could find discursive room to maneuver" in the show, ultimately rendering its politics ambivalent.[17] So while today's liberals often celebrate *All in the Family*, the show also provides room for Tim Allen to be able to proudly compare his patriarch character in *Last Man Standing* to Archie Bunker.

As the media map began to expand in the 1980s and '90s, a variety of takes on the sitcom format emerged along a spectrum of cultural identities and political affiliations. *Family Ties* retreated to the conservative comforts of home in the Reagan '80s, while an explosion of Black cultural production on the FOX network in the 1990s generated transgressive hits like *Martin* and *Living Single*. Today, given the explosion of comedic TV programming, it is impossible to generalize about sitcom politics.[18] However, as media scholar Alfred L. Martin Jr. puts it, the sitcom brings with it an "understanding" of its audience that encourages writers and producers to stick to a certain set of contained, nostalgic, and politically conservative ideas.[19] Yes, they may take on a controversial topic or even offer a momentarily unorthodox take on a subject, but such aberrations tend to be swept quickly away to meet audience expectations and mollify advertisers.

Regardless of political content, the traditional sitcom form itself can create a sense of romanticized, white-washed domesticity via set design, camera work, or even a well-placed laugh track. This connection between conservative form and nostalgic affect is perhaps best illustrated in contrast. In the early 2000s, some producers sought to challenge the staid, "stable form of the genre"—its artificial studio settings, multi-camera shooting style, and "live" audience supplemented with that hoariest of

sitcom tropes, the laugh track.[20] Shows such as *Arrested Development,
The Office, Parks and Recreation,* and *Modern Family* invoked a realistic,
"verité" documentary style that flattered the sensibilities of presumed liberal viewers who had sat through a film class or two.[21] Laugh tracks were
out, the sly stares of Jim Halpert were in. And it's no accident that the
narratives of verité sitcoms trafficked in liberal sensibilities, whether root-
ing for a bright-eyed girlboss working in local government (Leslie Knope
from *Parks*) or an upper-middle-class gay couple longing for same-sex
marriage legalization (Cam and Mitch from *Modern Family*). To signal
their more progressive politics, these outlier sitcoms eschewed the staid
aesthetic markers of the traditional sitcom genre.

For Tim Allen and his most recent sitcom *Last Man Standing,* however,
staidness is a Huckabeean ideal, as is the traditionally old, laugh-tracked,
multi-camera domesticom format. *Last Man Standing* falls back on old-
school sitcom conventions, knowing that they both invoke the good old days
and suggest a safe space for viewers tired of being challenged by changing
cultural norms and mores. When *Last Man Standing* debuted in 2011 it
did so at the critical peak of verité sitcoms. The show proudly embraced
its lack of cool in the hopes of tapping into a more conservative viewership
than *Parks and Recreation* could ever aspire to. This would prove to be a
good bet, as the rise of Donald Trump a few years hence would serve to
emphasize the political and purchasing power of right-wing comedy audiences. As we note below, Tim Allen has been making—and winning—this
bet from his early standup days through to today's sitcom success.

TIM ALLEN FROM STANDUP TO *LAST MAN STANDING*

Tim Allen is the very best example of a paleocomedian whose work underscores the viability and reach of this form of conservative comedy. The
Last Man Standing star has been a fixture of American humor for several
decades, touring as a standup and regularly appearing onscreen in sitcoms and film comedies. He's also a fixture in the sense of an old house
appliance, planted firmly in the floor, refusing to budge even as the world
changes around him. An actor of limited range, Allen has long held to
a specifically masculine, conservative comedy style that equally fits the

narrative universes of domesticoms and nostalgic children's fare. If Dennis Miller's comedic persona is one of searching for his home in a rapidly changing political comedy landscape, Allen has stayed stuck in place, waiting for a newer version of the right-wing comedy complex to be built around him.

Allen's regressive aesthetic is perhaps best exemplified in an early standup bit that sets the tone for his future work. In the act, Allen describes his upbringing in a home with six brothers and how his mother would call them pigs. "She said, 'Don't even bother speaking, just grunt like the pigs you are.'" He then emits an aggressive, guttural grunt that sounds like an ape and swine battling for a banana in slop. The crowd roars with laughter. Of course, that grunt became the catchphrase for his Tim "The Tool Man" Taylor character on the hit ABC sitcom *Home Improvement*. Like Allen's family and the jokes in his standup, Taylor and his wife in *Home Improvement* have all boys. He juggles raising them with hosting duties on a successful cable show about, well, home improvement. Humor on the show frequently arises from benign domestic disputes (after his wife implores him not to, Tim intentionally breaks the dishwasher in order to make it more "manly") and sexual temptations (Tim's cable show is cohosted by a rotating cast of busty assistants played by the likes of Pamela Anderson). Although a conventional domesticom, *Home Improvement* was a kind of proto-paleocomedy celebrating traditional masculinity amid the culture wars of the '90s. The feel of the show is certainly conservative, but Allen wouldn't yet display any of the overt political inclinations that punctuate much of *Last Man Standing*.

All of Allen's projects have the feel of his famous primal grunt: a yelping attempt to corral and commodify a boy-man's understanding of what once was. There are the three *Santa Clause* movies, in which Allen embodies and reanimates a version of St. Nick straight out of a 1930s Coca-Cola ad. There is *Wild Hogs*, in which Allen's character joins three fellow midlife-crisising boomers on a cross-country motorcycle adventure in search of their lost virility. And of course, there are the *Toy Story* movies, the massively successful Pixar franchise that pathologically seeks to seize and embalm the innocence of youth. *Last Man Standing* represents the logical end of such a screen career, with Allen returning to ABC in 2011 to reclaim his lost not-quite-youth with another standard format domisticom.

In *Last Man Standing* Allen plays Mike Baxter, a reboot of sorts of his "Tool Man" character, but now an executive at a fictional sporting goods store, Outdoor Man. Instead of gleefully trading "UUUEEGGHH?!?!" grunts with his three *Home Improvement* sons, Allen's *Last Man* character argues with, scowls at, but eventually loves his three teenaged daughters and devoted wife. The characters are boiler-plate television women specifically designed to aggravate Mike: eldest daughter Kristin waits tables and raises her son Boyd with on-again off-again boyfriend Ryan; middle-child Mandy is vapid and girly; and youngest Eve is athletic but hard-headed. Mike's wife, Vanessa, smiles and takes it all in stride, when she's not working as a geologist and attending to the domestic labor. Overall, the Baxters create a dynamic in which contemporary political issues and cultural conflicts can always be resolved through standardized story arcs and the familiar invocation of sitcom families past.

In the opening scene of the show's pilot episode from 2011, Mike's family awaits his return home from a photoshoot in Alaska for Outdoor Man's catalog. He barges through the door with a huge fish—dinner!—and plops it on the kitchen table. "What am I supposed to do with this?" Vanessa wonders. You half expect Mike to reply with confused exasperation, or perhaps with Allen's signature grunt. Instead, he cheerily instructs her to slice the fish mouth to anus, kisses her, and trudges off-screen, grinning that it's "great to be back home." It's a throwaway line, but one that establishes the familiar, nostalgic comforts of home as the thematic, paleocomedic core of the series.

Mike's happiness to see his television family hints at Allen's joy at returning home to a primetime domesticom on ABC. The Baxter home anchors the show in a conservative safe space, shielding Mike and like-minded viewers from an increasingly complicated outside world and reasserting his man-of-the-house authority as the one to which all others defer. Beyond Allen and the show, the home metaphor takes on even more weight. It's not just *Last Man Standing*'s domestic setting that hails conservative viewers, then, but also its multi-camera, laugh-track format. The combination of these factors—*Last Man*'s traditionally domestic narrative arcs, its production style, and television industry commonsense about viewer tastes—reinforce the paleocomedic worldview of nostalgic, white, patriarchal, "father knows best"-ness. You might say that Allen and *Last*

Man Standing are the televisual embodiment of a deep-seated desire among a once culturally prominent male archetype to, yes, make America great again. While liberals' have directed much critical acclaim at hipper sitcoms like *Parks and Recreation* and *The Good Place*, Allen has felt right at home in the warm embrace of the genre's traditional production practices and storylines. As denizens of the right-wing comedy complex age out of the targeted audiences for the edgier right-wing comedy discussed later in this book, paleocomedians like Allen are there to remind them that they can always go home again.

LAST MAN STANDING MAKES THE SITCOM GREAT AGAIN

For much of its first season, *Last Man Standing* centers stories around inter- and intra-familial conflicts within the paleocomedic setting of the Baxters' suburban house and neighborhood. Again and again, the show creates conflict out of presenting Mike with some new (to him) social or cultural phenomenon, then allowing him to navigate it through the creature comforts of home. Not unlike Phil Hartman's "Unfrozen Caveman Lawyer" character on *Saturday Night Live*, Mike is equal parts terrified by the modern, politically correct world, and yet strangely adept at navigating it by relying on good old-fashioned masculine intuition. Mike's humor is steeped in exactly the nativist attitude that defines paleoconservatism as a political movement. He gripes that soccer is part of "Europe's covert war for the hearts and minds of America's kids." He takes grandson Boyd to daycare only to catch the class in the middle of "building a mosque out of pillows." Each storyline seems ripped from a culture war bit on *Watters' World* or *Gutfeld!* However, instead of an escalating series of outrages, *Last Man Standing* always cools things down by returning the story to Mike's castle, where there's nothing a good old family dinner can't solve. Just as paleoconservatism romanticizes hearth and home, paleocomedy finds relief and resolution among the three walls of the domesticom's kitchen stage set.

Even when he's got it completely wrong, patriarch Mike somehow gets it right. He is, of course, baffled by the internet, clinging to his store's old print catalog until declining sales force him online. When he relents, he records a vlog rant that, although ostensibly an ad for hunting gear, hits many of the get-off-my-lawn notes one might hear on *The Dennis Miller Option*. It even ends with a Jay Leno paleo-punchline:

> God. Who am I kidding? If you're watching this, you don't hunt. You're probably hunting for a tissue right about now, aren't you? And some girl at a soccer game where nobody can lose sprained your ankle! There's a guy named Jack Youngblood—played the Super Bowl with a broken leg! That's not fantasy! What the heck is fantasy football? I got a fantasy. Why don't you get off the frickin' couch, you morons? What happened to men? Men used to build cities just so we could burn 'em down. We got our hair cut by a guy named Hank. But modern man—what do you do? You run from stuff—responsibility, fatherhood. You can't even change a tire. A tire! [. . .] Why don't you get off the couch, you moron, and go outside?! You'll see something bright. It's called the sun. It's like a tanning bed, but it's free!

Mike is, like Mike Huckabee, both the butt of his own jokes and their purveyor. He is ridiculous but, in the conservative fantasy world of *Last Man Standing*, also victorious, having forced old jokes onto new media and gaining fans in the process. In doing so, Allen has proved the widespread appeal of paleocomedy and fortified its place as a key genre of conservative humor in the right-wing comedy complex.

Initially, press coverage characterized *Last Man Standing* as a "struggling comedy [that] failed to generate much buzz in its first season after getting off to a strong ratings start."[22] Overall, however, the show garnered a respectable 9.12 million total viewers, placing it in the top third of ratings for primetime network television shows that year.[23] Furthermore, the show delivered over 40 percent more total viewers than the shows occupying its timeslot on ABC the previous season, and the network renewed it for a second season.[24] Although not a critical darling like lauded liberal-courting sitcoms such as *Parks and Recreation* or *The Office*, *Last Man Standing* provided ABC with a reliable landing spot for the older, conservative viewers who remain a part of broadcast networks' audience coalitions.

In the 2012–13 season, *Last Man Standing* moved to Friday night, the least watched weeknight of television, but one associated with classic ABC domesticoms like *Family Matters* and *Step by Step*. Allen's strategy, as evidenced by his public statements, was to emphasize his show's political valence by overtly, if self-flatteringly, comparing Mike Baxter to Archie Bunker: "When didn't you talk about what Archie Bunker said?"[25] Allen's goal going into the second season seemed to be to make Mike Baxter's opinions more pointed, banking on the fact that conservatives were, in fact, increasingly looking to make comedy part of their media diet.

The show's second season premiere, "Voting," wastes no time in hailing right-wing viewers, opening on a shot of the Baxter's lawn covered in "Mitt Romney for President" signs. When Mike confronts his liberal daughter Kirstin about the Obama sign she placed on his lawn, she sarcastically says she thought he liked things "fair and balanced," a reference to the now-discarded slogan for the hilariously partisan Fox News. Wife Vanessa intermittently intervenes with self-deprecating jokes about how she keeps her vote private—the doting domesticom spouse certainly doesn't want to disrupt dinner with her political opinions. Kristin's boyfriend Ryan enters and immediately takes on the Meathead role—Archie Bunker's hippie son-in-law—grazing on Mike's hard-earned grub and defending Obama. Democrats like Ryan, Mike argues, want to take his money and "throw gay weddings for illegal aliens."

Later, after Mike sings the virtues of using land ownership as a requirement to vote, he rants in a vlog that George Washington and Thomas Jefferson got it right: "We didn't call them the founders. We call them the founding *fathers*. Because we respected fathers. Now nobody listens to fathers." Again, Mike works the conflicts of the outside world through the narrow frame of patriarchal authority and domestic amity. The episode closes with his daughters voting for Obama, but Mike concedes that he's proud to have raised two strong, independent women whom he's happy to drive to the polling place in his "vehicle that gets four miles a gallon." This veer directly into electoral politics served as a clear signal to audiences where Mike and the show would stand in subsequent seasons. Future episodes tend toward more subtle, but no less political territory, with racial and other social conflicts resolved by the easy embrace of orderly, patriarchal domesticity and a little bit of car talk. Storylines like these neatly align with conservative audiences' presumed tastes while operating just out of view of liberals, providing light-hearted comedic relief for right-wing comedy complex denizens increasingly ignored by hipper sitcoms' pandering to trend-setting liberals.

RACE CARS AND THE CONSERVATIVE
TROPES OF PALEOCOMEDY

Cars hold a special symbolic value in many paleocomedies. *Last Man Standing* is infatuated with cars. Particularly old, loud, impractical cars that aren't any fun for anyone but the driver. This makes sense, as paleo-comedians have long loved cars as symbols of patriarchal authority. Dennis Miller, of course, spent his early years playing up his erudition and literary acumen. During his career's paleocomedic third act in *The Dennis Miller Option*, however, Miller often longs wistfully for the muscle cars of yore and spends hours talking to the high priests of the paleocomedic gearhead subculture. The comedian Adam Carolla, for instance, always began his visits with Miller with a series of light, funny jabs at the libs, before touting his business producing dramatic car-racing films such as *The 24 Hour War* and *Winning: The Racing Life of Paul Newman*. These films aren't funny and yet, through the demographic affinities between paleocomedy and car culture, they pair seamlessly with Carolla's conservative brand of humor. Jay Leno, as noted above, pulls the same trick on *The Dennis Miller Option*, unleashing a torrent of anachronistic one-liners before eventually revealing his true purpose: promoting the streaming show *Jay Leno's Garage*, in which the multimillionaire comic simply shows off his collection.

Tim Allen is also a car guy. In *Last Man Standing*, he uses automotive comedy to craft jokes, complete narratives and, above all, avoid the more difficult aspects of contemporary American life. Cars in *Last Man Standing* represent a romanticized patriarchal past in which the conservative cultural capital of cars smooths over pesky issues like prejudice, racism, and systemic inequality. They also serve as a winking opportunity to reassert the centrality of whiteness in the show's universe. Car jokes subtly alienate and mock Black characters before quickly retreating into safe "just a joke" territory.

For example, Mike Baxter refers to his Black neighbors, Chuck and Carol Larabee, as "the Tahoes" next door, in reference to the giant Chevy SUVs in their driveway. This is a laugh line, and probably for more than one reason. Ostensibly, it is a reference to Mike's car obsession. There is also a class component, as a Tahoe is an expensive vehicle that Mike clearly approves of. At a somewhat deeper level, it jokingly suggests that Mike doesn't see race, evoking the outmoded colorblind discourse that took hold among conservatives and well-meaning liberals alike after Obama's election. And then, perhaps buried in the subconscious of the writers and laughers, is the fact that *Tahoes* rhymes with an anachronistic, racist term for Black Americans. In any case, the rhetorical flourish of referring to minority residents of a white neighborhood as "The _____s" winks at a time of open redlining and racial prejudice. In *Last Man Standing*'s paleo-comedy, these meanings all swirl together, giving plausible deniability of racism as viewers enjoy problematic pleasures.

Even when it isn't directly dealing with race through the metaphor of cars, *Last Man Standing* is a good illustration of how paleocomedy brushes off larger cultural and social issues in America. Allen's comedy targets an audience seeking an excuse to turn away from liberal social justice activism and identity politics. For example, in the episode "High Expectations" from season two introducing the new Black neighbors, the Larabees, the plot initially creates space for soft-core political incorrect-ness. After Mike's wife Vanessa frets that recent neighborhood vandalism might be targeting the newly moved-in Larabees, she invites them over for a happy hour. Mike—true to his newfound Archie Bunker form—dismisses her concern: "Vandalism happens to everybody, guys. Why is it if you're black, or gay, or a midget you think stuff happens to you just because you're black, or you're gay, or you're a midget?" Again invoking the now commonplace practice on the right of minimizing cultural iden-tities, Mike claims not to see the Larabees' race and continues to make clumsy race jokes. When the Larabees gift the Baxters a large, cylindrical object wrapped in a paper bag, Mike worries that it's a bottle of malt liquor (it's a candle). Chuck senses Mike's uneasiness and playfully tricks him into thinking his son excels at water polo. Hey, Mike's face reads, Black folks aren't supposed to be good swimmers! Just kidding, Chuck reassures him, his son is actually a great basketball player. Their happy hour ends with humorous acknowledgment and release of racial tension through a (weirdly violent) retreat to their shared class symbols—their homes:

MIKE: I'll tell you right now, if your house was on fire, I would call the fire department.

CHUCK: And if someone was breaking into your house, I'd call the police. Except if it's a white guy. Then you go ahead and shoot him.

MIKE: Yeah, but what are the odds?

As this exchange illustrates, the episode leaves the complexities of racial identity just outside the Baxters' front door, something that, in this house, we don't need to get all worked up talking about. This dynamic is visible in other episodes as well—in "Voting," the season's opening episode, for instance, one of the storylines suggests that political conflict can simply be resolved through family loyalty. In this way, *Last Man Standing* longs for a time when father knew best and when neighbors were just neighbors, before they were racially marked people who might dare to put up a Black Lives Matter yard sign. In fact, once the happy hour begins, there is no mention of the potentially racially motivated vandalism. In a generous reading, this plot convenience functions in the name of racial harmony. In the context of the domesticom's history of privileging white patriarchal authority, however, it has the effect of flattening any salient differences between the families and erasing the Larabees' uniquely raced experiences. It doesn't matter if or how the Larabees might have overcome structural disadvantages like redlining or racist policing in their ascent to the upper-middle class. They have snot nosed kids, a nice house, and, most importantly, a giant SUV in the driveway.

Of course, when the show inevitably invites viewers behind the wheel again, there's an appearance from Jay Leno. In the season five episode "The Road Less Driven," Leno guests as Joe, a gearhead who can't fully let go of a classic car after selling it to Mike. When Mike brings Chuck Larabee to Joe's garage, Chuck introduces himself saying he "paid his way through college" working in an auto shop. "You mean a chop shop?" Leno's Joe retorts, in a bit of brazen racist stereotyping punctuated by a laugh track. By the end of the episode, however, everything drives smoothly. The men reminisce about the cars from their youth, framed in a wide shot of Joe's tricked out garage. Again, *Last Man Standing* subsumes any potential racial tension through its male characters' lusting for the symbols of their youthful vibrancy. Cars evoke an era in which the systematic aspects of racism were absent from debates about the class mobility that would provide someone the ability to buy a car or go to college. If a Black man

Paleocomedians Tim Allen and Jay Leno long for the cars and politics of their youth in the FOX sitcom *Last Man Standing*. (FOX)

like Chuck could work (on cars!) up to the middle, then upper-middle class, why should *Last Man Standing*'s viewers be concerned with the complications of the millions of Black people who did not? Instead, the show offers a comforting retreat to right-wing comedy complex visitors who want a light-hearted chuckle unburdened by the increasingly visible rifts in contemporary American race relations.

Last Man Standing additionally shows how paleocomedy can directly incorporate some of the uglier aspects of paleoconservative philosophy. For example, depictions of immigration on the show often have strong parallels with nativist, anti-immigrant paleoconservatism, highlighting the domestic setting as a safe space for anti-immigrant jokes. In one episode, for example, Mike is offended that his grandson Boyd is learning Spanish in school. And although the show does not take a strictly hostile approach to immigrants, *Last Man Standing* presages a Trumpian immigration policy that frames "good" migrants as ones who patiently, gratefully work through a system designed to keep them out, while "bad" ones seek shortcuts and threaten domestic stability. In the season two episode, "The Help," for instance, the Baxters hire Guatemalan migrant Blanca ("White" in Spanish, perhaps not coincidentally) to help with cooking and

Last Man Standing portrays nonwhite characters as subservient to white ones, creating moments of paleocomedy when Tim Allen must wait on his Black neighbor and Latina maid. (FOX)

cleaning. Blanca loves working for "Mr. Mike," fetching him a frosted mug of beer and fending off the annoying requests of his daughters. Blanca is so good at her job that it makes Vanessa insecure, so she insists on vacuuming while Blanca takes a break to enjoy tea with Carol Larabee. In a perfect bit of timing that seems only to exist in the alternate universes of sitcoms, Mike walks in to find his wife doing housework, while his Latina maid and Black neighbor relax in his living room. This raced incursion into Mike's property is, ultimately, OK. Carol Larabee already shares the Baxters' class status—she is a Tahoe, after all. Blanca is a "good" migrant who has her green card and whose labor supports the greater good of a smoothly functioning Baxter household. The scene's central paleocomedic premise is Blanca play-acting at upper-middle-class leisure time while Vanessa vacuums instead.

This episode also illustrates how paleocomedy collapses neoliberal markers of the present—employers disingenuously treating wage laborers as "family"—with paleo-longings for the past, a time when men identified as providers, not ethnically marked subjects. The episode discussed above, "The Help," clumsily contrasts Blanca's experience as a legally employed domestic worker with that of JJ, an undocumented Latino migrant who works at Mike's store, Outdoor Man. Inspired by Blanca's happy servitude, Mike decides to make sure that the other Latino workers at Outdoor Man are there legally. He discovers that all are except JJ, whom he unceremoniously fires, despite lamenting that he's "practically part of our family." JJ cheerfully accepts his fate and informs Mike that he's taken a dishwashing job elsewhere because "It's honest work. I do what I do for my family." Inspired by JJ's invocation of this paleoconservative trope of Family First, Mike notes that "illegal aliens" can stay in the country "under sponsorship if they're vital" to a business. JJ, however, isn't apparently all that vital, and he disappears for the rest of the episode. Since the character of JJ is undocumented, it is fitting that—despite Mike's characterization of him as "family"—JJ is never able to ingratiate himself into the Baxter home the way Blanca does. Ultimately, the episode depicts how JJ's legal status and subsequent firing underscore the fact that for Mike, family is a legal construct, one which centers his own patriarchal authority. In the end, Mike embraces his role as legal defender, firing JJ, while also gazing metaphorically backward to a time when migrants labored quietly and cheerfully in the service of the Mike Baxters of the world.

LAST MAN STANDING FINDS A HOME IN THE RIGHT-WING COMEDY COMPLEX

For six seasons, Last Man Standing threaded a needle for ABC. Its ratings were solid and it courted viewers yearning to see overt conservative representation on their TV screens without flipping to Fox News. Then came Trump's election in 2016. Widespread, intense opposition to the president shifted the political climate in which television network executives operated. Press reports hinted that Allen was increasingly angry about network censorship whenever his character tried "to go after liberal icons."[26] Furthermore, during this stretch, ABC's parent company, Disney, was spending heavily on other media properties to add to its content library in advance of launching its Disney+ streaming service late in 2019. Last Man Standing was a successful show, but a tough fit for a brand hoping to skew younger and go digital.

Allen drove this point home all too forcefully when he went on ABC's *Jimmy Kimmel Live!* in March—a mere three months into the Trump presidency—and said that being a Republican in Hollywood is "like 1930s Germany. You gotta be real careful around here, you know. You'll get beat up if you don't believe what everybody believes."[27] Such language was jarring, perhaps shocking, in the center-left space of *Kimmel*. It sounded much more like, perhaps, a segment Dennis Miller might offer on *Hannity* or *Gutfeld!* Luckily for Allen, by 2016 FOX had begun to appreciate the ways in which comedy could enhance the interplay between their main broadcast network and Fox News. When ABC officially cut ties with *Last Man Standing*, FOX picked up Allen's show, plugged it into their Friday-night schedule, and promoted it aggressively. Allen began showing up all over the Fox News schedule, promoting the show and serving as a cultural pundit. The show's September 2018 premiere earned 8.13 million viewers, "FOX's most-watched Friday telecast in 18 years" and *Last Man Standing*'s highest season premiere mark since its very first episode.[28] As the show opens, Mike addresses the camera in perfect paleo fashion: "No matter how long you haven't seen me, I'm still the same old guy."

Though perhaps counterintuitive, Allen's move to the FOX broadcast network encouraged the show to tone down some of its more aggressive and offensive rhetoric. When Allen shot his last ABC episode in the summer of 2016, few could have envisioned the election results that were around the corner. By the time he began shooting with FOX in 2018, Trump was entrenched in power. With his guy in the White House and a steady flow of conservative viewers coming from the Fox News big box store to his paleocomedy cigar shop, Allen comfortably sank into the leather couch and lit a victory smoke. In the run up to *Last Man Standing*'s FOX debut in the fall of 2018, Allen began to distance himself and the show from any explicit connection to conservative ideology: "It's *not* a political show. I encourage the people who say I'm some closeted Hollywood conservative to forget about Tim Allen and what his politics are."[29] Instead, the FOX run of *Last Man Standing* ditched the loud, liberal-baiting jokes in order to focus on Allen's comfortable, domestic dominion over the traditional family home. With many conservatives already aware of Allen's politics, there was no need to over-signal them in the show itself and alienate more moderate audience members.

In the show's 2018 season premiere, "Welcome Baxter," Mike tries to tune out the political infighting in his house when his daughters scream that, politically, "there is no middle anymore!" There is little mention of Trump himself, and although it's clear who Mike voted for in 2016, he waxes nostalgic about "the good old days when we were all on the same page." This rhetorical tack is a savvy move by the show, one that establishes soft-focus nostalgia as its defining characteristic, leaving the harder edges of racist nationalism to corporate sister channel Fox News. At the same time, however, *Last Man Standing*'s MAGA-ian longing for the past normalizes Trump's extremism by equating it with any other political position of the moment. You can't fix the big, political messes of the present, the show suggests, and the best way to preserve the status quo is by preventing friends and family from venturing too far off into an unknown future.

As the Baxters' political infighting reaches a boiling point, daughter Kristin and son-in-law Ryan burst into the living room to inform every-one that Mike's grandson Boyd has gone missing. In a delightfully paleo-comedic touch, the family scrambles to check for Boyd in kid hideouts drawn straight out of a 1980s PG-rated comedy—the arcade, comic book store, etc.[30] It turns out that Mike and Boyd have been secretly fixing up a dirt bike together against his parents' wishes, and he's stolen away to the Outdoor Man store to spend time alone with the bike. Suspecting this, Mike finds Boyd and chides him for running away. Boyd, with the most doe-eyed, heart-string-tugging line reading in the show's history, tells his grandfather that he "just wanted a quiet place to think [because] every-body's fighting about everything." Mike then launches into a cringe-worthy parable about how no one wanted the busted old dirt bike, but "We saw something worth saving, and we were willing to do the work together to fix it." The episode ends with Mike giving a speech to his family that boils down to the kind of "agree to disagree, but do it respectfully" sentiment that grandparents around the country have invoked for ages when all they want is the kids to quiet down for a bit. No one's political concerns have been addressed in any meaningful way, but Mike's home has returned to a pre-Trump, pre-Obama, pre-*all of this* status quo for the moment. With Trump in power at the time and Fox News on his side, Allen could win simply by avoiding the argument altogether.

THE LIMITS OF PALEOCOMEDY

Paleocomedy is at its funniest, and least dangerous, when it remains bounded in conservative spaces that are committed to polite, if still anti-progressive, decorum. There is, for example, Rob Long, a former show-runner for the hit sitcom *Cheers*, who operates the right-leaning podcast platform Ricochet. On one Ricochet show, *GLoP Culture*, Long is joined by fellow right-wing voices Jonah Goldberg and John Podhoretz. They are lions of pre-Trump conservative thought, noted in their world for jocularity and wit alongside traditional conservative positions in support of small government and outsized military spending. The jokes on *GLoP Culture* are meant to feature a little spice, but in the way of an old school standup comedian like Dennis Miller, as opposed to a modern-day edgelord troll. Racial minorities, women, and the libs don't need to be targeted or triggered, because in this cigar shop, they just don't exist. It's a group of old guys leaning back, smoking a stogie, and remembering how funny Bill Murray was before he got all serious. *GLoP Culture* is conservative comedy built around a culture that is indifferent to conservatism's lack of diversity. At the same time, the podcast does not stray too far from basic bourgeois social mores. It is paleo because it harkens back to the days of elite consensus, in which high-ranking liberals and conservatives spent far less time performing ideological differences and more time attending each other's cocktail parties.

Paleocomedy is, however, rarely so neatly contained. ABC learned this lesson all too well when, despite its misgivings with Allen and *Last Man Standing*, the network attempted to reach back to the early 1990s and revive the long-retired hit sitcom, *Roseanne*, in 2017. On paper, the move was inspired. The election of Trump in 2016 foregrounded all too well the cultural and commercial power embedded within working class, white America. If they can stuff the ballot box, this thinking goes, then they can also draw advertiser interest. *Roseanne* promised to address just this crowd, while harkening back to an era of imagined broader public consensus and reduced political polarization. Of course, the show's star, Roseanne Barr, had always been a controversial figure. She was not necessarily perceived as divisive, however. Yes, her singular persona was best known for an iconoclastic streak, and she had spent the previous decade touting conspiracy theories often laced with right-wing ideology on Twitter. But at the same time, Barr represented a certain sort of feminist rebellion, harnessing the power of what scholar Kathleen Rowe describes as "disruptive," "unruly," femininity.[31] Her reemergence was intended to reconvene the days of big-tent television by taking working-class domestic conflicts and resolving them through stories of family consensus. Ideally, Trump-supporting conservatives would be intrigued by Barr's cantankerous online persona, more liberal viewers would remember her as a boundary-breaking woman, and all would be lulled into long-term viewership through the comforts of old-school sitcom stories and aesthetics.

It nearly worked. The reboot was heavily touted as a show that voiced the concerns "of the white exurban Trump voter."[32] The first episode takes pages straight out of the middle-season *Last Man Standing* playbook, introducing hot-button political issues before offering the cooling bath of domestic resolution. Like *Last Man Standing*, *Roseanne*'s revival premiere plays politics explicitly and ham-fistedly. There is little plot to speak of, just characters invoking ripped-from-the-headlines talking points to provoke one another. "What's up, deplorable?" Roseanne's sister Jackie says to her while donning a pink knit hat and "nasty woman" shirt—all references to Hillary Clinton's losing presidential bid to Trump in 2016. The sisters butt heads over politics, gender fluidity, and economic hardship until eventually—like any good paleocomedy—they express longing for a bygone era of happiness based in familial stability. In theory, the show presented both sides of a political fight, but reaffirmed the lesson that Trump—like births, weddings, and funerals—was simply a thing that happened, eventually to be tucked away in the family's box of faded polaroid memories.

The results were, from a financial standpoint, stellar, as the *Roseanne* reboot premiere scored over eighteen million viewers in late March 2018 and made countless headlines in the process. Subsequent episodes of the revival season found similar success, with episodes using traditional sitcom plotting to make comfortable the severe political tensions arising throughout the Trump presidency. This romantic consensus was, however, false. Unlike the guys at the *GLoP Culture* podcast, Barr was not a true paleocomic. Although her show emphasized detente, Barr's Twitter feed kept on fighting Trump's online war. The last straw came in May of

2018 when Barr tweeted an explicitly racist remark about former Obama advisor Valerie Jarrett. The comment, which received vast media coverage, laid bare the thin layer of old-timey, domestic consensus-laden paleocomedy around which the new *Roseanne* was ostensibly built. By making her racism explicit, Barr exposed not only herself, but also the nastier elements embedded in her show's reboot as it refused to pass moral judgment on Trumpist policy and rhetoric. ABC fired Roseanne and rebranded the show *The Conners*, keeping some part of the audience but losing what was, briefly, a profit-driving cultural phenomenon.

The fundamental problem with paleocomedy is that the past is, of course, not even past. There are real, nostalgic pleasures in Dennis Miller rehashing old comedy bits and making podcasts that sound like drive-time radio. The sitcom format, particularly when it indulges its most conventional conventions, can be fun and funny in the same way a worn-out blanket feels good to the skin even when it can't provide much warmth. But today, there is little audience for a version of Dennis Miller who keeps the old school aesthetic but skips the reactionary politics. Instead, he shows up on *Hannity* and chums the water with whatever Fox News is serving up that day. Tim Allen tells old fashioned stories, but laces them with racist innuendo and ensures through his other media appearances that many viewers see his show as a rebuke to those with more contemporary moral concerns. And Roseanne, well, eventually just came out and said the quiet part out loud, exposing the underlying ideas that were propelling some of her show's success.

Ultimately, a closer consideration of paleocomedy reveals how raced, classed, and gendered power structures have long been with us and persist today. To invoke the cultural scholar George Lipsitz's description of televisual nostalgia, paleocomedy uses "the experiences of the past to lend legitimacy to the dominant ideology of the present."[33] When Trump implores supporters to Make America Great Again, or Huckabee knowingly tweets a dad-joke pun straight out of the good old days, they do so to invoke not the actual lived experiences of mid-century America, but the whitewashed televisual representations of that time. Of course, believing that life before *all of this* was all *Father Knows Best* is a fool's errand. You can't go home again, and you certainly can't go home to a place that only existed in the fictional confines of a sitcom. And yet, Tim Allen and Dennis Miller prove that the ideologies espoused by paleocomedy do have a home in the present day, with some support from neighboring storefronts in the right-wing comedy complex. Those of us passing by are left with that strange, atemporal feeling of trying to understand jokes and references that are two and three generations removed, akin to a present-day teenager watching a movie from the '80s about the '50s like *Back to the Future*. But for those comfortably relaxing in the exclusive confines of paleocomedy's old white men's club, right-wing ideology continues to fill the air like so much cigar smoke and half-remembered *Caddyshack* quotations.

3 Religio-Rational Satire

OWNING THE LIBS ONE FAULTY
SYLLOGISM AT A TIME

WARNING TO LIBERAL READERS: Please, for the sake of your fragile, snowflake, special selves, skip the introduction to this chapter unless you want to be OWNED!!!!!

Right-wing media star Ben Shapiro is a staunch conservative. As such, he is committed to private property rights—he loves owning things. For example, in 2019 his website, *The Daily Wire*, posted a ten-minute super-cut of Shapiro "owning SJWs [social justice warriors] and Liberals" with facts and logic.[1] It begins with him owning the transgender reporter Zoey Tur by deploying his catchphrase, "Facts don't care about your feelings," and then going on about X and Y chromosomes for a while. It ends with Shapiro responding to a group of college student protestors by writing "Morons" on a chalkboard.[2] Fade to black. Owned.

To be fair, Shapiro doesn't just own people and things with his arguments. Sometimes he DESTROYS them. For example, on YouTube you can find Shapiro destroying: Hillary Clinton, transgenderism, the minimum wage, Piers Morgan, Karl Marx, Every College Snowflake, institutional racism, climate change, Rachel Maddow, Black Lives Matter, John Oliver, and "leftists FOR ALL ETERNITY," which should save him some time, if you think about it. Each discursive destruction or act of ownership follows a certain formula. He begins with assertions that often derive from his traditional (and in his case, Jewish) religious beliefs regarding definitions of life, basic moral principles and, yes, property. He then moves into debate club mode, deriding his opponents and steering them toward his conclusion with carefully selected facts and figures. In doing so, Shapiro crafts a unique form of political entertainment that merges the fiery passion of a religious believer with a Vulcan logical affect.[3] The result has been tens of millions of viewers and listeners, a key place in conservative culture, and a surprisingly important role in the right-wing comedy complex.

Shapiro does not call himself a comedian, instead relying on his oft-mentioned Harvard Law degree to add gravitas to his more or less conventional political punditry. He is, however, a vocal proponent of conservative humor, wading into cultural debates surrounding comedy and promoting right-wing satire on his platforms. In 2017, for example, he posted to *The Daily Wire* a highly controversial video that was a representative example of contemporary right-wing satire. The video in question is a very bad history lesson that uses an animated narrative to depict Native Americans as furious savages who were saved by the arrival of Christopher Columbus. It begins with a title card setting the scene: "The Americas, before Columbus c. 1491." A light drum beat, meant to evoke Native American rhythms, fills the soundtrack. The image then cuts to a crudely drawn Native American family sitting by a campfire, gentle evergreens and snow-capped mountains lining the background. A Native American boy runs in, carrying a flower, denoting the romanticism about peaceful pre-Columbian American life that the video's creators ascribe to liberals. A caption sardonically reads "The North American Indigenous people are a noble people." A second later, warriors in feathered headdresses decapitate the boy and shoot an arrow through a mother as she holds a baby, her black eyes converting to cartoon Xs. A visage of the liberal Democratic Senator Elizabeth Warren, who controversially claims Native American heritage, pops up to cheer the violence on. Then, in close-up, one of the warriors takes a bloody bite out of the dead boy's leg, exuding a satisfied "mmm" sound as he chomps.

At this point, a map pops up, depicting Columbus's voyage across the Atlantic. He lands in the Caribbean, which is historically correct but

Ben Shapiro's and *The Daily Wire*'s racist Columbus Day video depicts Native Americans as violent savages before the arrival of Europeans. (*The Daily Wire*)

contextually confusing, as the explorer jumps off his boat, gives a handsome smile, and enters the previous scene, snow-capped mountains and all. He then single-handedly teaches the surviving Native American family members about agriculture, construction, and animal husbandry, receiving adoring oohs and ahhs in response. The story then accelerates to the present day, showing a modern city complete with cars, planes, and rocket ships. It ends with a chart of facetiously framed "accomplishments." Under "Pre-Columbus" it lists "Dreamcatchers," "Tomahawks," and "Cannibalism." The "After-Columbus" column scrolls quickly, running down a potpourri of modern marvels ranging from "Mathematics" to "Women's Suffrage" to "Velcro" to "Not-Scalping." It ends with text reading "Happy Indigenous People's Day!" The ironic exclamation underscores the satiric argument that has just unfolded over the video's interminable forty-seven seconds.

Shapiro didn't produce this video, but as *The Daily Wire*'s chief editor, he let it stay up for a full day, first defending it before eventually admitting that it "engaged in broad-based stereotyping" and "skipped over the grave injustices visited upon Native Americans."[4] This vague, tellingly passive-voiced semi-apology underscores the ambivalence with which Shapiro approached the video. It, or at least the response to it, did cross a line for him. But just barely, and only after it accrued thousands of hits and significantly raised *The Daily Wire*'s brand recognition across the political social media spectrum.

The Columbus Day video, in fact, played a key role in one of Shapiro's main political projects: claiming that comedy has died on the left and is ascendant on the right. He made this point explicitly in an hour-long *Daily Wire* special, *No One's Laughing: Cancel Culture Is Killing Comedy*.[5] In the special, right-wing comedy complex all-stars Greg Gutfeld, Dennis Miller, Joe Rogan, Adam Carolla, and Steven Crowder (whom we discuss in this chapter) argue that liberal comedians have become political panderers while conservatives do the real work of getting laughs. The Columbus Day video, for Shapiro, was therefore an opportunity to make his point in a concrete, if not terribly convincing way. Before making his non-apology and reversing course by taking the video down, Shapiro defended it by noting that "conservatives are allowed to make satire, too."[6] With this statement, Shapiro, armed with the meagerest of counterexamples, took aim at the liberal psychological complex that encourages left-leaning media consumers to assume that satire belongs only to them. To be sure, the Columbus Day video is both racist and comically inept. But it is, just as certainly, ideologically right-wing, satirically ironic, and existent. For years, center-left media dominated the world of comedy, while right-wing outlets such as *National Review* embraced the staid, lucrative approach of dry, erudite conservatism. Shapiro's project today is to keep the audience for the latter while using just enough of the former to create a bigger, younger, more digital-friendly audience. *The Daily Wire*'s tagline is "hard-hitting, irreverent news and commentary" for "a new generation of conservatives." The Columbus Day video attempts just this, putting ostensibly comic, undeniably racist, material in an incendiary satirical mode of address that Shapiro claims those politically correct liberals are too afraid to try.

The Daily Wire's Columbus Day video represents a notable example of what we call "religio-rational satire," a form of right-wing comedy using purportedly rational arguments based on questionable, often religiously inspired facts to "own" liberals with reason. In this case, conservative laughter is supposed to emerge from the video's spotlighting of liberal hypocrites who say they love peace and women's rights but would still rather celebrate patriarchal Indigenous cannibals over the Christian,

God-fearing Columbus. Never mind, of course, that Columbus's arrival would lead to immense suffering and genocide among Native populations, or that it would take centuries for anything even approaching gender equality to develop in the West.

The Columbus Day video starts with the religious principle that the Christian West is fundamentally civilized in a way that other cultures are not. While the video does not assert this claim directly, it is this faith-based assumption that allows a sympathetic viewer to ignore what should be the bald-faced nonsense of Columbus as a peacemaker. From there, the video employs the cringeworthy argumentation of a high school debate club, using a certain sophomoric, bullying progression of logic to prove its case. "Isn't it true that Native Americans fought wars before Columbus came?" and "Isn't it true that now Native Americans don't fight wars and that we have rocket ships?" and "Isn't it true that you, a liberal, are anti-war and are more or less pro-rocket ship, other things being equal?" Well, yes, right? Oh, lookie what we have here. Seems like someone just got OWNED!

RELIGIO-RATIONAL SATIRE'S CULTURE WAR CONSERVATISM

Religio-rational satire is, we argue, the main product for sale at the right-wing comedy complex's religious bookstore. In addition to the Columbus Day video, this form of comedic address is also the basis for the comedy of major right-wing media figures such as Steven Crowder and the influential conservative satire site *The Babylon Bee*. As we discuss in this chapter, this form of comedy starts with religious ideas, and then mobilizes those ideas into comedy that mocks liberals by owning them in an ersatz debate. To some readers, this combination of religion and reason may appear itself ironic, and perhaps even contradictory. After all, so much of the liberal tradition involves separating the realm of faith from the purview of science. Religio-rational satire, however, takes its cue from long-standing right-wing political traditions. American conservatism has often taken a much more synthetic approach to faith and reason, whereby revealed religious truths are used as building blocks for ornate forms of political argumentation.

In addition to his podcasts and social media videos, Ben Shapiro has written several books that illustrate this melding of faith and reason, emphasizing his knowledge of and commitment to biblically inspired morality. For example, in his 2019 book, *The Right Side of History: How Reason and Moral Purpose Made the West Great*, Shapiro devotes several pages to explaining how the "self-evident" rights spelled out in the Declaration of Independence owe their genesis to Hebrew scripture.[7] Not coincidentally, this combination of faith and reason informs much of right-wing intellectual history. For example, George W. Bush–era neoconservatism took to the philosophy of Leo Strauss, whose "Athens and Jerusalem" thesis argued that "Western man became what he is . . . through the coming together of biblical faith and Greek" rational thought.[8] The neocons used this thinking to argue that individual, natural rights and liberties should be defended with an "aggressive position toward any global forces which threaten" them, including, of course, the perceived threat of an Iraqi attack on America and its interests.[9] In 2003, in the run-up to the second Iraq War, the neocons mounted fierce, verbal assaults against those who disagreed with their arguments for invading Iraq, using questionable facts meant to be taken on unearned faith, to try to make their case. From the neocons' perspective, it seems, like minded Americans were a fleet of modern Columbuses, armed with righteous wisdom as they sailed off to faraway lands. The infamous result of neocons' efforts, however, was the horribly botched invasion of Iraq, an atrocity ostensibly enacted as a logical means of spreading the gospel of free markets and free elections to the unenlightened parts of the globe.

Neoconservatism may be going out of style even on the right these days, but Shapiro is himself of this lineage, and his religio-rational satire plays a crucial role in fusing together yesterday's Iraq war supporters with today's newer generation coming of age in the Trump-inflected Republican party. Shapiro is, of course, a post-Iraq millennial neocon, born in 1984. Bush-style neoconservatism was largely discredited before Shapiro could legally hoist a toast to Dick Cheney. He has aimed his religio-rational, Athens and Jerusalem instincts down a more insular and, it turns out, lucrative path. For figures like Shapiro, the new battleground has been that of American popular culture. Driven by his mentor Andrew Breitbart's famous slogan, "politics is downstream from culture," Shapiro has refitted neoconservative instincts toward the domain of new media.[10] He creates entertainment that includes political ideas, but he spends just as much time trying to look fun, funny, and smart to younger right-wing audiences. He doesn't advocate for imperialist adventurism underpinned by faith-based arguments with severely racist overtones. But he does post animated videos about them, evidently. He couldn't invade Iraq with the 173rd Airborne, but he succeeded in occupying thousands of Twitter feeds with a cartoon *Santa Maria*. In the contemporary culture war, jokes like those in the Columbus Day video are, yes, conservative weapons of mass destruction.

Shapiro's approach to both comedy and politics is steeped in his literal religious faith as well as a more metaphorical commitment to the religion of conservatism. It is at this intersection that the right-wing comedy complex's religious bookstore courts its customers. *The Babylon Bee*, another mainstay in the complex's bookshop, began as an explicitly Christian alternative to the liberal satirical website *The Onion*, later developing into a more generally accommodating space for conservative satire. Mimicking *The Onion*'s mocking, combative style, it starts with a fundamentalist perspective on Christian ethics and argues out from there with headlines such as "Dems Recommend Drinking Bleach after Learning It Could Cause An Abortion."[11] The website's arguments are dressed in irony, but they are still attempts to merge faith and reason in order to court right-wing laughs. And then there is Steven Crowder, the onetime abstinence advocate turned YouTube star and very online comedian-provocateur who now racks up millions of views by stomping onto college campuses, plopping down a sign that says "There are only 2 Genders-Change My Mind" and editing the resulting debates for maximum ownage.

TRIGGER HAPPY: THE RELIGIO-RATIONAL SATIRE OF STEVEN CROWDER

In HBO's comedy *The Righteous Gemstones*, Adam DeVine plays Kelvin Gemstone, the youngest in a family of ultra-wealthy southern televangelists. As the Gemstone siblings vie for power in the family megachurch, baby Kelvin is relegated to youth ministry. With vices like sex, drugs, and

Comedian Steven Crowder tries to appeal to young conservatives with religiously informed right-wing arguments, a dynamic parodied by the character portrayed by Adam DeVine on HBO's *The Righteous Gemstones*. (HBO; YouTube)

alcohol unavailable to him, Kelvin instead uses video games and ATVs to awe and appeal to young Christians. The only problem is that Kelvin—clearly in his mid-thirties—isn't really young anymore. His tight-fitting V-neck plunges a little too deeply, his faux-hawk stands a little too stiffly, and his use of social media-slang is a little too forced. Early in one episode about the salvation of a promiscuous teenage girl, Kelvin initially wins her over by wowing her with an acrobatic routine at a trampoline park. The girl shows enthusiasm and joins Kelvin's youth group, but in the very next scene, she skips out for a drug-fueled party with a Satanic sex cult.

Steven Crowder is the Kelvin Gemstone of the right-wing comedy world. Crowder, though, is trying to get clicks, not converts, with his seemingly cool, Christian conservative comedy. Starting out as an abstinence advocate and finding a foothold in Fox News's early flirtations with comedy, he now thrives in the distracted attention economies of Facebook (roughly six million likes and followers) and YouTube (over five million subscribers) with the viral "Change My Mind" video series. He does so with an initially amusing gospel of young conservatism centered on family values, chauvinistic nationalism, and Shapiro-esque debate club harangues. But after luring potential apostles to his social media channels with shock comedy, his sweaty, strained rants quickly become obnoxious, officious, and repellant. Like Kelvin Gemstone, he's just a little too old and doughy to be wearing a Henley that tight, a little too white to be doing comedy sketches in ethnic dialect, and a little too thirsty for fame to make credibly populist appeals. Upon anything more than an initial consideration, his argumentative acrobatics fall flat and retreat into sophistic, contextless data. For liberal comedy fans, he's anathema from the start. For many conservatives just looking for a quick diversion, however, Crowder's rough approximation of youth and intelligence somehow succeeds.

Crowder's early 2010s viral editorials and appearances on Fox News provide another excellent example of the way religio-rational satire connects to other storefronts within the broader right-wing comedy complex. His Obama-era culture war op-eds for the Fox News website had lib-triggering titles like "The Trouble with Hipsters," "Is Liberalism Killing the Manly Man?," and "Why NOT Having Sex Might Be Good for You." The latter piece opens with a knowing, comedic misdirection meant to bait half-interested young readers and perhaps shock the website's elderly demo: "Sex. Some of us do it, most of us like it and we all think about it. . . . A lot." The rest of the piece is, of course, dedicated to singing the praises of abstinence with suspiciously sourced data and instantly dated jokes about how "I can rest easy knowing that my dame won't be trying to bed *Jersey Shore*'s The Situation anytime soon.—Though he does have great abs."[12] Crowder discussed the piece on Greg Gutfeld's *Red Eye* in a 2010 roundtable conversation with the feminist standup comic Amy Schumer before her mainstream fame. In the appearance, he immediately takes on a Shapiro-esque, debate club persona and tries to position his Christian moralism as a shocking and taboo counterpoint to the depraved world of standup comedy. After Schumer questions his comedy bona fides ("I go fishing a couple times a year, but I don't introduce myself on TV as a fisherman."), Crowder retreats to specious statistics, a tack he takes over and over again in the later "Change My Mind" videos. "87 percent of people who wait until marriage are happier," Crowder plainly states, as though both sex before marriage and marital happiness were the only two things couples never lie about.

Despite his questionable credentials, Crowder quickly ascended to the role of house comic in the right-wing media world. The *Red Eye* hit inspired a series of groan-inducingly titled "Tough Crowder" segments on Fox News, during which the young whippersnapper hilariously tells it like it is. He emceed the Conservative Political Action Conference in 2013, doing bits in between speakers like Mitch McConnell and Sarah Palin. His role was to appeal to younger Republicans by taking conservative talking points and converting them into comedic owns. In one such joke he combines Shapiro-style gotcha argumentation with a strained pop culture reference to make a particularly ugly point: "Ashley Judd just tweeted that buying Apple products is akin to rape . . . from her iPhone. Now she knows how my brain felt after *Divine Secrets of the Ya-Ya Sisterhood*. What is this obsession with Ashley Judd and rape?"[13] Judd, of course, would be one of the earliest and most prominent voices accusing movie mogul Harvey Weinstein of sexual assault. Crowder's schtick eventually wore thin at Fox News, both because the network hadn't fully paved the way for comedy yet and because Crowder began feuding with older, established stars like Sean Hannity.[14] Since then, Crowder has become a highly visible YouTube personality and mainstay on Glenn Beck's Blaze Media service with the daily streaming program *Louder with Crowder*. Even though the show is little more than Crowder and companions filming a glorified podcast, extended excerpts routinely rack up millions of views on YouTube, with full episodes and premium content hiding behind a paywall.

Crowder's real prominence in the right-wing comedy world comes in the social media circulation of videos of him on college campuses and in urban centers confronting young lefties, ethnic minorities, or other liberal archetypes scapegoated by the right. Though each video is structured as a serious investigation or debate, they are all peppered with funny moments of demeaning ownage. One early viral (thirty million views) example of Crowder's religio-rational satire is a 2015 video called "#SJW Feminist Festival Crashed by Crowder . . . in Underwear." Standing under a marquee for the Grand Rapids Feminist Film Festival, Crowder sarcastically says into the camera that he hopes to prove "once and for all that not all feminists are fat, unattractive, boy-cutted, androgynous, amoebas." Both the video's algorithm-friendly title and Crowder's introduction set an immediate expectation of liberal-triggering debate. Clearly, though, Crowder is not there to do any sort of sincere investigation of his ideological opponents, but to bait them into bad-faith arguments and logical dead-ends. Upon entering the movie theater lobby, he quickly points out a greatest hits of Obama-era right-wing grievances. When one young woman describes her conservative Christian upbringing, Crowder asks her why there are no films or panels examining the "Islamic oppression of women." He grills another woman about the gender-neutral restrooms.

Exasperated, he takes a break outside of the theater in order to peruse the festival program and bemoan the many trigger warnings included in film synopses. A concerned festival worker politely confronts Crowder's crew. She begins, "Some people—"

"Feel triggered?" Crowder interrupts. Owned.

Clearly, for Crowder and other practitioners of religio-rational satire, triggering is the whole point. There's never any real payoff to Crowder's conversations with the festivalgoers, no real exchange of ideas. Instead, each interaction provokes them into exasperated, angry reactions and provides conservative viewers of the video the smug satisfaction of laughing at the supposed excesses of liberalism run amok. Later in the festival video, Crowder works through the tortured logic of how feminism flies in the face of religiously informed gender roles. Apparently tired of owning feminists in person, he addresses the camera and delivers this mind-boggling thesis statement: "It's the biggest irony that feminists want to claim female empowerment, yet they are so weak that they demand legislation and cultural censorship in order to protect them." Of course, Crowder's argument blithely ignores the largely invisible structural barriers preventing women from claiming female empowerment. Moreover, his framing conflates feminists' apparent cultural victories with political power—why do they demand legislation, this thinking goes, when they've already got their own film festivals, for heaven's sake? Finally, the video displays one of religio-rational satire's favorite tactics when it reframes men as the real victims of liberals' cultural transgressions. To drive this point home, Crowder takes up one more act of shocking, comedic ownage by parading around outside the festival in his underwear, proudly showing off his dad bod in an attempt to lampoon feminist fat activists.

In subsequent viral videos, Crowder continues to claim victimhood and attempts to call bullshit on the injustices visited upon allegedly marginalized cultural groups. Like its abrasively stylized title suggests, the 2017 video "HIDDEN CAM: 'Stealing' Illegal Immigrant's [*sic*] Jobs!" has all the comedic subtlety of a sugar-addled eight-year-old with his first book of Mad Libs. It begins with clips of various liberal personalities—Chuck Schumer, Joy Ann Reid, the women of *The View*—defending the civil rights of undocumented migrant Latino laborers. Aha, Crowder quickly implies, but if these "aliens" are here illegally, what basic human rights or decent pay could they possibly be entitled to? As he's filmed from afar, Crowder approaches groups of Latino men in big-box store parking lots looking for work. After one explains that he wants $160 for six hours of work, Crowder (in voice-over) comedically exclaims "Damn bro!" This interjection is supposed to be a cue for viewers to laugh, relieving their shock and preparing them for the line of argumentation that follows.

The video quickly cuts to graphics explaining how that amounts to $26.66 an hour, or $1,066 for a forty-hour work week—tax free. "Wow," the incredulous conservative viewer might be thinking, "that's way more than I make, and I pay taxes!" Of course, Crowder's logic ignores the reality that many migrant day laborers don't really string together their dangerous, precarious jobs into anything close to resembling a forty-hour work week (to say nothing of the health benefits and protections that legal, full-time work often includes). But providing useful context is not Crowder's objective. What he wants, and presumably what his viewers want, is to see these illegal aliens get DESTROYED! After slogging through several suspicious, context-free data points to prove just how devious and prosperous these migrants actually are, the video closes with Crowder picking several of them up for a job. While a mariachi horn plays in the soundtrack, he pulls over and shouts to the migrant workers in his truck bed: "Hey, you guys have papers? I'm gonna call ICE, you motherfuckers!" The migrant workers climb down and hurriedly walk away.

At a superficial level, "'Stealing' Illegal Immigrant's Jobs!" resembles MTV's hidden camera prank show from the mid-2000s, *Punk'd*. That program featured sitcom star Ashton Kutcher plotting elaborate schemes to frame celebrities for accidentally wrecking cars, starting fires, or some other illegal or embarrassing spectacle. As pranks unfold, the show frequently cuts to Kutcher and his cohort off-set in a production trailer, laughing uproariously and giving on-set confederates further instructions via an earpiece. These shots, crucially, prompt audiences to laugh at the targeted celebrities, both because the latter are never in any real danger and because they hold positions of higher cultural and economic power than viewers do. In other words, *Punk'd* was a classic case of satire punching up. Crowder, by contrast, punches down, engaging in what the comedy scholars Peter Stallybrass and Allon White describe as the "displaced abjection" of a carnival show gone bad.[15] As opposed to mocking those in authority, Crowder's populist attack instead degrades those who are already most vulnerable in society. Lacking the clear guidance to direct viewers' laughter upward at those in power, Crowder's comedy relies on cruelty and the faulty syllogisms of religio-rational satire. If migrant laborers are here illegally, and if we should be comedically targeting illegal things in order to defuse their potential harm, then it must be OK to—BOOM! DESTROY!—migrant laborers. Crowder's labored, pedantic proof—they're actually making over $4,000 a month tax free!—disingenuously repositions the migrants from a low to a high position of economic authority. Like the Native Americans in Ben Shapiro's Columbus Day video, Crowder's laborers are portrayed as lawless savages for whom an ICE raid or a colonial conquest should be seen as just desserts. "'Stealing' Illegal Immigrant's Jobs!" mimics satire's familiar function, but by falsely elevating a marginalized group in order to laugh at it, Crowder provides a fleeting, lib-triggering victory to a contemporary conservative movement struggling to win cultural terrain.

Crowder's favored comedic tactic of puffing up and punching down is perhaps the best example of a particularly prominent strain of joking among the American right since the Trump era, one that also speaks to the fusionism at the core of the contemporary conservative movement. As Crowder's antics illustrate, the right is often bound less by a common ideological thread than by a shared antagonism to its political opponents. The title of Adam Serwer's much-discussed 2018 editorial for *The Atlantic*, "The Cruelty Is the Point," captures this sentiment, which had been roiling over decades of political division but came to a head in the first two years of Trump's term. Owning migrant Latino laborers as Crowder does, or separating them from their children as Trump does, serves, in Serwer's conception, as "a vehicle for intimacy through contempt" that inspires a "spectacle of cruel laughter."[16] Crowder and Trump don't just serve as another mundane example of the superiority theory of humor, then. Their cruel humor additionally fortifies bonds among conservatives, makes these relationships highly visible and available via social media, and spreads them throughout the rest of the right-wing comedy complex.

BACK TO SCHOOL: STEVEN CROWDER'S "CHANGE MY MIND" CAMPUS CRUSADES

No cultural battleground has proven more fertile for Crowder's religio-rational satire than college campuses, especially in his viral "Change My Mind" video series. The first installment from February 2018 announces its comedic intent by seating Crowder behind a folding table with a cheap, duct-taped banner stating "Male Privilege Is a Myth: Change My Mind." Of course, the invitation is disingenuous, and the mere thought that some college kid could waltz straight out of a Gender Studies class and talk Crowder out of his position is quite obviously laughable.[17] During the hour-long bit, several young people try, doing their best to marshal half-remembered Wikipedia facts and talking points from their classes, only to be—predictably, hilariously—owned by Crowder. One of Crowder's favored tactics is to steer the conversation to derisive counterpoints aimed at making him look reasonable while evoking laughter from the gathered crowd. When a young Black woman argues that Black men receive harsh jail sentences for possessing small amounts of marijuana while white men are throwing "weed parties," Crowder draws a big laugh from observers by simply asking what a "weed party" is. Another young woman bemoans the overwhelming whiteness of her campus's student body in order to argue for affirmative action. Crowder deliberately points to a young Black man standing feet away as the camera slowly pans for a comedic, objectifying reveal. Ownage complete, the crowd bursts into laughter. The exchanges mimic the type of crowd-work a standup comic might do in a live stage performance in order to warm up the audience or defuse a tense heckling situation. They have a nervous, improvisational energy, which is precisely Crowder's goal—to knock his young interlocutors off balance and overwhelm them with prepared material.

As arguments heat up, Crowder loves to put his conversational combatants on the spot by asking for empirically backed answers to vague questions like "What systematic racism do we have today?" Of course,

Steven Crowder shot to right-wing fame with his viral "Change My Mind" video series in which he debates liberal college students. (YouTube)

students don't walk around with prepared lectures and thus fall silent as they are forced to comically visualize their ignorance by frantically scrolling through their phones. This is when Crowder launches into his prepared act, often signaled with Shapiro-style prefaces like "What the data actually say . . ." or "The facts simply are . . . ." If a social inequality or cultural phenomenon isn't observable (to him) and quantifiable, it doesn't exist, according to Crowder. Never mind that racial and gendered privilege fester in the silent, immeasurable interstices of everyday life, often in felt ways that can't be articulated succinctly. Remember, for practitioners of religio-rational satire, facts don't care about your feelings. Facts aren't even facts unless you happen to walk around with them on a notecard in case someone shows up to bait you into an argument. Moreover, Crowder's marshalling of facts serves the comedic purpose of portraying his interlocutors as willfully ignorant and narrow-minded. The result is what the philosopher Thomas Hobbes describes as "Sudden Glory Laughter" that occurs when one watches another flounder and "by comparison whereof they suddenly applaud themselves."[18]

The zealous devotion to facts and data in "Change My Mind" bolsters Crowder's broader brand as a savant whose apparent command of statistics gives him cover to comedically bully vulnerable populations, a dynamic not unlike Jesse Watters's vox populi bits on Fox News. And though some of the principles he asserts are not literally religious, they reflect his long-standing commitment to bedrock ideas upon which conservative arguments can be built. If men are jailed at a much higher rate than women, how can male privilege be a thing? Back to the kitchen and child-rearing with you, ladies! Crowder's favored rhetorical tactic in this regard is to retreat to lawyerly terminology and to legal interpretations of cultural and social phenomena. In "There Are Only 2 Genders: Change My Mind," he begins by asking each college student, "How many genders are there?" immediately framing any answer other than "two" as flying in the face of centuries-old legal institutions. When one young man says he doesn't know and that people ought to be able to declare their own gender identity, Crowder retorts "Isn't that important? We have to function within certain parameters." Again, never mind that the "parameters" themselves are patriarchal, capitalist constructions. Crowder wants to know what's to become of us if there are no narrowly defined rules, setting up a moment of comedic ownage. "What if I told you that I believe I am a bobcat?" Having backed himself into a corner, the flummoxed young man simply says, "I hope you're the best bobcat on the fucking earth, man." Crowder guffaws, inviting viewers of the video to laugh at this wacky liberal college kid. Crowder closes the conversation by doing his best impersonation of a television lawyer: "This is a very emotive argument you're making . . . the ramifications of saying that we have to acknowledge somebody legally who identifies as a bobcat would be insurmountable . . . all sorts of new legal identifications would be required which don't currently exist."

Crowder's recourse to legalese gives him a cudgel to wield against anyone who finds his tactics distasteful or offensive. Any feminists, Marxists, or gender nonconformists who call him out are denying his right to free speech and engaging in that unholiest of liberal desecrations: cancellation. This is best exemplified by his 2019 fight with the journalist Carlos Maza, whom Crowder called several ethnic and homophobic slurs in his shows. After initially determining that Crowder hadn't violated its antiharassment policies, YouTube quietly demonetized (removed advertising support from) his channel for a little over a year. While decrying the move as tyrannical censorship, Crowder also wore it as a badge of honor, proof that he had so triggered the libs that they had no choice but to silence him. Of course, Crowder made a meal of his demonetization, railing against the liberal bias of tech giants like YouTube and rallying conservative comedy fans to his cause. As we explore in the case of libertarian comedy podcasters in the next chapter, Crowder's mode of provocation is ultimately an economic ploy. He knows that his brand of comedic ownage sticks out in the din of online chatter, driving clicks and revenue both to him and to hosting platforms like YouTube and Facebook. As Maza put it, "YouTube has a tremendous profit incentive to keep hate speech on the platform. Hate performs well and drives up the company's numbers."[19]

Importantly, critical media scholars have echoed Maza's observation in ways that highlight key aspects of how disparate strands of humorous content circulate throughout the right-wing comedy complex. It's not just the sheer, cold, political economy of social media that drives internet traffic, though that is a key factor. What leads users into and around the complex—from something like Fox News to Dennis Miller to Steven Crowder to the darker corners of right-wing comedy we explore in the next two chapters—are the subtler ways that social media platforms shape both cultural objects themselves and viewer reactions to them. The result of these more insidious practices is that platforms amplify the most emotional, inflammatory content and stories, moving them farther and faster than others in pursuit of user engagement. Facebook, for instance, makes its content, whether from Crowder or the *New York Times*, visually uniform. This impedes users' ability to assess sources and determine the veracity of a given claim. By leveling news sources aesthetically and optimizing them for emotional impact, Facebook's platform gives a considerable leg up to the Crowders of the online world—digital shock jocks whose feigned outrage and bad-faith argumentation stimulate a right-wing social media conversation that is largely unknown to the left. As Siva Vaidhyanathan notes, this framing of Facebook content creates "filter bubbles" that reward users with more of what they say they want, "narrowing fields of vision and potentially creating echo chambers of reinforced belief."[20] The more a piece of incendiary content zips around among the targeted audience of a particular filter bubble, the more incentivized creators will be to make more of it.

Intuitively, one might think that mainstream right-wing outlets like Fox News reign supreme in the conservative Facebook echo chamber. However, it's actually the comedic ownage of Ben Shapiro, Steven Crowder, and company that are most successful at engaging right-wing Facebook users and exposing them to the ever-expanding comedy complex. In July 2020 leading up to the election, for instance, Shapiro's *The Daily Wire* was the top publisher of content on Facebook.[21] In August, the *New York Times* reported that Shapiro's Facebook page had more interactions that month than those of mainstream news outlets ABC News, NBC News, the *New York Times*, the *Washington Post*, and NPR combined.[22] And the two most shared Facebook posts about the George Floyd protests that summer were from The Hodgetwins, Black right-wing comedians who are frequent guests on Crowder's various programs.[23] Conservative Facebook, then, seems to be less of a bubble and more of a biome, with religio-rational satire seeding ever-growing thickets of right-wing comedy.

THE COMPLEX CASE OF *THE BABYLON BEE*

Although Ben Shapiro and Steven Crowder are two of the tallest trees in Facebook's right-wing comedy forest, another humor outlet has recently sprouted without the prickly, provocative approach of the religio-rational satirists we've discussed so far. *The Babylon Bee* started early in 2016 as, simply, a satirical news site for Christians. The *Washington Post* framed the site in terms more familiar to fans of liberal satire by asking: "What would *The Onion* look like if it were written for the godly?"[24] Early headlines like "Local Family Attending Church on Easter Just in Case God Is Real"[25] evinced a gentle, self-deprecating wit, the kind that might get a good chuckle out of *Last Man Standing*'s Mike Baxter when he attends Sunday services. The site's devout Evangelical founder sold the *Bee* in 2018 out of a concern for the power that social media platforms like Facebook held over content creators, citing in particular a perceived bias against Christians.[26] With the increased Trumpification of the religious right, the *Bee* has since stepped up its efforts to generate partisan political satire from a conservative perspective. The move was clearly intended to expand the *Bee*'s reach beyond a purely religious readership, attracting the social media users lurking just a few clicks away on Shapiro's and Crowder's Facebook pages. Whereas once the *Bee* was the church across the street from the right-wing comedy complex, it's now part of the complex's religious bookstore, bringing pithy, topical humor to those inclined toward both Jesus and the pleasures of ownage. This transition has included, for instance, hiring creative director Ethan Nicolle, who recently adapted his *Axe Cop* webcomic into a successful animated sitcom starring Nick Offerman for the hip cable outlet FXX. That show's tone of absurd, reflexive irony informs much of the *Bee*'s current comedic targeting of high-profile figures both on the political left (like Joe Biden) and religious right (like celebrity televangelist Joel Osteen). The *Bee* has since grown its following to over three million across social media platforms, but not without bumping up against some of their structural mechanisms of censorship, ones both real and imagined.

The *Bee* and its proponents often argue that social media companies unfairly target the site, creating problems for it that would never be visited upon the liberal *Onion*. There is a complicated, but illuminating, mix of truth and fiction in such claims. As political scientist Richard Hofstadter famously argues, there is a distinct, recurring "paranoid style" of politics that is popular in the United States.[27] According to Hofstadter, a small but passionately persistent minority of Americans refuse "to accept the ineluctable limitations and imperfections of human existence," preferring instead to believe that national and personal failures derive from invisible, omnipresent forces of conspiracy.[28] Hofstadter is careful to clarify that this American instinct reaches broadly across the political spectrum. However, writing during the height of the cold war, he emphasizes how the anti-Communist right-wing in America rushed giddily to embrace the paranoid style, blaming cultural changes and electoral losses on sinister forces controlling the world through media manipulation, educational indoctrination, and, somehow or another, water fluoridation. This was the paranoid style of Barry Goldwater's Republican Party in 1964, and it echoes through to today's Trumpified GOP. During the 1950s and '60s, paranoiac right-wing voices blamed communists, Masons, and Jews for their shortcomings. Today, it is tech giants, social justice warriors and Jews that sundry right-wingers say are secretly undermining their efforts to set America back on the righteous path. These forces are also, according to the paranoid right, intent on destroying *The Babylon Bee*, America's most popular right-wing satire website.

Today's most common right-wing media conspiracy is that of "shadow banning," a process by which Facebook, Twitter, Instagram, and other social media platforms allegedly reduce the visibility of undesirable political positions through a secret, liberal-biased filtering process. Run by liberal Democrats, these sites are assumed to be part of a coordinated effort to undermine conservative values and unfairly depress Republican electoral success. Gleefully tweeted about by Trump, shadow banning remains little more than a conspiracy theory whose primary function is to obscure the relative lack of popularity of certain right-wing positions on mainstream social media.[29] Supporters of *The Babylon Bee* often say the site is shadow banned, implying that its satiric content reaches fewer users than it should due to big, liberal tech interference. For this, like all shadow banning, there is little actual evidence. Another form of potential online chicanery, however, has a less fictionalized relationship to the *Bee*: fact-checking.

For years, *The Babylon Bee*'s Facebook profile described the publication as "Fake news you can trust." It is impossible to dispute the site's open commitment to satire and its intent to mock, as opposed to mimic, real-life journalism. It is not, by any reasonable interpretation, akin to the sort of fake news infamously pumped out by teams of Macedonian teens (Pope Francis endorses Trump!) during the 2016 election cycle.[30] And yet, as conservative outlets have spilled much virtual ink bemoaning, the *Bee* is constantly subjected to seemingly serious fact-checking by mainstream news and research websites such as Politifact and Snopes. A search for "Babylon Bee" on Politifact, for example, helpfully clarifies that "No, ISIS didn't lay down its arms after Katy Perry encouraged world peace" despite a *Babylon Bee* headline to the contrary. The *Bee*'s obviously satirical effort to mock the inefficacy of symbolic celebrity activism earned the comedy publication a "Pants on Fire" rating from Politifact, as well as a healthy number of eyerolls from conservative pundits. Similarly, a search for "Babylon Bee" on the myth-busting outlet Snopes brings up dozens of fact checks, each one sillier than the next. "Did U.S. Rep. Ocasio-Cortez Repeatedly Guess 'Free' on TV Show '*The Price Is Right*'?" No, she did not, but thanks for making sure, Snopes. "Is Playing Christmas Music before Thanksgiving Now a Federal Crime?" Snopes is on it! Turns out, no, "Rudolph" on Veterans Day remains gauche but legal, sadly. These *Bee* headlines are, of course, satirical, a fact that Snopes acknowledges. The fact-checking site approaches them jauntily, rating each as "labeled satire," while completely forgoing the inapplicable categories of "true" or "false." According to Snopes, the site checks these articles because they "circulate" widely on social media and can be "puzzling" to some readers, leaving them "confused" about real-life events.[31]

The influential conservative writer David French, however, offers a different, more insidious explanation for the level of self-serious scrutiny the *Bee* receives from mainstream fact-checkers. The *Bee*, he writes, is "distinctly conservative," "distinctly Christian," and "very, very funny."[32] The site's sin, he argues, is crafting "viral satire of progressive politicians [that] is apparently intolerable" to the presumably liberal Snopes editorial staff. Listing out a number of obvious joke headlines investigated by Snopes, French accuses the site of targeting "satire that stings its [progressive] allies," and demands that fact checkers get their "hands off the Babylon Bee."[33] *The Onion*, French points out, does the very same thing as the *Bee* from a liberal, secular vantage point. Instead of scrutiny and scorn, however, *The Onion* receives plaudits and praise.

French is largely correct on the first count: *The Babylon Bee* operates in nearly direct parallel to *The Onion*, using satirical headlines as shorthand for logical arguments meant to mock, own, and destroy liberal hypocrites and fools. Take, for example, *The Onion* article "Billionaires Buy U.S. from Millionaires." Published in 2005 but presented as though it were a front page from 1927, the article offers an obviously ironic headline in the service of making a broader argument. No, the United States was not purchased by a small group of ultra-wealthy elites in the years leading up to the Great Depression. *The Onion* article argues, however, that for all intents and purposes, it was. By presenting the headline both in the present moment (in 2005) and in the past tense, *The Onion* asks viewers to assent to the claim that the wealthy have written the rules in the United States for generations. Of course, if you are persuaded by *The Onion*'s argument, you are not terribly likely to find *The Babylon Bee*'s Alexandria Ocasio-Cortez's *Price Is Right* headline terribly funny. For its intended conservative audience, however, the *Bee*'s story serves a parallel function to *The Onion*'s "Billionaires" piece. In this case, the *Bee* posits that projects like the Green

New Deal, with its taxpayer-funded programs that conservatives deride as "free stuff," will fatally undermine the notion that things need to be paid for at all. Alexandria Ocasio-Cortez, the *Bee* piece implicitly argues by ironically claiming she doesn't know that Rice-A-Roni costs currency, is dooming America to a future of entitled ignorance. Liberal readers may not agree with the argument, but it is hard to deny French's claim that the *Bee* and *The Onion* are two sides of one satiric coin.

But as to the more right-wing conspiratorial claim that only the *Bee* gets fact checked, French is wrong, coming dangerously close to acting out Hofstadter's politics of the paranoid. He is simply incorrect in his misleading implication that watchdog sites only fact check conservative satire. That "Billionaires" story from *The Onion*? Politifact deemed that "pants on fire," too.[34] Snopes has also fact checked and labeled dozens of *Onion* pieces, including "Judge Rules White Girl Be Tried as Black Adult,"[35] and "WWE Staff Forced to Shoot Aggressive Wrestler after Child Climbs into Steel Cage."[36] There is, quite plainly, no evidence suggesting a specific, intentional targeting of right-wing comedy by fact checkers like Snopes. Conservative defenders of the *Bee* tend to conveniently leave this information out of their op-eds, feeding into the same sort of mindset that encourages shadow banning hysteria among right-wingers.

There is, however, still more to this story of mainstream news sources misrecognizing *The Babylon Bee* as right-wing satire. Paranoids do, to tweak the old saying, sometimes have enemies. Although the conservative *Bee* is not uniquely targeted by liberal fact checking sites like Snopes, right-wing satire provokes a greater level of confusion among social media administrators. In March of 2018, *Babylon Bee* CEO Adam Ford posted a message he received from Facebook, warning him: "A page you admin (*The Babylon Bee*) recently posted the link (CNN Purchases Industrial Sized Washing Machine to Spin News Before Publication) that contains info disputed by (Snopes.com), an independent fact checker. Repeat offenders will see their distribution reduced and their ability to monetize [suspended]."[37] Certainly, some stories from *The Babylon Bee* have created public confusion, just as *Onion* stories are occasionally taken seriously by the uniformed.[38] Putting fake words into the real mouths of Alexandria Ocasio-Cortez or Katy Perry is funny in no small part because it creates a sense of ambiguity.

But if you claim the headline "CNN Purchases Industrial Sized Washing Machine to Spin News before Publication" is an attempt to create misinformation about cable news, well, we're no Politifact, but we know burning pants when we smell them. Even if you were to somehow be completely unaware of the colloquial meaning of "spin" invoked by the headline, you would still be left to explain what exactly you think the duped reader pictures when CNN literally places "News" into a "Washing Machine." Then there are the logistics of drying said news. CNN certainly doesn't want the news to shrink, with the demands of filling a full 24/7 news cycle. Only someone suffering from a serious case of the liberal psychological complex that obscures right-wing comedy could possibly be confused by what's going on in this instance.

Although it is not clear exactly what led to Facebook's admonishment, the tech giant's reaction to the *Bee*'s "Washing Machine" headline highlights the blind spot liberals have for right-wing comedy. It appears that the washing machine story was flagged first by Facebook users. Very likely, this was an act of intentional provocation by liberal users of the site. Given Donald Trump's consistent, over-the-top attacks on news media, one might justify a disingenuous flagging of the story as a resistant clap back on behalf of journalism. Alternatively, there may have been a large number of users who, themselves knowing it was fake, assumed their conservative friends wouldn't get it, they being humorless conservatives and all. In any case, the user reporting process set off an automated request for a Snopes fact check. The check, of course, determined that CNN does not literally launder the news. At this point, someone at Facebook was faced with a decision. *The Onion* posts countless "fake" stories, a high number of which are fact checked, but none of which cost them advertising revenue by being censored or de-monetized on social media. Somebody, it would seem, looked at the case of the *Bee* and couldn't—or wouldn't—see what was directly in front of them: a joke.

Liberals' myopia to religio-rational satire is grounded in both popular and academic thinking surrounding the world of comedy. Magazine articles tell us that "Conservatives just aren't into comedy."[39] Think piece after think piece appears online asking why there are no conservative satirists on TV, ignoring both the existence of Greg Gutfeld and the fact that there are countless, mostly economic, reasons that networks prefer to showcase center-left worldviews. Psychologists produce studies and twist data to make points such as "conservatives really do lack a sense of humor!" when right-wingers prove unimpressed by the mostly left-leaning comedy that researchers present them.[40] It is not our place to say whether, on the margins, there are factors beyond the economics and history of the media industry that point to liberals being more engaged by funny content. Perhaps there is, though any study of the subject ought to ask conservatives what they do laugh at, as opposed to investigating why they don't find funny what others do. Doing so will reveal both expected and unexpected results, including *The Babylon Bee*'s tendency to satirize figures from across the political spectrum, including on the right.

THE BABYLON BEE SWINGS
THE DOUBLE-EDGED STINGER OF IRONY

When an argument and a joke love each other very much, sometimes they become intimate and create an irony together. Unless, of course, some sort of birth control is in effect, but neither abstinence-only Steven Crowder nor the Evangelical *Babylon Bee* are much into that. And whereas those blinded by the liberal psychological complex that cloaks conservative comedy believe the right to be ironically barren, an honest look at the *Bee* proves it extremely, if not quite immaculately, fertile with jokes. Ironic address uses humor and contempt in order to craft implicit arguments that render opponents not only incorrect, but also "laughable."[41] Saying something other than what she means, the ironist argues through clever inversion and sarcastic opposition to both amuse and convince. This unusual form of persuasion depends on the audience's "knowledge" of communication "conventions" and its "intuition" of the ironist's intent.[42] Properly placed and uttered, a single, stinging line of irony can be more compelling than a full-length dissertation. Whereas Ben Shapiro and Steven Crowder use hour-long videos to prove their points, *The Babylon Bee* trades in pithy, fake news stories to craft its religio-rational satire.

The *Bee* also differs from Crowder and Shapiro in another core attribute: the *Bee*'s arguments, while certainly inclusive of right-wing red meat, also feature critiques of the right. Just as the *Bee*'s relationship to online censorship proved complicated upon close analysis, so does the publication's engagement with partisan politics. Certainly, the *Bee* uses its ironic form of argumentative satire to mock the liberal world, sometimes drawing upon racist and sexist stereotypes. In the era of media silos and the interconnected right-wing comedy complex, the real money is in feeding the partisan beast. At the same time, it is undeniable that the *Bee* uses irony as a pan-ideological tool, equally well suited to rhetorically dismembering targets from left to right. The resulting material considerably expands the scope of American satire, producing, on occasion, right-wing jokes aimed at the right that even *Onion* readers won't want to "that's not funny" away.

The Babylon Bee is particularly adept at focusing its satire on the internal inconsistencies of contemporary Evangelical Christianity. According to scholar Zachary Shelton, *The Babylon Bee* engages with a long-standing tradition of devout Christian satire that uses humor to attack "superfluous structures and practices in the church."[43] So while liberal readers of the site might focus on the way it mocks their own left-wing positions on abortion or transgender rights, conservative Christians might appreciate the *Bee*'s ability to ironically admonish its own right-wing community. In particular, the site takes a merciless approach to the celebrity pastor Joel Osteen, upon whom the aforementioned *Righteous Gemstones* is at least partially based. According to the *Bee*'s understanding of Evangelical Christianity, faith requires a deep respect for "the authority of God's Word."[44] The *Bee* thus aims its satirical slings at those who use the "Bible as a prop for a lifestyle or worldview."[45] Joel Osteen, in the eyes of his critics, does just this in marketing his prosperity gospel, putting forth a "theology not centered on God and his glory, but an anthropocentric psychological message aimed at making individuals merely feel better about themselves."[46] For the *Bee*, this makes Osteen a more deserving target than even Alexandria Ocasio-Cortez, Joe Biden, or any other Democratic politician. These liberal figures all unambiguously announce who they are to conservatives. Osteen, however, is an Evangelical wolf in sheep's clothing, leading right-thinking, right-wing Christians astray. The *Bee* therefore sends more stings his way than anywhere else. In the midst of the COVID-19 crisis in 2020, for example, the *Bee* ran the following stories:

"Joel Osteen Warns It Is Far Too Soon to Reopen the Bible"

"Joel Osteen Encourages Congregation to Continue Scriptural Distancing"

"Joel Osteen Tests Negative for Christianity"

And to tie things all together sarcastically: "AOC Is a Strong, Intelligent Woman, Snopes Is an Excellent Fact-Checker, and Joel Osteen Is a Biblically Faithful Preacher."[47]

Crucially, the *Bee* is America's only consistent stop for satire aimed at this particular conservative public figure. Despite possessing one of the country's most powerful religious voices, Osteen goes unremarked upon in *The Onion*, America's satirical paper of record.[48] *Onion* writers, one suspects, are particularly ill-equipped to critique Osteen because they likely lack the religious worldview that makes available the most biting, rational critique of his power. Viewed from outside the Christian faith community, Osteen appears rather similar to a long line of famous Protestant preachers who enthrall millions but strike the liberal world as alien curiosities. For the *Bee*, Osteen is a singular figure with a specific weak spot at which satire must be aimed. In the "Too Soon to Re-Open the Bible" article mentioned above, the *Bee* uses COVID-era buzz language to argue that Osteen's prosperity gospel Christianity fails the most basic scriptural test, joking that simply opening the Bible causes "sudden heart change, reduced fear and anxiety, and the destruction of every tenet of the prosperity gospel."[49] Such in-group aimed satire fills much of the *Bee*'s stories, with dozens of articles taking aim at the indulgences, hypocrisies, and indiscretions of people from within the world of Christian belief like Osteen. This fact may fall short of convincing a liberal that the right-wing comedy complex isn't so bad. It does, however, indicate that the hegemonic liberal comedy industry fails to cover all of its satiric bases.

If Osteen is too niche or obscure a case, consider the *Bee*'s relationship to Donald Trump. Famously, Trump finds tremendous support among self-professed Evangelicals, despite what appear to be some, let's say, tensions between their stated beliefs and his behavior.[50] Trump, a professed Christian, often seems unaware of the rudiments of Christian doctrine.[51] He gets the names of Bible books wrong ("Two Corinthians"), and apparently he was so confused about church practice that he once put money on a communion plate, which is especially odd given his tendency not to pay for things in other contexts.[52] And this is just the silly stuff. He's also famously immodest, possessing a stomach-churning approach to women and sex, including, but not limited to, bragging about grabbing women's genitals. Yet white Evangelical support remained strong throughout his presidency, with roughly 75 percent of Evangelicals voting for his reelection in 2020.[53] If you find this state of affairs both astounding and risible, then you, as a liberal, may be shocked to learn that you agree with *The Babylon Bee*. Despite its largely right-wing fan base, the *Bee* has consistently taken a critical approach to Trump, particularly toward the hypocrisy he inspires among Evangelicals. Yes, the *Bee* is a proudly right-wing outlet, but its commitment is to a certain brand of Christianity that refuses to impose a partisan binary onto a spiritual worldview.

In December of 2019, the *Bee* scored one of its most viral hits with the headline "Trump: 'I Have Done More for Christianity Than Jesus.'"[54] Shared five million times on social media, the headline serves as a comic defense of *Christianity Today*, an Evangelical news magazine that decided in December of 2019 that "Trump should be removed from office," due to the conduct leading to his first impeachment.[55] Trump, of course, attacked the notoriously conservative outlet, calling it "radical left" and implying that he and his supporters know more about Christianity today than the editors of *Christianity Today*.[56] Published just days after the very serious *Christianity Today* op-ed, the *Bee*'s article ridicules the pro-Trump argument, highlighting its absurdity in a way that could only emerge from an authentic conservative voice. If Trump-supporting Evangelicals excuse Trump's inveterate lying, braggadocious infidelity, and assault on the other eight commandments, then they must, the *Bee* suggests, see something very special about the forty-fifth president. How special? Well, if he can defy Jesus's word and still get their vote, he must be more Christian than, yes, Jesus Christ Himself. In the *Bee* article, fake Trump says "I appointed judges to help protect religious rights."[57] Thus he parrots a thousand right-wing talking heads who excuse the president's excesses. He goes on: "How many judges has Jesus appointed?" The fake Trump then says he's "protecting churches," while Jesus "has disappeared," suggesting Evangelicals who support him care more about culture war politics than the death of their savior. Finally, fake Trump says that he "saved Christmas," and asks "What has Jesus ever done for Christmas? Be born? He wants credit for that? Come on." Certainly, *The Onion* takes its shots at Trump, but there's a little extra honey for the reader when stings like this come from a right-wing, Christian source.

The Babylon Bee warns against what happens when religious believers put aside their bedrock principles in order to reach a convenient, partisan conclusion. Ultimately, Christian Trump supporters are forced to raise convenience above principle. If Trump trumps Christ even for a moment, and Christ is, to Evangelicals, the embodiment of eternal truth, then perhaps these churchgoers need to trade in their wooden crucifixes for solid-gold toilets. The Trump article is a prime piece of religio-rational satire, this time used to take down, as opposed to build up, a conventional right-wing position. Coming from the central, faith-based principles of Christian belief, the *Bee* uses observation and exaggeration to own churchgoing Trump supporters in the same way that Shapiro or Crowder try to own their liberal debate opponents. Considered more broadly, the *Bee*'s coverage of both Osteen and Trump proves that conservatives can do reflexive, intra-ideological satire. Liberal satirists like *The Onion* can't do the *Bee*'s jokes for lack of knowledge and religio-political positioning, and liberal comedy fans can't see what the *Bee* does because of the liberal psychological complex. Additionally, the *Bee*'s conservative critique helps in mirroring the fusionistic aspect of the American Republican party, inviting some Evangelicals into the right-wing comedy complex. For liberals, this side of the *Bee* shows the potential value inherent in some right-wing comedy.

THE BABYLON BEE, BACK TO DEVOUTLY OWNING THE LIBS

All that said, we apologize if the liberal reader just wasted their time tuning up the acoustic guitar for a round of "Kumbaya." Yes, the *Bee* has scored viral hits by taking aim at hypocrites on the right. But its main business, like any good religio-rational satirist, is owning the libs. Although the *Bee* spends lots of time skewering the Christian world, most of its money-making stories are greased up in order to slide most effectively throughout the corridors of the right-wing comedy complex. Sure, a well-crafted Trump joke might get impressive crossover attention. Such successes are exceedingly difficult to come by, however. A better business can be built around comedy that is politically, and algorithmically, similar to that produced by existing neighbors in the right-wing comedy complex such as Steven Crowder, Greg Gutfeld, or Tim Allen. Why work to earn clicks and shares with lots of nuanced, nonpartisan jokes when social media platforms are just giving them away via "You Might Also Like" recommendations? So, the *Bee* primarily uses its religio-rational satire to indulge in familiar conservative mockery of marginalized groups and the spreading of wild, irresponsible conspiracies.

Among the most popular of the *Bee*'s stories is a satirical news brief headlined "Motorcyclist Who Identifies as Bicyclist Sets Cycling World Record."[58] Posted in October of 2019, the article has been shared over four million times, primarily on Facebook. The argument it makes—that transgender identification is foolish, potentially dangerous, and fundamentally unfair to cisgender women—is a favorite right-wing talking point with particular resonance in the world of religious conservatism from which the *Bee* springs. The *Bee*'s metaphor in the story functions as both an argument and a cruel joke, exemplifying the incongruity-resolution model of humor. In this conception of comedy, pioneered by the Scottish philosopher James Beattie, laughter arises when seemingly unrelated things are unified in a satisfying, surprising way.[59]

So, what do motorcycles have to do with the politics of gender identity? *The Babylon Bee* piece implicitly references a number of cases in which transgender girls have been permitted to compete against cisgender girls in athletic competitions. The most famous such instance occurred in June 2018, when a transgender girl won the 100- and 200-meter dashes at the Connecticut Interscholastic State Athletic Conference Track & Field Championship. Making headlines across the country, right-wing media presented the result as a model of slavish liberal devotion to political correctness over common, traditionalist, sense. The *Bee* article argues by metaphor, funhouse mirroring the champion sprinter with a motorcyclist who defeats his peddling competition by multiple hours. Those who question his identification as a bicyclist are deemed "bigots" and "banned" from the sport in metaphorical reference to the alleged cancelling of those who publicly challenged the Connecticut result. The *Bee* story adds egregious cruelty to the metaphor by noting that the motorcyclist "painted the word

'HUFFY' on the side of his bike, ensuring he had no advantage over the bikes that came out of the factory as bicycles." The metaphor here points, one presumes, to the external markers of normative femininity that transgender runners might add to their appearance, twisting the pursuit of adolescent self-expression into an image of slapdash superficiality. For some liberal readers, there is no doubt something distasteful, and perhaps fundamentally unfunny, about the article. It does, however, create a successful, theoretically comical, resolution of its apparent incongruity by extending out its metaphor for transgenderism at such length. And it pairs perfectly with right-wing comedy complex hits such as a Crowder's forty-million-view blockbuster video "There Are Only 2 Genders: Change My Mind."

The *Bee* has found similar success with pure conspiracy dressed up as facts and logic. For example, nearly six million people have shared the article "CDC: People with Dirt on Clintons Have 843% Greater Risk of Suicide."[60] This headline is, of course, aimed squarely at expanding the *Bee*'s base into the broader, uglier world of conservative, conspiracy-laden media. The headline indulges in and amplifies one of the most damaging right-wing conspiracies, arguing that people associated with the Clinton family regularly die under suspicious circumstances. Baseless, the charge has nonetheless been highly profitable in online media spaces that are adjacent to the right-wing comedy complex. In particular, the webhost, charlatan, and self-admitted "performance artist" Alex Jones has run with the theory.[61] He posted a "Clinton Body Count" on his website as early as 2008.[62] Jones is not quite a comedian (though he does engage in the type of right-wing trolling we examine in chapter 5), but he successfully creates a sense of grotesque ambiguity in his outrageous, over-the-top web shows and podcasts. Alongside the Clinton suicide conspiracy, he has garnered millions of clicks by claiming that the government controls the weather, is populated by actual demons, and, somehow, makes frogs gay.[63] These latter examples are perhaps tinged with irony and explain why some viewers may consider his show a form of comic entertainment. The Clinton conspiracy, along with the even more disgusting claim that the tragic Sandy Hook Elementary shooting in 2012 was a "hoax," however, show the dangers of laughing him off. The *Bee*, with its Clinton headline, plays up the entertainment appeal of Jones's derangement, drawing attention to it while remaining, at best, ambivalent about its truth value.

In the Trump and Osteen stories, *The Babylon Bee* engages with un-knowable, unprovable religious ideas. In doing so, they offer a nuance that can be apprehended, and perhaps even appreciated, by people who take different approaches to religious truth. You may reject Christianity but appreciate the moral and ethical values the *Bee* is upholding as they satirize Osteen or Trump. In the Clinton body count piece, however, the *Bee* indulges in a different variety of faith: the fully partisan. To believe in Alex Jones–style conspiracies even so much as to laugh along with them requires a quasi-religious faith in the most extreme of conservative, conspiracy-laden, talking points. It is to put partisan advantage above basic reason and apparent empirical reality. To an outsider, Jones appears deranged and exploitative. For the *Bee* to play off of Jones is, perhaps, a violation of its own principles akin to that which they accuse Evangeli-cal hypocrites, as they choose right-wing clicks over right-thinking satiric critiques. As opposed to being a unique voice of satiric religious introspec-tion, the *Bee* becomes merely another preacher representing the Church of Right-Wing Reaction.

Of course, *The Babylon Bee* is not a church. It is a media and entertain-ment business whose success depends on a consistent flow of customers from the rest of the right-wing comedy complex. Certainly, some shoppers at the complex's religious bookstore are stopping by after a nice morning of Bible study and a potluck church picnic. Far more, though, are coming through because a certain algorithmic friend suggested that if they like videos of Steven Crowder owning minorities, they might like the *Bee* too. It is true that if you read an interview with the *Bee*'s creators, you'll find a sincere devotion to jokes critiquing those who misuse the Christian faith. If you see a *Bee* story going viral, however, it is much more likely to be of the Clinton body count variety.

PRIMING POLITICAL ARGUMENTS WITH PUNCHLINES

In her analysis of liberal irony, political communication scholar Dannagal Young notes that left-leaning satirists have a tendency to joke in a man-ner that comes just short of making their true political point. For example in 2016, liberal late-night hosts constructed forms of comedy that, while never stating that Donald Trump is a fascist, asked viewers to read between the lines and "come to the argument" for Trumpian Totalitarianism on their own.[64] For example, she cites Conan O'Brien's joke that, while Trump sometimes lags in the US election polls, he's always "number 1 among Germans of the 1930s." This is, of course, a stark joke, and one that (just barely) hides within it the most serious of allegations. It is also, obviously, only a joke, and only one among countless efforts to satirize, send up, and assault the forty-fifth president. As Young notes: "One joke implying that Trump and his supporters are Nazis isn't going to suddenly persuade someone that Trump and his supporters are actually Nazis. But getting an audience to entertain such a proposition without explicitly making that argument could be a powerful step in the persuasive process, as is getting an audience to entertain that proposition while suspending their resistance to it."[65] Here Young makes a point about partisan comedy, suggesting such two-step irony-argument tactics are exemplary of the "psychological roots of humor's liberal bias."[66] Young's broader insight—that extreme ideological jokes might be understood as preparation for more serious forms of political argumentation—is astute and absolutely crucial to understanding our current political moment. However, having considered the content and breadth of existing, successful right-wing comedy, it becomes much harder to see satire in terms of fundamental, partisan distinctions. The normalization of extreme ideological positions on the American right does, undoubtedly, benefit from the increasing ability of the right-wing comedy complex to circulate outlandishly partisan positions in the form of satiric comedy.

A joke about Trump being a Nazi is not, on its own, an important political statement. Similarly, one joke that implies that the Clintons and their supporters are complicit in the murder of dozens of innocent people is not going to persuade someone that Alex Jones had it right all along. However, just as Conan's Hitler gag asks the audience to understand an extreme anti-Trump joke by filling out its obvious internal logic, so does the *Bee*'s Clinton "body count" joke discussed above. It does not take Ben Shapiro's Harvard Law degree to realize that the *Bee*'s joke asks the reader to understand that the "suicides" are not suicides at all. As Young argues, this bit of inference is an excellent primer to encourage a fuller line of reasoning. If nothing else, it gives the reader an excuse to contemplate the apparently extreme without immediately committing to taking it seriously. Logic, as it so often does, may arrive late to the party. It only needs an invitation.

Furthermore, the structure of the right-wing comedy complex is well suited to nurturing conspiratorial seedlings. In our consideration of the religio-rational satire on display at the complex's religious bookstore, *The Babylon Bee* represents the purest form of comedy. Whether you appreciate it or not, the *Bee's* fake stories directly parallel those of *The Onion*. They are, accordingly, clearly marked as jokes. Yes, they use logical satire to make a political point but, in doing so, they remain in the relatively humble realm of the comic.

Steven Crowder and Ben Shapiro, by contrast, have greater, more profitable ambitions. Yes, the millennial Crowder proudly identifies himself as a young comedian and does whatever possible to brand his rambling own-age videos as youth-oriented humor. At the same time, he understands himself as a serious person for whom jokes offer a gateway to the greener pasture of political punditry. Shapiro, in turn, takes this movement one step further. Though he works hard to be associated with humor, this remains a mere marketing tool for Shapiro, differentiating him from other brands of conservative pundits and allowing him to tap into the right-wing comedy complex's emerging generation of conservatives equally versed in both comedy and sophistry.

Steven Crowder and Ben Shapiro thus take priming jokes like the ones found in the *Bee* and develop them as more serious, and more profitable, political punditry. Take, for example, a brief exchange from Crowder's *Louder with Crowder* program from 2016.[67] With Shapiro as his guest, Crowder takes on the Clinton body count "question." Though lacing the segment with jokes, Crowder goes one argumentative step further than the *Bee*, offering "evidence" of Clinton perfidy via reference to information he gleaned in "off-air" discussions with Mike Huckabee, who no doubt previously joined the show to try out some of his new Twitter jokes. The totality of Crowder's argument is, per usual, quite bad. However, for viewers primed by the *Bee's* Clinton-conspiracy jokes like the one discussed above, the Crowder-Shapiro exchange gives viewers a more robust permission structure for believing outlandish conspiracies about the Clintons' criminality.

Shapiro's response to Crowder on *Louder with Crowder*, however, is more telling and, in some ways, more disturbing. Shapiro quite clearly does not support the Clinton body-count conspiracy, and says so. Almost. He may not believe that Hillary ordered hits on a dozen low-level Democrats, but he certainly believes in the juicy, revenue-dripping clicks that can come from those who do. Shapiro himself panders to the right-wing only slightly less pathetically than Crowder, saying that he is "not a big buyer" of the grand Clinton body-count conspiracy. He does, however, go on to say that it's reasonable to believe that long-time Clinton associate Sydney Blumenthal may have killed a number of people in Libya on behalf of the Clintons.

In the course of a single minute, Steven Crowder and Ben Shapiro move *The Babylon Bee*'s Clinton joke up the argumentative and economic chain, making it a seriously (if still ridiculously) reasoned argument while expanding its appeal throughout and beyond the right-wing comedy complex. By the time Crowder and Shapiro are done talking, they've given viewers two iterations of the Clinton conspiracy argument, both the garden-variety Alex Jones version as well as a more sophisticated-sounding one that relies on Shapiro's knowledge of Hillary Clinton's involvement in Libya. Crowder and Shapiro then return viewers to the comfortable realm of sophomoric humor, having been both entertained and (mis)informed.

Shapiro's shifting of the Clinton body count conspiracy into something related, different, and only slightly less outlandish has, like most of the things discussed throughout this chapter, a certain religious feel. It is as though he were a fundamentalist leader confronted with a troubling scriptural inconsistency. From a moral perspective he probably ought to simply explain that the facts in this case do not add up and that the conservative belief that the Clintons slaughter opponents like Samson savaging so many Philistines is certainly not *literally* true. But, where's the money in that? Instead, he squirms and justifies, keeping his content as close as possible to the preconceptions of the intersecting fan bases who, with the help of social media filter bubbles and internet algorithms, frequent both the right-wing comedy complex and the wider world of conservative political media. In the next chapter, we explore fundamentalist belief of a slightly different stripe, one grounded not in devotion to religious first principles or to owning the libs with logic, but one devoutly worshipping at the altar of the sacred conservative principles of free markets and free speech.

4 The Legions of Libertarian Podcasters

Like any full-service shopping center, the right-wing comedy complex features a healthy selection of bars and restaurants. These are spaces of both consumption and invitation, slinging drinks to complex regulars while also attracting people who may just be passing by. Visitors are enticed with a quick beer or bite, but are always asked to stay a bit longer. A nightcap is just one questionable decision away from a pub crawl and a few more from a full-on bender. It's true of drink and it's true, as we argue in this chapter, of right-wing comedy podcasts. A shot of whiskey and a link to *The Joe Rogan Experience* have a lot in common. Both might seem like a good idea but then have you staring at the clock hours later, wondering where the night went, and what happened to that self-care plan you spent so much time on. Right-wing comedy podcasters, particularly those of a libertarian bent, have a knack for serving up just the right substances to keep listeners coming back for one more, regrets be damned.

Podcasts, notoriously, excel in creating a sense of ersatz intimacy.[1] Done well, they feel like a nearly perfect watering hole, your own personal Cheers. You feel invited, included, and validated, as the bounty of podcast options means you can find the one that's just right for you. On the downside, they're always BYOB, or, perhaps in the case of libertarian podcasts,

BYOP (Bring Your Own Politics). Nonetheless, podcasts, and particularly comedy podcasts, have a way of making listeners feel like they are a part of something bigger, crafting an unusual sort of brand loyalty in the process. Built on recommendations and cross-promotions in which hosts become guests on each other's shows, podcasts develop, like bar districts, as rows of interrelated establishments. This approach is central to the podcast business. For example, Joe Rogan, the podcast medium's dominant voice, often fills his schedule by interviewing other podcasters, who, in turn, spend most of their shows talking to one another. Once a listener stumbles into this part of the right-wing comedy complex, they're liable to stick around, sampling drinks at the various neighboring establishments.

And it's no coincidence that libertarianism is the political mixer of choice for the world of right-wing and right-friendly comedy podcasting. Crucially, this ideology, which combines traditional free-market conservatism with laissez-faire approaches to social issues and vice laws, has the capacity to connect beyond the bounds of mainstream right-wing media. The libertarian movement's long-held positions on marijuana legalization, free speech absolutism, and decriminalization of sex work give listeners from other, more liberal parts of town an excuse to drop into the right-wing comedy complex and slum it. Furthermore, these ingredients of drugs, profanity, and sex, are key components in many a comedian's arsenal, making the transition from politics to comedy particularly seamless for many libertarian podcasters.

And, perhaps just as importantly, libertarianism appeals to a demographic blend that is valuable, coherent, and attractive to podcast advertisers. There may not be a large number of self-described libertarians but, according to Pew Research, they are overwhelmingly male, white, and between the ages of eighteen and forty-nine.[2] They also disproportionately represent the high end of the salary scale, with about half of libertarians earning over \$75,000.[3] This profile makes libertarian audiences highly desirable to certain advertisers. It also helps explain why so many libertarian comics use their freedom of speech to pursue jokes that offend minority groups, women, and LGBTQ communities.

As economist Walter E. Block argues, libertarianism's fundamental philosophical basis, the nonaggression principle, asks only a single moral question: "What is the proper use of force?"[4] The answer, generally speaking, is that force is only appropriate in the realm of self-defense and personal property protection. This means that no one, including the government, has the right to restrict the personal choices of individuals who are not direct threats to anyone else. It also, as Block notes, ignores other potential moral goods, including "opposition to sexism, prejudice, and racism."[5] To be clear, libertarian philosophy does not espouse these pernicious attitudes; it simply declares them to be beside the moral point. In other words, when Joe Rogan goes for a laugh by making light of black-face or using a racial slur, a strict libertarian will find no moral fault. Despite the many good arguments one might make against such language, Rogan has not *directly* aggressed against an individual. As a result, libertarian comedy podcasts often offer an intellectual and economic justification to court a valuable young male audience through the deployment of racist, sexist, and homophobic comedy.

A considerable number of podcasters operating today have a notable relationship to libertarianism. In this chapter, we look at three successful libertarian podcasters to help shine a light on how libertarian comedy podcasting plays an important role in the right-wing comedy complex. We look first at the influential podcast *The Joe Rogan Experience* (*JRE*) and host-comedian Joe Rogan, whose personal politics defy easy categorization, but whose comedy and guest list often veer into avowedly libertarian spaces. Rogan's style on the show and branding across social media are exemplary of an approach to comedy that is particularly successful today among libertarian audiences, as well as among right-wing curious young men intrigued by Rogan's masculinist ethos. Next, we look at the rowdy and debauched *Legion of Skanks*, which features an evangelizing libertarian cohost, Dave Smith, and takes the cause of free, deeply offensive speech to new heights (or should we say, lows). *JRE* and *Legion of Skanks* often share guests, jokes, and worldviews, but *Skanks* is a much more extreme form of libertarian comedy than Rogan's and hails young male libertarian listeners in a much more targeted way. Lastly, we consider Andrew Heaton, a different sort of libertarian comedian who, despite (or perhaps because of) his commitment to both libertarianism and decency, must embrace a more modest approach to the comedy business in order to maintain his integrity. Heaton highlights the dilemma of trying to deliver principled jokes within a libertarian comedy marketplace dominated by unrelentingly offensive appeals to the lowest common denominator.

JOE ROGAN, POLITICS, AND THE BUSINESS OF PODCASTING

Joe Rogan is particularly hard to pinpoint on the political spectrum. The same can be said for the podcast medium he dominates, where iTunes charts and Spotify ratings display a wide range of political affiliations. American talk media, however, has an undeniably conservative heritage. Since the 1980s, politically conservative radio hosts—even reactionaries—have dominated America's political talk radio programming. In 1987, the Federal Communications Commission repealed a regulation known as the Fairness Doctrine, which mandated that broadcasters balance their political content over the course of their weekly schedule. The impact of this deregulation was made even more dramatic when the United States Congress passed the Telecommunications Act of 1996, a law that allowed large media companies such as Clear Channel to syndicate talk shows across the country, reaching literally thousands of stations simultaneously, and undermining the variety of programming around the country.[6]

Freed from any requirement to balance their political content, stations across the country loaded up on bombastic right-wing voices—like Rush Limbaugh, Sean Hannity, and Michael Savage, along with a cadre of lesser known and often more extreme right-wing hosts—who appealed to the older, whiter, and more male audiences that tended to listen to radio in the first place. Making matters worse, talk radio tends to drift toward what scholars describe as the "genre," of "outrage," meaning that what starts as garden-variety Republican conservatism may well morph into radical, conspiratorial anti-liberalism in short order.[7] However, the arrival of podcasting in the early 2000s—which circumvented many of terrestrial radio's technological limitations—allowed for new voices to emerge and reach increasingly siloed listeners across the country in an even more politically targeted fashion. Those new voices also showed that political talk programming could have an audience well beyond just conservative listeners. The past half decade has seen an explosion of successful liberal podcasts featuring ideologies ranging from Democratic establishmentarianism to dirtbag socialist leftism.

In the beginning of the Trump era, for example, the success of shows from former Obama White House staffers (*Pod Save America*), NPR (*Code Switch, This American Life*) and the *New York Times* (*The Daily*) reflected a leftward trend within American talk media. In August of 2017, *Vice* argued that "Podcasts are becoming the left's right-wing radio," citing with both excitement and trepidation the format's ability to extend popular discourse leftward in the same way AM radio expanded it to the far right.[8] A month later *The Week* put it bluntly, claiming that liberal podcasts were "dethroning Rush Limbaugh."[9] Despite these claims, however, today's podcast charts suggest that there is no single dominant political view among podcasters. The right-wing *Ben Shapiro Show* rivals the liberal *Pod Save America* both in total downloads and cultural relevance. Today there are also numerous voices from the world of AM radio, including older arch conservatives such as Mark Levin, who have successfully gone digital.

It is in this context that the comedian Joe Rogan, a unicorn in the world of contemporary talk media, emerged onto the podcast scene with *The Joe Rogan Experience*. The politics of *JRE* defy simple categorization. But the show, nevertheless, regularly promotes right-wing politics and comedy, leaving his podcast—which is the true powerhouse of the medium today—very much wrapped up into the larger right-wing comedy complex. From his humble beginnings as a stoner standup and character actor on shows like *NewsRadio*, his podcast now holds a massive audience while remaining politically heterodox. As of 2022, *The Joe Rogan Experience* had over eleven million YouTube subscribers and was being streamed nearly two hundred million times per month.[10] And despite this era's trend toward increasingly partisan branding, Rogan refuses to pick a lane. Sometimes, he'll position himself on the left. He'll tell you that he's "always been" progressive and back it up with proclamations in favor of gay rights, women's rights, and even a series of interviews in which he pushes politicians across the spectrum to support Medicare for All.[11] In 2020, he endorsed Democratic presidential hopeful Bernie Sanders and argued, even when talking to right-wing politicians, that health care must be considered a human right.[12] The case that he is a rare liberal voice with crossover appeal is a superficially compelling one and was marshalled by the Sanders campaign as they touted Rogan's endorsement in the Democratic presidential primary.[13]

And yet, a polar opposite case can be made similarly persuasively. For all of Rogan's self-professed liberalism and confessed commitment to certain progressive positions, his career and podcast are littered with jokes, remarks, and declarations that give pause to liberal listeners. His right-friendly comedy approach began with his star-making turns as the host of *Fear Factor* and *The Man Show* in the early 2000s. The latter program was exactly what its name suggests: a show for young, horny men. In Rogan's first *Man Show* episode in 2003, two out of four segments is devoted to jokes about breast implants. If that weren't enough, every commercial break begins and ends with zoom-ins on the show's bikini-clad "Juggies." Another bit from Rogan's first *Man Show* episode features an offensively stereotyped Black man who counsels Rogan to follow his "penis's heart" and spend more time with an exotic dancer. The bit is steeped in racist and sexist iconography that, while supposedly ironic, remains quite racist and sexist.

The Man Show's style proved even more successful when podcasting came around and let it roam free. Historically, comedians could either have a lot of recurring time with a small nightclub audience or an occasional "tight-five" with a national audience on a late-night television show. The growth of standup on Comedy Central and HBO loosened this bind a bit, but not much, given the fierce competition for slots. All of these venues limited the appeal of politically unconventional comedy, including humor aimed at libertarians. Podcasting relieves both temporal and spatial constraints, freeing comedians like Rogan to gather often and go off on extended riffs about whatever is in the pop culture or political ether that week. Tight-fives give way to long digressions, with audiences often tolerating forays into politics, so long as a lighter, comedic vibe eventually returns. Although Rogan's politics may not be easily categorized, they remain anchored to perspectives popular with his key demographic of young men. This is why a typical week of *The Joe Rogan Experience* looks as eclectic as it does—four to five episodes stretching past three hours each with comedian, politician, mixed martial artist, academic, and/or tech entrepreneur. Not all will voice right-wing perspectives, but quite a few will.

For example, Rogan engages seriously with questions of race and IQ that are deeply offensive and out of step with contemporary liberal morality.[14] He says he's for gay rights, but makes light, or worse, of LGBTQ issues, casually using antiquated, hurtful slurs and nomenclature. He invites on voices associated with right-wing extremism and, when the conversation starts getting provocative, is happy to embrace and even encourage the most extreme aspects of their worldview. For example, in the run up to Trump's 2016 election, Rogan interviewed former *Breitbart* writer Milo Yiannopoulos. At one point during the nearly three-hour interview, Yiannopoulos idly mentions that he is thinking about appearing in blackface in order to prove some ill-defined point about free speech. Not missing a beat, Rogan goads him on, saying "you can, and you must." [15]

Rogan's politics are so messy that it is hard to even credit them with being contradictory. Really, they are not even politics, in the sense that they don't necessarily try to align with any electoral outcome. Instead, Rogan's political positions are the distilled essence of the podcasting industry's financial model. They are appeals to straight young white men looking for jokes that scratch their libertarian or otherwise antiestablishment itches. In other words, Rogan isn't as clearly right-wing as some of the other figures we discuss in this book, but he is the loud, boisterous doorman at the right-wing comedy complex's bar, beckoning you in with cheap shots (at liberals) and the promise of connecting with other free-thinking, free-wheeling public figures.

Thus, when Rogan takes a political position, he's really deploying the logic of the podcast industry to attract and appease his key demographic. His approach to the 2020 election illustrates the point. He began with a strong endorsement of Sanders, a figure who enjoyed overwhelming support among young voters and particularly young men.[16] Rogan cited the candidate's consistency and support for health care rights as his concerns. Upon Sanders's exit from the race, Rogan's stated preference swung to Donald Trump over Joe Biden, despite the fact that the former had lived a life of extreme political inconsistency and showed no interest whatsoever in the expansion of health care rights.[17] Perhaps not incidentally, Biden was, at least at the time, exhibiting weakness among young male voters.[18] What first looked like a series of political endorsements from Rogan turned out instead to be a great strategy for selling boxes of raw meat and pubic hair trimmers to his target audience of young men.

The Joe Rogan Experience's treatment of politics—or at least the vague whiff of whatever political discourse filters through the broader cultural zeitgeist—is part of Rogan's long-standing comedic strategy of pursuing young, mostly male audiences who have money to spend but tend to be hard targets for advertisers to reach. Whether he chases, embodies, or even accelerates the political tendencies of young male Americans is hard to say. Rogan is perhaps only partially and only sometimes right-wing. Nonetheless *The Joe Rogan Experience* is a major part of the right-wing comedy complex. Though Rogan may look and feel like an odd counter-cultural character, in the diffuse world of contemporary media he still offers one of the biggest platforms. He thus offers unprecedented audience exposure to the many marginal right-wing figures with fringe right-wing ideas that appear on *JRE* as guests. Sometimes Rogan's comedy and commentary appeal directly to right-wing fans, as when he jokes about blackface with clownish Trump supporters. Just as importantly, however, Rogan's comedy provides an access point for young men and others to visit more extreme parts of the right-wing comedy complex's bar.

THE DARK UNDERBELLY OF LIBERTARIANISM
AND THE *LEGION OF SKANKS*

There are different ways to get to the titillating, regret-filled part of the right-wing comedy complex bar that is the *Legion of Skanks* podcast. One of the easiest is just to skip over from the main party that Joe Rogan is hosting at the front of the venue. Surrounded by an audience primed for heterodox humor and proven willing to enter promotional codes at a comedian's request, Rogan has real power to drive podcast success.

The *Legion of Skanks* hosts Luis Gomez, Dave Smith, and Big Jay Oakerson are regular guests on *The Joe Rogan Experience*, appearing both as individuals and as a unit. In their appearance from a March 2018 episode, they push Rogan as far as he can go on a show that, while committed to a controversial sense of cool, must stay in bounds enough for widespread appeal. As the episode unfolds, the Skanks quickly establish both their individual and group branding, making it clear that they can play along with Rogan, but still promising listeners that if they want to get at the really dirty stuff, they'll need to take a more adventurous scroll through their podcast app. Smith is the brainy ideologue who won't get a dumb tattoo and, whenever possible, wants to interject serious libertarian philosophy into a discussion about how hot former Democratic Congresswoman Tulsi Gabbard is. Gomez plays a regular guy's guy, but one who can pull out his Puerto Rican heritage (though everyone on the show anglicizes his name as "Louis") to either deflect or introduce racism as needed, guiding the show toward Rogan's golden mean of edgy but advertisable. Oakerson is the neanderthal gone self-aware, dipping into various genres of offense but evincing a sense of irony and even occasional masculine vulnerability. To call them diverse would not be quite right, but they do serve to consolidate different flavors of young male listenership that can be pointed at select podcast advertisers.

The conversation between Rogan and the three hosts of the *Legion of Skanks* is revealing, and it illustrates how Rogan is willing and able to serve as an amplifier for fringe libertarian ideas. They weave in and out of various topics friendly to a young, male, libertarian audience, opening with some harmless potty talk and discussing a mutual friend's bout with hemorrhoids. They indulge Rogan's obsession with fighting, both in the mixed martial arts arena and on the street. They riff on the downside of drug prohibition, making relatively cogent, funny observations about the appeals of heroin and the futility of the drug war. And then they talk about women. Oakerson's ex-girlfriend is, of course, so dumb she literally does not know her own name. They talk about the success of their comedy festival, Skankfest, lauding an appearance by the disgraced comic Louis CK and gleefully recounting another comedian's bit which included a mock sexual assault. As good libertarians, Smith, Gomez, and Oakerson are willing to say anything that will bring them a listen. If you like *Rogan's* willingness to flout the rules of propriety, they suggest, then you will love the anarchic, gleefully offensive *Legion of Skanks* podcast.

But the Skanks aim for more than an audience hungry for dirty jokes and racial slurs. So, if you're of a more overtly ideological mind, there is a different, more austere place to be introduced to *Legion of Skanks*: libertarianinstitute.org. Specifically, there's a link on one of the institute's web pages featuring a large, black-and-white headshot of the long-deceased Murray Rothbard, hero of orthodox libertarian economists and politicians. Bow-tied and contemplative, Rothbard stares wistfully

The Legion of Skanks indulge in obscene gestures and racial epithets all in the name of free speech. (GaS Digital)

through his thick-rimmed glasses, a picture of serious thought. The caption reads in plain white-on-red text: "Dave Smith [. . .] on why Rothbard matters." The main link is to a recording of Smith talking to another podcaster about how Rothbard inspires his politics and his comedy. They go through Rothbard's books, with Smith gushing about his genius. They discuss a variety of radical but coolly rendered libertarian arguments ranging from the case for abolishing drunk driving laws to the purpose of creative destruction in the advancement of global living standards. Smith's main role is that of the charismatic proselytizer attesting to the idea that one can be simultaneously funny, informed, and libertarian.

And between the airy photo of Rothbard and Smith's audio dissertation is a link to the *Legion of Skanks* podcast. Click it, and the calm plain text of libertarianinstitute.org is traded instantaneously for bold graffiti-style graphics, a huge photo of Smith giving the middle finger to the camera, and a promise of "shit" talk and "filthy stories" on the "most offensive podcast on Earth." The juxtaposition is shocking and amusing, but also of strategic and political significance. For one, it gives the *Skanks* a sense of gravitas, both tying their show into the popular space of political podcasting and creating a hook for higher-educated, higher-income listeners. One can easily envision free-market, tech-sector disruptor bros coming for Smith's Austrian economics and staying for the *Skanks'* no-rules humor, complete with all varieties of sexism, homophobia, and abject racism. If it seems morally abhorrent, there is always the libertarian's nonaggression principle to point to. For those who enter the right-wing comedy complex's bar through this side door, sophomoric, racist jokes become defiant acts of free speech. A premium subscription morphs into a voluntary contribution in the defense of liberty. A drunken party, however improbably, becomes a movement.

The libertarian values of free markets and free speech are present in virtually every comedian we examine in this book, but none embody these values quite as brazenly as the *Legion of Skanks* podcast. The show was misogynistically named after Oakerson's ex caught him cheating, threw him out, and told him to take up with his "legion of skanks." Each week's episode features a raucous, inebriated discussion among Smith, Gomez, Oakerson, and other guest comics trading war stories about the standup world, as well as the dirtiest of jokes they can bounce off of one another. The Skanks' audience is a fraction of *The Joe Rogan Experience*'s. However, both the aesthetic of *Skanks* and the financial approach of its parent company, GaS Digital, are quite similar to Rogan's. Like *The Joe Rogan Experience, Legion of Skanks* creates intense loyalty in its young male audience by embracing an anti-PC community-building ethos, underpinned by Dave Smith's more explicit libertarian philosophy. Ultimately, this community is united by a crude embrace of the most regressive instincts of shock comedy and aligned with the tastes of the young male audiences so sought after by advertisers and entrenched media industry powers.

Legion of Skanks is the flagship show of GaS Digital, a podcasting network founded in 2016 by *Skanks* cohost Gomez and broadcaster Ralph Sutton. The network hosts dozens of podcasts and web series, with topics ranging from libertarian politics to hair metal to pornography. Recent episodes of most programs are available for free on the GaS homepage, or via streaming services such as Spotify and YouTube. GaS Digital also makes monthly, premium memberships available for customers desiring exclusive content. The podcast that Sutton cohosts with the *Skanks'* Oakerson, for instance, *The SDR Show* (*SDR* stands for *Sex, Drugs, and Rock &*

Roll), welcomes guests from the raunchiest reaches of the worlds of sex work, the alcohol industry, and music. An episode from May 2020, for instance, features a rambling interview with four adult performers there to compete in a "squirt off" to see who could visibly ejaculate the most and fastest. Audio of the interview is available in one window, but video of the sexually explicit material is only available uncensored to users who have the "High Octane All Access" subscription of around $10 per month. The sexually explicit stunt might seem like pure shock value, but it aligns with the free-speech libertarianism of pornographers like Hustler founder Larry Flynt.[19]

GaS Digital's business model of mixing free free-speech-protected comedy with paid subscription-protected obscenity certainly isn't unique. Scores of podcasters and internet content producers thrive with a similar setup on any number of subscription platforms. GaS Digital's explicitly branded embrace of this business model, however, is born of a key moment in social media history. In March 2017, not long after the launch of GaS Digital, YouTube (and parent company Google) announced "expanded safeguards for advertisers," making it easier for them to pull ads from objectionable content.[20] The platform did so after threatened boycotts from several multinational corporations like AT&T and Walmart, whose advertisements were showing up in videos from extremist groups. By making it easier "for brands to pull their advertising from content that was 'potentially objectionable,'" creators whose videos didn't fit neatly into this group—like comedians—saw a near-instant drop in revenue.[21] The invisible hand of the market, it seemed, tightened its grip around what was permissible online, much to the chagrin of YouTubers flustered by the punitive and often arbitrary decisions of sponsors. Even though GaS shows were and continue to be regularly hosted on YouTube, Gomez decried the decision as "anti-art," "anti-comedy," and "anti-creation," echoing long-standing libertarian arguments for free expression.[22] A wholly owned-and-operated network like GaS afforded Gomez and the Skanks the digital playground that would not only be free of tech company mandates, but also allow them to build a specific comedic brand identity based in liberty and transgression.

Comedy podcasts like *Legion of Skanks* and the GaS Digital network manifest the two media industry phenomena we described in the introduction of this book—convergence and audience siloing. Spotify's deal in 2020 to bring Rogan exclusively onto the platform, for instance, is one example of how "the fragmentation in podcasting is slowly giving way to platform consolidation in the service of monetization and audience maximization."[23] It's not just that streaming audio giants like Spotify are luring big talent. They are also using that talent to target increasingly narrow audience groups, siloing them into easy-to-sell-to segments. The service now "algorithmically generates podcast playlists and has launched its own advertising tool called Streaming Ad Insertion that lets targeted ads be placed into shows as people stream them."[24] This reorganization of audiences is intentional, displaying and selling back to them their own identity through the podcasts they're listening to. Media scholar Sarah Florini has demonstrated how this dynamic can induce in Black listeners, for instance, a desire to "reproduce a sense of being in Black social spaces."[25] In a very different but parallel fashion, fans of right-wing comedy podcasts like *The Joe Rogan Experience* and *Legion of Skanks* forge identities based on opposition to what they view as politically correct, liberal, mainstream culture.

In many cases, podcasters now aim to form these tight affiliative bonds with listeners first, and worry about monetization later. As the journalist Jamie Lauren Keiles notes, podcasters' parasocial relationships with fans are often their primary business. The intimate, everyday nature of podcast listening establishes deeply personal—though one-sided—connections between performers and listeners, allowing the latter to network and bond with other fans sharing a particular comedic worldview. This worldview is turned into data for podcast advertisers, then sold back to listeners in the form of ad-reads for off-brand Viagra and CBD supplements from Smith, Gomez, and Oakerson. As Keiles puts it: "Today's podcast hosts are not just on-air personae, but community managers, designers of incentives, spokespeople for subscription toothbrushes and business-to-business software. The worth of a podcast is no longer just its content, but rather the sum of the relations it produces."[26]

In other words, *Legion of Skanks* and GaS comedians have intentionally set out to connect their opposition to authority with a specific fan base already receptive to that worldview, then foster loyalty in that fanbase through premium content and live events. Media scholar Michael Curtin describes this practice as "edge," clearly defining and intensely courting a small, lucrative audience segment with tailored, often incendiary content.[27] For Curtin, the appeal of edgy content to a niche audience is precisely its ability to repel larger audience groups. In the case of podcasting, comedians utilizing "edge" intentionally make their targeted viewers feel marginalized (whether that is the case or not) in order to imbue in them a sense of hostility toward mainstream cultural institutions. The Skanks' aggressively offensive humor creates a largely male, libertarian in-group at the same time that it repulses anyone looking on from the mainstream outside of the GaS Digital family.

For Gomez, the impulse to start his own network came from sharing with listeners the sense of oppositionality—however manufactured—built into edge. Several of his early podcasting projects couldn't get off the ground, Gomez claims, because their audiences weren't *already* big enough to attract conventional advertisers. As Gomez said in 2018: "Our fans love us, so I hate that networks would imply there's no value in our fan base."[28] Although *Skanks* started modestly, Gomez now claims the show "gets a quarter of a million downloads per episode," and its YouTube channel draws anywhere between twenty thousand to fifty thousand views per episode.[29] For comparison, *The Joe Rogan Experience* routinely garners millions of views per episode on YouTube. Rogan's most-watched YouTube video, for instance, is a 2018 interview with Elon Musk that has amassed nearly fifty million views.

The *Skanks'* audience is thus smaller, but also more coherent, having been forged in a proprietary platform born of an ideological commitment. Both on *Skanks* and in interviews, Gomez and his cohorts pair libertarian complaints about big government with Trumpian conspiracies about tech companies shadow banning their non-progressive ideas.

> When you watch what's happening in the world, no matter what side you're on with net neutrality or any of that bullshit. . . . there's no doubt about it, one day somebody's coming for us. One day somebody's coming to say "you can't say that." Whether it's the FCC, whether it's Comcast, Verizon, or the SJWs . . . it doesn't matter if they are the good guys or the bad guys. The truth of the matter is . . . *it's all of them* . . . they're all going to come. So for me . . . I'm building my storm shelter. I'm creating these projects that are mine. No one is going to take away my podcast or my podcast Network.[30]

As we explore in the following examples of segments from *Legion of Skanks*, their unrelenting appeal to the lowest common denominator—to always take bits to the most racist, sexist, homophobic place possible—is both a branding mechanism and an intentional testing of free speech. This branded humor fortifies both their bond with listeners and their aggrieved resolve against anyone who's not down with the Skanks' provocations.

HOOKING UP WITH THE *LEGION OF SKANKS* IN THE RIGHT-WING COMEDY COMPLEX BAR

Explicit discussions of American electoral politics are rare in most *Skanks* episodes. Occasionally, someone will joke about Trump or another high-profile politician. Or Smith (clearly unable to restrain himself) will inter-ject thoughts on a recent political event, only to be good-naturedly shouted down by his cohorts. When party politics do enter the *Skanks* universe, they do so mostly to be dismissed as too highbrow, in much the same way that the boisterous group of drunks at the bar jeer the quiet gentleman in the booth sipping his martini and reading a book. Instead, political content serves as one of many reference points off of which the Skanks riff, always in ways that support the show's (and GaS Digital network's) broader brand of bawdy, base bro humor. This brand also has the feel of natural connectedness to a broader libertarian ethos, one that extends out beyond the *Skanks* and GaS Digital through the lurid back-alleys of the right-wing comedy complex.

In an episode from May 2020, for example, the Skanks begin by riffing about whether Oakerson or Gomez would make for a better "president of Skanks." It's a silly bit, but one that allows the comedians to build the sort of self-branded world that makes its young male listeners feel like one of the guys, just talking shit about who is better qualified to be the fictional leader of "Skankonia." Oakerson makes fun of Gomez for being too eager to interact with fans, while the latter prods Oakerson right back. "And then Dave [Smith] could be the weird third-party candidate," guest comic Dan Soder adds of the third Skank. "Dave's the treasurer," says Oakerson. "Because he's a fucking Jew," Gomez adds. Over the course of 2020, the Skanks would extend the bit into a running gag complete with a rigged election. However, the joke largely remained apolitical and only served as a conduit for the comics' broader commitment to libertarian principles and offensive free speech.

Later in the same May 2020 episode, the "Skankonia" bit returns with even more edge, doubling down on its appeal to young male listeners and repelling others outside of that demographic at the same time. After a lengthy, graphic discussion of various sexual conquests and the joys of sleeping with large women, the comedians riff on the ethics of ejaculating inside a woman during unprotected sex. A very stoned Gomez contradicts himself about whether or not he will intentionally climax inside a woman in certain situations, leading to this exchange with guest (and *Joe Rogan Experience* regular) Tony Hinchcliffe:

HINCHCLIFFE: So if you're having sex with a hot chick that you just met that night, and you're fucking her, and she goes, "When you cum, I want you to cum inside of me," you'd be like, "No"?

GOMEZ: No no no, I would 100 percent say, "Of course."

HINCHCLIFFE: That's the fastest track to becoming president of the Legion of Skanks, by the way.

GOMEZ: "I took off that condom when you weren't looking." Do you guys think that that should be a sex crime? I said yes recently to that question—

OAKERSON: It is!

GOMEZ: Not in my country, not when I'm president, not in Skankonia!

Oakerson then initiates a bit using an Atticus Finch accent in a mock trial about whether or not it's illegal to ejaculate inside a woman without her knowledge or consent.[31] He takes the joke to its most extreme, chauvinistic place before Oakerson ends it by urging the fictional woman in the scenario to "Come on in for a 'fill-er-up!'" Not coincidentally, this canned catchphrase—"Fill-er up!"—plays at the top of all GaS Digital podcasts. The exchange is a disturbing, yet instructive, look into the world of libertarian podcasting through the eyes of the Skanks. It is a subtle reinforcement of GaS Digital's brand identity and independence from more mainstream podcasting and advertising institutions. It's also a button to an unrelentingly graphic discussion of male sexual indiscretion and prowess. It's not enough for the Skanks to, say, brag about sexual conquests. But in order to fit the brand, that conversation must routinely go to the most base and regressive place, positioning the women of those conquests as worthless, voiceless receptacles of male sexual power. They must say these things, it seems, because they can.

To be clear, our analysis of *Skanks* isn't a call for libertarian comedy podcasts to do better, or to be more polite, in the same way professional political commentators were forever waiting for Trump to act more presidential. Our goal is to make clear that the repeated choices of the Skanks—and podcasters like them—to steer bits into the most controversial, incendiary places is intentional and driven by the commercial imperatives of the podcasting industry. It is a financial ploy, not a plea for free speech protection. What's more, the Skanks' financial motivations do not exist in a vacuum. They're part of the same discursive network of sexual domination and humiliation by many American men in positions of power, be they leaders of college athletics programs, major broadcast networks, or the United States of America.

It is no coincidence, for instance, that the Skanks' semiannual standup comedy festival, Skankfest, served as the venue for an unannounced comeback performance by former liberal hero turned libertarian cause célèbre Louis C.K. in the summer of 2019. The massively successful standup had kept a relatively low profile since admitting to masturbating in front of women comics without their consent in 2017. He found a friendly audience, however, in *Legion of Skanks* fans, who gave him a standing ovation. Given the flippantly graphic nature of *Skanks* bits like the one described above, C.K. ought to have been relieved the fans that night didn't jeer him for not having done something worse.

Skanks is political, then, in how it uses the guise of libertarianism in order to welcome the cultural concerns of aggrieved straight white men who believe they no longer have a place in today's world of political correctness. To the Skanks, PC-culture is their ultimate asset and enemy, and any mainstream institution that plays it safe gets a middle finger. In their minds, they are fighters against a system that tamps down their freedom of expression and, by extension, their freedom to maximize profit. Their overt hostility to contemporary identity politics comes through in many other recurring bits from the show, ones that lead further away from the realm of a cohesive electoral project to the ugliest, unwashed corners of the right-wing complex's libertarian watering hole.

One recurring bit is the racist and misogynist game "Who's More Justi-fied ... ?" in which the Skanks watch viral internet videos of people hitting women or using racial slurs. They then argue over who is most justified doing these egregious acts. We've covered the Skanks' attitudes toward women in the previous example, so suffice it to say that they very often find women getting punched, kicked, and beaten up to be hilariously justi-fied. No one should be surprised to hear, then, that Oakerson, Smith, and Gomez have an unrepentantly graphic and unfiltered style of joking about race and using racial epithets, too.

In addition to their casual, routine use of racial slurs, the trio regularly engages in extended bits grounded in ugly racial stereotypes, especially ones centered on African Americans. In one infamous *Skanks* riff, Oaker-son has (for reasons too dumb to explain) a Black infant doll that he uses to improvise the baby's version of a standup set from *Def Comedy Jam*, the extremely influential 1990s HBO show featuring Black comics. Here, though, *Def Comedy Jam* is reduced by the Skanks to mere minstrelsy. After some free-associative uses of the n-word, Oakerson launches into a bit inviting the white women in the audience to fellate the Black baby standup comic. "I be long-dicking bitches!" he screams, mixed with jokes about how the baby is excited to be treated to name-brand cereal because "daddy out of jail." Once again, at every turn, the Skanks use their free-dom to take their humor straight into the gutter, indulging in the most racist of stereotypes about how Black men are impoverished, lascivious criminals.

In another bit from 2019, Oakerson, Smith, and Gomez watch a news segment about gendered pronouns from NowThis, a progressive social media–focused news organization targeted at young viewers. The video's host is a young Black woman named Foluke Tuakli, a name that predict-ably sends Gomez into a fit of derisive giggles. "I'd Fol-ook her right in her Tuakli," he says, straining for a way to sexually objectify and degrade her. As she explains the problematic nature of using "guys" to address a mixed-gender group, Oakerson quips that he "hopes this bitch gets AIDS." "Would I be justified calling her the 'n-word'?" guest comic Jim Florentine chimes in to rousing applause from the live audience in atten-dance who surely recognizes the nod to the *Skanks'* recurring bit. By now, you've gotten to know the Skanks enough to guess where the rest of the segment goes—Smith homophobically calls the NowThis staff "f*****s,"

Oakerson imitates Taukli through the racist "mammy" stereotype, and Gomez decries her pronunciation as "cunty."

In writing about the rise of right-wing standup comedy in the Trump era, the comedy journalist Seth Simons notes, "Media consumption today is so plentiful and so specialized that it's easy to never encounter comedy outside your own tastes. . . . Comedians can forge whole, quite successful careers within walled gardens where the ones who engage in bigotry and hate speech face no meaningful repercussions."[32] Importantly, Simons points out, the media industry structures bolstering liberals' psychological complex and siloing them into their own enclaves are the same ones siloing *Legion of Skanks* fans with one another. These structures usher right-wing comedy fans from the complex's bar to more scaled-up locales, where Dave Smith debates libertarian theory with journalists at *Reason* magazine. Some libertarian comedians, however, resist being pulled into the dirtier parts of the complex's bar entirely, salvaging their self-respect but making it much harder to stay in business.

A KINDER, GENTLER (LESS PROFITABLE) LIBERTARIAN COMEDIAN

Andrew Heaton would love to get his little drink stand out of the right-wing comedy complex. If only it would let him break his lease. His current project, *The Political Orphanage* podcast, is built around a nonpartisan perspective and employs that not-so-neon tagline, "Good and intelligent people can disagree on matters of substance." The *Legion of Skanks'* "Fill 'er Up!" it is not. Heaton is, we argue, evidence that libertarian comedy need not rely on extreme rhetoric in order to create laughs. It also, however, emphasizes how little economic potential exists in the realm of responsible right-wing comedy. Heaton knows this and keeps looking for a way out. "So I start a funny sci-fi podcast, no politics," he tells us over a spotty Oklahoma cell phone connection. "It's going great, but then I do an episode on space robots and I still get iTunes reviews about my 'libertarian humor.'"[33] Heaton, both for personal and professional reasons, no longer identifies as a conservative. But whether he likes it or not, he always ends up playing one on TV.

To be fair, Heaton's resume is dominated by right-branded comedy efforts, including stints as the comedian-in-residence at such deeply ideological outlets as Fox Business, Reason TV, and Blaze Media. After nearly ten years in the right-wing comedy complex, he knows which demographic pays his bills, even if he desperately wishes to expand it: "mostly young, mostly male, pretty educated and very, very into being libertarian." *The Political Orphanage*, for all of its admirable interest in eschewing partisan hackery, features plenty of guests and topics that appeal to his accrued fanbase. Certainly, Heaton goes in directions that Dave Smith or the *Legion of Skanks* never would, finding humor without giving offense and respectfully inviting feminist comics, transgender performers, and even progressive perspectives on his show. Nonetheless, he'll spend an hour with someone like David Frisby, a pro-Brexit British libertarian oddly intent on persuading Americans that the Civil War was not, in fact, about slavery. Heaton's media career is an exercise in the study of tradeoffs, his association with the world of right-wing comedy accelerating his career, but never quite in the correct direction.

Heaton's unusual path began in Washington, D.C., where he served as a legislative assistant for blue dog, pro-business Democratic congressmen, while moonlighting as a standup comic. In 2014, he escaped to New York City, making the path-determining decision to take a job as a writer and editor for the Fox Business Network talk show *The Independents*. Even at the time, Heaton felt ambivalence about the impact that Fox News branding might have on his career prospects. *The Independents*, however, was a unique project, taking up an explicitly libertarian angle and mixing an attention to civil liberties with the more predictably Fox Business Network issue of market deregulation. When the show rebranded as *Kennedy* in 2015, Heaton began producing a comedic segment called "Topical Storm" that reported on social media trends. Though made up largely of web memes and other ephemera, partisanship is apparent in its approach to Hillary Clinton, a frequent target, whom the segment describes as a "robot kraken" among other less-than-endearing terms.

After leaving the Fox Business Network, Heaton moved to Reason TV, a web video outgrowth of the long-running libertarian periodical *Reason* magazine. Producing his own videos, Heaton stayed away from political sniping or partisan cruelty, creating upbeat explainer videos advocating for traditional libertarian policy positions with a particular focus on reducing the size of government. In a video entitled "We Should Privatize the Post Office," Heaton makes just that case, wryly noting that the semi-public constitution of the USPS results in "the efficiency of government with the cuddliness of a large corporation." In "We're Spending Too Much on Defense" he observes that the United States' "kill-y thing" budget of $700 billion would be enough to buy "one Turkey" or, alternatively, "thirty billion turkeys." The videos are collisions of math problems, history lessons, and dexterous wordplay, which, even if you disagree with their conclusions, can be judged as honest attempts to amusingly argue a position. Certainly, they never aim to provoke offense, shock, or belittle anyone. At the same time, the association with *Reason* brings with it inevitable baggage, being supported in part by the radically libertarian Koch Industries.[34] *Reason* also has a checkered past that includes the publication of Holocaust deniers, and its critics accuse it of promoting both overt and structural racism.[35] Yes, Heaton's own programs are consistently respectful and comparatively inclusive in their rhetoric and guest lists. Nonetheless, his associations with Fox Business and *Reason* tend to create opportunities to work in the right-wing comedy complex while making him an object of suspicion in other parts of the media map.

Looking back, it seems all too obvious that Heaton's next career move was only going to make things worse. At the time, however, it sort of made sense. There was a moment, if one can believe it, when noted right-wing conspiracy theorist Glenn Beck was feted by political centrists for taking a principled, measured stand against the 2016 Trump campaign. After years of spouting anti-Semitic conspiracies about George Soros, calling Barack Obama a racist, and comparing left-leaning opponents to Nazis, Beck found brief but intense favor in the mainstream. *Rolling Stone*, the *Washington Post*, and *The Atlantic* wrote pieces about his conversion. Liberal satire icon Samantha Bee invited him onto her show, *Full Frontal*, for a bit in which the two talk through their differences and eat cake. And after Trump's victory, Beck published a *New York Times* op-ed headlined "Don't Move to Canada, Talk to the Other Side."[36] For a moment, Beck and his company, Blaze Media, exemplified the hope that the American right might come to its senses. It was during this halcyon phase that Beck approached Andrew Heaton with a job offer he could not, apparently, refuse.

And, for a while at least, it went pretty well. Heaton was given full editorial control over an hour-long daily talk show available to Blaze's decidedly right-wing subscriber base. The program, *Something's Off with Andrew Heaton*, was a shoestring operation, but one that allowed its host the freedom to develop his unique comedic voice. Inverting the model of *The Daily Show*, *Something's Off* opens with a short segment of absurdist sketch comedy, followed by an extensive, substantive interview focusing on policy questions of particular libertarian interest. Often, the comedy segment is topical and, though laced with Heaton's free-market perspective, it is by no means right-wing propaganda. In one episode Heaton reimagines the famous "Mueller Report" as a John Grisham thriller, describing the original version as "literary dreck" that lacks "ninjas, sex, a spunky sidekick" and "British seafaring vessels." Bemoaning the report's focus on a "bloviating orange guy falling all over himself," he sets out to rewrite a sexier version of the story. Heaton edits the report, inserting a variety of spy genre tropes, the most amusing of which is Mike Pence repeatedly emerging "from the shadows," to brandish a gun and utter the phrase "end of the line, Biff!" in hard-boiled reference to Donald Trump's uncanny resemblance to the villain from *Back to the Future*. It is very silly and very funny, while carving a clear distinction between Heaton's libertarian values and the baser instincts of the other libertarian comedians discussed throughout this chapter.

The interview segments on *Something's Off* are similarly nuanced, featuring a range of guests aimed explicitly at overcoming polarized, sensational rhetoric. Episode 62 from 2018 of the show moves quickly from an absurdist bit about spam filtering to a forty-minute discussion on transgender military service with the transgender comedian Carya Magyar. At the very start of the interview, Heaton tells his audience that the discussion requires both transgender and military perspectives and that he is choosing to begin with the former. In episodes 106 and 107 he facilitates a discussion on climate change that, while stopping short of endorsing progressive policy solutions, goes directly against the climate denialism often espoused by Glenn Beck on his own Blaze Media show. The serious, and often funny, debate confronts viewers with the reality of human-influenced climate change, with free-market solutions such as carbon taxes and nuclear energy emerging as favored policy approaches.

Something's Off illustrates a more pro-social vision of libertarian comedy, avoiding cruelty and challenging progressive thinkers in a manner worthy of consideration and response. It also, however, makes plain the long-term economic difficulties inherent in being both nuanced and open to conservative ideas. Although Heaton affirms that he never lost editorial control of *Something's Off*, he also notes the niche nature of his audience. In the world of Blaze Media, only a select subset of subscribers were willing to countenance his tempered, anti-bile approach to political humor. According to Heaton, he quickly developed about ten thousand viewers, but struggled to grow thereafter. Blaze, of course, took notice, suggesting he take up "culture war" issues and provide a bit more "red meat" to an audience keen on finding an intense, self-affirming alternative to what they perceived as liberal mainstream media bias.[37]

Heaton not only refused to do this but actively, even visibly, pushed back. As part of his contract, Heaton served as a panelist on the Blaze Media show *The News and Why It Matters*. Though nominally hosted by Sarah Gonzalez, the table talk program is dominated by Glenn Beck. As Beck moved away from his 2016 rebranding as a rational, liberal-friendly voice, his commentary grew in both outrage and pro-Trump partisanship, leading to a rather obvious incompatibility with Heaton's comedy. In a 2018 episode, Beck defends Megyn Kelly's defense of blackface Halloween costuming. Heaton sits stunned, blinking frequently before eventually offering that he "would be interested in hearing the opinions of Black people." Beck becomes near irate at Heaton's responsible rhetoric. Heaton finishes the show by offering a comic, well-articulated libertarian take on the perils of soybean tariffs. Heaton's brand was, quite clearly, no longer Beck's.

Unsurprisingly, Heaton's employment with Blaze Media lasted less than a year. Putting it succinctly, Heaton says "I'd be much richer if I were willing to go Alt-Right." Instead, he converted his *Something's Off* formula into the independent *Political Orphanage* podcast, financed exclusively through Patreon donations from listeners. The show maintains its libertarian perspective, interviewing prominent free-market politicians and writers. The comedy segments, however, grow increasingly abstract, drawing on wild, absurdist premises. A representative bit makes a sales pitch for an innovative product: transparent bagels. With a regular bagel, the sketch goes, how can you be sure your local deli isn't "using lower-quality meat which contains screws or bottle caps?" Transparent bagels, Heaton reads, are "essential to health and safety," particularly if you don't want to spend time and money "at the magnet doctor getting all those screws out."

The joke is very strange, very funny, and, in its own odd way, libertarian. Bits such as this one center around outlandish solutions in search of problems. They are logical if, but only if, you accept their comically faulty premises. If you grant that bagel screws are a real threat, it's certainly worth diverting some funding toward their mitigation. Though absurd, the sketch parallels how libertarian critics tend to view things like municipal health regulations or the ever-expanding military budget. If you accept without sufficient evidence that, for example, a certain country is aiming weapons of mass destruction in your direction, there's no end to what you'll spend to stop it. The same would go for expensive government social programs that libertarians believe to be counterproductive. They are ideas that make sense if, but only if, you accept a premise the libertarian critic finds fundamentally faulty. The transparent bagel joke is thus libertarian insofar as libertarians are committed to the idea that people and institutions tend to create problems—such as having to invent see-through pumpernickel—when they claim to be solving them.

This absurd comedy echoes a certain paradoxical element of Heaton's career. Every solution he comes up with in his quest to make a living as a comedian—Fox Business Network, *Reason*, Blaze Media—only creates further obstacles to future success. Googling his name brings up associations that liberal and even centrist comedy venues may find anathema. At the same time, he can never truly set up shop next to Joe Rogan, Dave Smith, and the *Legion of Skanks*. His demographic is too close to theirs, but his demeanor, moral code, and approach to generating laughs are too far away. He is inside the right-wing comedy complex, but not of it. As the rest of the libertarians sling stiff drinks and roll robust joints, Heaton's little stand next door is selling lightly spiked lemonade to the occasional open-minded customer who stumbles over.

INTO THE BASEMENT OF THE RIGHT-WING COMEDY COMPLEX

As we have argued in this chapter, libertarian comedy doesn't have to be ugly. Due to its economic ethos and relationship to the broader mediasphere, it just often is. Libertarianism's foundational nonaggression principle does not require racist jokes. It instead refers merely to the belief that speech ought to remain thoroughly unregulated. The connection between libertarian thought and racist joke-making, however, is more than coincidental. As the economic historian Quinn Slobodian argues, there is an intellectual through line that runs from dry libertarian philosophy to a disregard for economic inequality and, sometimes, straight into outright racism.[38] As Slobodian argues, libertarians are faced with the difficult reality that an unrestricted "universal marketplace" will often result in distinct inequities that correlate heavily with racial, ethnic, and other identity markers.[39] Forced with either criticizing the market or the identity groups within it, some libertarians choose the latter. Inequality, they argue, must result from the relative unfitness of the groups that are less economically successful. These groups, particularly Black Americans, are also often those targeted by the "anything goes" philosophy of Joe Rogan or *Legion of Skanks*.

In the realm of libertarian economics, this disturbing train of thought moves from one philosopher to another, sloping toward the ugliest elements of contemporary right-wing social theory. For example, Slobodian argues that Ludwig von Mises, a founding father of libertarian economics, allowed for "the possibility of race" as an explanatory factor in his economic analysis. Subsequent writers, including Dave Smith's hero Murray Rothbard, displayed an explicit "openness" to "racialist" arguments in explaining economic reality.[40] Today, far-right figures such as the white supremacist Christopher Cantwell engage rather directly with this line of libertarian theory as they develop avowedly neo-Nazi worldviews.[41] Certainly, not all libertarians go down this ugly path after finding an amusing video about reduced public spending or decreased governmental regulation. The path from freeing markets to justifying racial prejudice is, however, well-trodden for those who wish to explore it.

The right-wing comedy complex offers a similar pathway from the mainstream, above-ground libertarian bar to the dark, dank, subterranean basement of trolling, white supremacist comedy that we consider in the next chapter. The very logic of the complex, which aims to collect right-wing audiences and then move them among a variety of interrelated products, ensures this possibility. A listen to *The Joe Rogan Experience* might introduce you to Dave Smith. You then might check out Dave Smith's solo podcast, *Part of the Problem*, and come away feeling smart about your desire not to pay taxes. Recommendation algorithms from your podcast player then implore you to try out the *Legion of Skanks*, which turns up the heat as the gang casually slings the n-word and makes a series of Jews-in-the-oven jokes. Now you're into the GaS digital network, so you check out Michael Malice's podcast *Your Welcome*. On it, (the Jewish) Malice will no doubt promote his 2019 book, *The New Right*, which talks about "funny" responses to "the Jewish Question" found at alt-right gatherings and on the anarchic website 4chan.[42] From there, you can find a startling variety of racist, misogynist, and anti-Semitic material dressed in irony, including *The Daily Shoah*, a Nazi podcast whose name depravedly merges Jon Stewart's legacy with the Hebrew term for the Holocaust. Of course, most people do not follow this path. Some libertarians just take a sip from Andrew Heaton. Others get wasted with the Skanks. However, enough right-wing comedy fans are looking for more—sincere, direct, action-oriented violence, racism, misogyny, anti-Semitism and so on—that we must descend further into the right-wing comedy complex in order to understand just how deep it goes.

5 Trolling the Depths of the Right-Wing Comedy Complex

Jesse Watters, Greg Gutfeld, Dennis Miller, Tim Allen, Steven Crowder, *The Babylon Bee*, Joe Rogan, and the *Legion of Skanks* aren't hiding from anyone. They occupy the ground level of the right-wing comedy complex, selling their wares on YouTube and Facebook, even if the algorithms of social media keep their content safely hidden from liberal consumers. If you get your news primarily from a customized feed, you likely come across either all or none of these figures on a daily basis. For liberals, this social media filter bubble contributes to the psychological complex that creates a pleasant, conservative-free world of comedy. For the right, social media siloing fuses together a coalition and customer base that includes everything from establishment Republicans to Evangelical Christians to libertine libertarians. Contemporary media infrastructure also, as we detail in this chapter, allows the ugliest, most violent aspects of far-right culture to connect to the more conventional, if often abhorrent, ones we've discussed thus far. This dynamic creates pathways from the above-ground world of regressive conservatism to the subterranean realm of the more exotic purveyors of comedic hatred. We describe the latter in this chapter as the right-wing comedy complex's basement: a dark, dirty lair full of trolls.

Ironically, this deeper level is maybe the part of the right-wing comedy complex best known to most some liberal readers. There are a number of reasons for this. For one, there is tremendous, ostentatious racism in the world of online trolling, connecting it to histories of minstrelsy and offensive jokes that liberal discourse often recognizes as defining conservative humor. As scholar Whitney Phillips argues, self-defined trolls invoke outlandish, racist language in order to evoke a response and then disassociate themselves from their own words by offering an ever so unpersuasive "just trolling" defense.[1] Relatedly, the 2016 election of Donald Trump, fueled in no small part by supposedly funny—but definitely racist and misogynist— Pepe the Frog memes made the weird world of right-wing trolling impossible to ignore. Scholars such as Viveca Greene and Angela Nagle have offered incisive documentation of this phenomenon, with mainstream news outlets also devoting ample space to right-wing troll culture.[2]

Furthermore, liberals have far less reason to claim ownership of the world of memes and 4chan discussions in which right-wing troll humor thrives. As we discussed in chapter 1, it is demonstrably difficult for liberal discourse to conceive of a conservative doing the ironic, intelligent satire of a Jon Stewart. Morally bankrupt, ostensibly comedic right-wing meme masters, however, do align with liberal understandings of how conservatives aim to be funny. Nonetheless, few on the left, or even the center, have fully grappled with how exactly right-wing trolling circulates, how it connects to other forms of right-wing comedy, and just how ugly some of its most popular examples are.

A full understanding of the deepest, darkest level of the right-wing comedy complex requires a guide, an insider familiar with both the complex's above-ground and subterranean levels. This guide must be able to trace not only the ways in which irony, comedy, and hate speech intermingle, but also how they recirculate back up to the surface level of more mainstream forms of right-wing comedy. For that, we summon the enigmatic, problematic character of right-wing troll Michael Malice.

MICHAEL MALICE: RIGHT-WING COMEDY COMPLEX CONCIERGE

Michael Malice didn't build the right-wing comedy complex. But, somehow, he has collected all of the keys. Malice is the complex's concierge, perhaps the only person who really knows how the whole labyrinthine structure actually works. As we have discussed throughout this book, right-wing comedy includes a wide range of ideologies, some of which stand in apparent contradiction to one another. It is hard, for example, to see the connected, mutually beneficial linkages between the libertine excesses of the *Legion of Skanks* and the Christian gatekeeping of *The Babylon Bee*. Malice, however, shows up regularly in both spaces, connecting them and the rest of the complex, representing the hippest, strangest, and potentially most dangerous form of contemporary right-wing comedy: trolling. As we detail in this chapter, Malice's celebration of the troll not only brings together the various complex properties—from Fox News to Dennis Miller to Joe Rogan—we have already encountered. He also connects this above-ground, mainstream world of right-wing comedy to a subterranean domain in which hatred, abject racism, violence, and outright fascism reign.

Malice is, by his own admission, a troll. Although the media often use this term loosely and inconsistently, Malice offers a straightforward definition of the concept. As he says in his book, *The New Right*, a troll is someone who strives to turn "an audience into a performer by exploiting their flaws for comedic effect."[3] Citing the comedian Andy Kaufman as the progenitor of the style, Malice sees trolling as the art of comedic reversal. Whereas most comedians aim to keep the spotlight, trolls turn their audiences into spectacles of embarrassing emotionality. His Twitter feed, with well over three hundred thousand followers, routinely demonstrates such trolling through its mixture of seemingly serious, ultra-libertarian anarcho-capitalist philosophies and absurdist jokes aimed to provoke naïfs from across the political spectrum.

His humor is very, very online—to the point that it is nearly impossible to translate to the page. We'll give it a shot, nonetheless. For example, when a Twitter user responded, "You're not funny" to one of Malice's many tasteless jokes about Joe Biden's mental fitness, Malice replied "my not funny what." We'll give you a moment with that one. OK, it's a joke with a few layers, but nothing approaching a traditional comedic payoff. Malice's "my not funny what" mimics the knee-jerk response of many online grammar police types who choose to correct their interlocutor's use of "your" and "you're," as opposed to engaging with the actual topic of debate. "My not funny what" would be just a dull schoolyard retort if the respondent had actually used "your." But she didn't. She used "you're," which means "you are," and she meant to say "you are not funny," which she did with perfect clarity, if little panache. What then to do with Malice's "my not funny what"? Well, nothing really, and that's the point. A third-party observer is made to imagine the frustrated, grammatically proficient attacker now stuck with no choice but either to explain to Malice a fact he evidently already knows—that she used the right word—or to shrug a silent "touché," having been bested by someone who refused to even argue. The comedy emerges entirely from a sketch that only exists in the reader's mind, with Malice forcing the respondent to play the fool by first playing one himself. This, for Malice, is the essence of a successful, comic troll.

Sometimes, Malice calls his shot, tweeting out, "The following tweet will be a troll," before posting something he knows is incorrect. In the wake of Supreme Court Justice Ruth Bader Ginsburg's death in September of 2020, Malice announced a troll that would cause "boomercons" (conservative baby boomers) to melt down.[4] He then tweeted that *Roe vs. Wade* can never be changed because it is "part of the Constitution," a claim that can be disproven with the most cursory of googles.[5] Like clockwork, old-school, square right-wingers went nuclear, demanding that Malice explain himself and offering self-satisfied "nu-uhs." The joke, of course, is on anyone who takes the bait. As the cliché goes, you can't wake up someone who is pretending to sleep. Malice knows his statement is false and is just enjoying the havoc he has wrought. Again, Malice plays the fool in order to also play the puppeteer. The "that's not funny" liberal is forced into a stony, comedic silence, and the "well actually" boomer is worked into a harried ALL CAPS-lather, both because Malice was happy to be wrong in the service of being, if you enjoy him, funny.

And it is this oddly nihilistic, ideologically flexible style of comedy that makes Malice such an important part of the right-wing comedy complex. He shows up, literally, everywhere that we have toured in the preceding pages. At the big box store of Fox News, he plays a hip consulting comedian, brought in for the benefit of Fox's older, conservative audience to shed light on what the kids are up to these days. He joins Greg Gutfeld, who none too awkwardly asks Malice to rate President Trump's "troll game." Malice gives Gutfeld and his viewers exactly what they want:

Trump is the "best troll we've seen."[6] He goes on the *Dennis Miller Option*, where Miller frames Malice's podcast *Night Shade* in paleo terms, comparing him to the legendary, if nearly forgotten, AM radio host Art Bell. After Malice offers a banal joke about the death of Jeffrey Epstein, Miller calls him "fucking hilarious." For Miller, Malice is hip and pretty much just like him, a flattering combination that makes the old pro feel just a bit younger. On *The Babylon Bee*'s podcast, the Jewish atheist Malice teaches the guileless Evangelical hosts about QAnon and other dirty parts of the internet. When Malice corrects them about things they are proud not to know, the *Bee* hosts ironically declare that he's "owned them with facts and logic." Talking to Dave Smith of the *Legion of Skanks*, he elaborately spells out where libertarianism ends and anarcho-capitalism (his brand of right-wing politics) begins. On *The Joe Rogan Experience*, he forgoes philosophy and Austrian economics, instead spending hours talking about psychedelic drug use while peppering in a few egregious moments of playful homophobia. Malice can be something to everyone because he is, in reality, no one to anyone. He is the right-wing comedy complex's most basic and profitable algorithm personified. He moves from storefront to storefront, bringing a youth-friendly, stylish aesthetic and the endlessly flexible comedic mode of trolling with him wherever he goes.

There is, of course, something else that connects Malice and the other storefronts in the right-wing comedy complex: a willingness to embrace, or at least excuse, racism, misogyny, homophobia, and other forms of hatred used in the service of comedic brand identity. As humor scholar Viveca Greene argues, trolls, despite their "playfulness, and their capacity to generate laughter," often serve a "serious sociopolitical function."[7] And it's not a pretty one. Malice is not nearly the worst offender, but like many other trollish voices on the right, he offends in disturbing ways in order to provoke a response. As the scholar Angela Nagle puts it, the Malice-style trolling that populates websites such as 4chan is often just "old-fashioned racism dressed up as Internet-savvy satire."[8] Malice himself admits as much, noting that much trolling involves racist language and ideas. He defends this practice, however, noting that trolls use racism only because race is "such an easy way to get the sensitive to act out."[9] Sure. And whacking people with a crowbar is a great way to make them scream, but to say so is much closer to a confession than an excuse. Malice, it would seem, is arguing that people are *too* sensitive about race. And trolls—practitioners of the art of pushing people's buttons in order to watch them squirm, squeal, and seethe—can't be asked to pass up their most inviting opportunities just so a few people can be spared offense. If this sounds like a sophomoric excuse for people itching to say the n-word or give a steaming hot phrenology take, that's because it is. Malice excuses racism, homophobia, misogyny, transphobia, and anti-Semitism all too easily. Hey, it's just trolling, he says, why so serious?

Malice's self-interested, morally dubious commitment to the art of trolling allows him to pull one last key off of his concierge's ring, opening up the door to the truly dank vice den in the basement of the right-wing comedy complex. In the introduction of his book, *The New Right*, Malice offers a colorful portrayal of his infiltration of young, right-wing social groups. He describes his first meeting with one gathering of entry-level Nazis as full of "highly educated and very bright" men making elaborate internet in-jokes over a nice steak dinner.[10] He also notes that, incidentally, in settings like this, the "JQ," or "Jewish Question," is a "never-ending topic."[11] Malice, somehow, does not think this anti-Semitic, Nazi "question" is reason to leave the room. Instead, he regales the crowd, playfully confessing that, as a Jew, he is a part of "ZOG," the "Zionist Occupied Government" of the United States, referring to a prominent anti-Semitic conspiracy theory about Jewish control of American politics. Most of the party goers burst into laughter. For Malice, it is just a big, playful gambit, as he offers a self-targeted bit of anti-Semitic humor in order to secure the biggest of troll-prizes: a grand reaction. In this room, anti-Semitism gets a bursting, if very ambiguous, laugh; on Twitter, it would get thousands of incensed, offended responses. But it always gets something, which is the point. Yes, sure, *some* of the party attendees sincerely entertain genocidal Nazi rhetoric but, hey, there are books to sell and clicks to bait and, also, why so serious?

Malice's friendly theories and descriptions of trolling all too often provide the weakest of excuses for basement-dwelling troll comedians to articulate the most hateful racist, anti-Semitic ideas. And there is, it seems, a market for such debased, abhorrent humor. This chapter thus descends down the right-wing comedy complex basement stairs, with Malice playing Virgil, guiding you into the trollish inferno. It begins, as our book did, at Fox News, where Gavin McInnes introduces just-kidding comedy that, by chance, also expresses some of the most virulently misogynist and racist ideas on cable news. We then move on to the cable television programming block Adult Swim, where the show *Million Dollar Extreme Presents: World Peace* (2016) courted racists, misogynists and Holocaust deniers while representing itself as cutting-edge, ultra-high-grade ironic comedy. And we end in the complex's ninth circle, the realm of true neo-Nazism, with *The Daily Shoah*, a news and comedy podcast that, while vilely hate-filled, nonetheless compels listeners out of the right-wing comedy complex's basement and back above ground through the other comedy storefronts we have outlined throughout this book.

GAVIN MCINNES FROM PROUD PAPA TO PROUD BOYS

In *The New Right*, Michael Malice introduces Gavin McInnes as a fun guy he meets at a party for the libertarian magazine *Reason*. He gushes with glee about a story in which McInnes asks some ex-junkie employees to score heroin for him, only to intentionally spill and spread it all over the floor in front of the former addicts to watch them freak out. The incident perfectly captures why Malice sees McInnes as a leading voice in a new frontier of right-wing thought—he's an expert troll, turning his targets of comedy into active participants in their own consternation, as he does with the ex-junkies.

McInnes lives, and trolls, from a state of carefully cultivated self-contradiction. As the cofounder of *Vice* magazine, McInnes is conversant in hipster-left aesthetics, drawing in liberals and then assaulting them with anti-PC humor and, sometimes, actual violence. He hangs out with New York's liberal media elite, then gets fired from writing gigs for deeply misogynistic and transphobic editorials. The street gang he founded, the Proud Boys, dresses in neat Fred Perry polos as they roam the streets picking fights with liberal activists. They then cry foul when they are identified as a hate group. McInnes largely abstains from electoral politics, but when President Trump infamously told the Proud Boys to "stand back and stand by" for future violent directives, they plastered the phrase on T-shirts. McInnes then took to his podcast *Get Off My Lawn* to complain how no one understood that "there's a sense of humor to this, there's an irony, there's a sarcasm to this."[12] In other words, McInnes loves to create a mess with his trolling until he has to clean it up. He jokingly endorses hate and violence, right up until the point that someone gets their nose broken. When that happens, he falls back on "just kidding." He's the schoolyard bully who grabs your hand and whacks you with it while asking why you won't stop hitting yourself.

Although McInnes is perhaps best known as the Proud Boys' spokesman, his early media career is full of the edgy, ironic comedy more commonly associated with the left. In the first decade of the 2000s, he helped shape *Vice*'s transgressive, punk aesthetic and libertine attitudes toward drugs and sex. As the magazine's popularity expanded beyond New York City's hipster subculture and into a mainstream, marketable brand, it (and McInnes) pioneered a proto-trolling sensibility. In retail stores, for instance, *Vice* sold women's underpants with the slogan "I Don't Have AIDS . . . Yet."[13] In interviews, McInnes would suggest that women simply want to be dominated by men in one breath, then tout his credentials as a women's studies major in college in the next.[14] Elsewhere, he expressed happiness that the trendy Brooklyn neighborhood of Williamsburg was predominantly white.[15] When called out for the comment, he claimed it was a joke meant to prank old-guard media like the *New York Times*.[16] See, just kidding! Edgy comedians like Sarah Silverman defended McInnes and *Vice* as supposed equal-opportunity offenders, while other liberal political comedians like Patton Oswalt and Samantha Bee provided blurbs for his memoir *How to Piss in Public: From Teenage Rebellion to the Hangover of Adulthood* (2012).

The book and other post-*Vice* efforts bolstered McInnes's burgeoning media celebrity as an angry, ironic, cool dad. They displayed a healthy sense of self-deprecation, but one always belied by a lingering resentment for the mounting (perceived) pressures to perform political correctness. For instance, his short internet comedy sketch from 2008, "Sophie Can Walk," builds on the idea that new father McInnes wants his infant daughter to walk within her first year on earth. He grows increasingly angry at (amateur actors playing) doctors and physical therapists, who tell him it's normal that Sophie—just a few months old—can't walk yet. The video's most memorable bit is a sequence of McInnes carting Sophie around in a tiny wheelchair, bemoaning New York City's inhospitality to the disabled. "Even going to the bodega to get cigarettes was a chore, because I would have to wheel in her chair backwards," he complains in deadpan voiceover. The video is a representative early example of DIY internet comedy, but its main idea transcends silly sight gags. Our guide Michael Malice loves the video, describing it as "irreverent . . . odd, and original."[17] It is also a case study in trolling. One can see a disability rights advocate taking issue, and getting righteously angry, with the false equivalences upon which it is built. At the same time, the video relies upon traditional comedic notions of absurdity, parody, and cute babies doing stuff.

For much of his early media career, McInnes probed these edges of comedic propriety. Upon reaching the metaphorical limits, though, he found a crowded field of like-minded performers using transgressive humor to critique discourses of race, gender, and sexuality.[18] McInnes, for all his efforts, paled next to the likes of contemporaries such as Dave Chappelle, Sacha Baron Cohen, and Sarah Silverman. So, instead of staying within the mainstream boundaries of edgy liberal humor, McInnes blew past them and turned to the right, where ample discursive—and economic—space remained. Why compete with left-friendly superstars when the field of right-wing comedy was wide open? Obama's second term provided trolls like McInnes with more fodder for increasingly reactionary humor focused on issues such as same-sex marriage and transgender rights. He regularly wrote articles for the far-right *Taki's Magazine* with titles like "Feminist Witch Hunts Are Rape" and "Taking Back Our Country from the PC Police."[19] In 2014, he penned a searingly offensive op-ed titled "Transphobia Is Perfectly Natural."[20] The piece led to his departure from the advertising agency he'd cofounded, but it fed his growing popularity among right-wing media outlets in New York City. Around that time he landed a podcast on the shock-jock comedian Anthony Cumia's Compound Media network and began making regular appearances on Fox News. It was there, in the right-wing comedy complex's big box store, that McInnes's true troll came out.

Greg Gutfeld offered McInnes a consistent platform on *Red Eye*, and it's easy to see why. Gutfeld, who flamed out of the New York men's magazine world that McInnes successfully subverted at *Vice*, saw him as the right kind of reactionary hipster. McInnes had both the work history and

Right-wing troll and Proud Boys founder Gavin McInnes rose to prominence parodying liberals on Greg Gutfeld's *Red Eye*. (Fox News)

aesthetic markers (tattoos, beard, and coke habit) of commodified punk rebellion, but he also had the angry, gender traditionalism and Islamophobia that Fox News has traded in for decades. Indeed, in Gutfeld's aptly titled 2014 book, *Not Cool: The Hipster Elite and Their War on You*, he calls McInnes "one of my best friends," like a paleocomedy sitcom dad whose cool new neighbor lets him help tune up his Camaro.[21] McInnes's *Red Eye* bits featured him doing drawn-out characters that befuddled co-panelists but sent Gutfeld cackling. In one, Gavin plays his fictionalized brother, Miles, a "Househusband/Blogger" and author of (the made-up) *Bush Lied, Babies Cried, and a Panda Died*. The character is meant to be a parody of soft, liberal beta men more interested in virtue signaling their sensitivity than in embracing their traditional masculinity. In another, Gavin plays his father, Jimmy, dressed in full Scottish regalia and affecting a brogue in order to—you guessed it—complain about how unmanly men are today. Gutfeld loved McInnes so much that when he left to start *The Greg Gutfeld Show* in 2015, McInnes served as a regular guest host of *Red Eye* for two more years.

McInnes's most contentious and trollish commentary for Fox News, however, came when he was simply himself, seething at the idea that feminism had actually improved women's quality of life. Rather than shouting into the televisual void as many Fox News pundits are wont to do, McInnes trolled, playing co-panelists and viewers against themselves as he ratcheted up the ironically framed misogyny. Gutfeld introduces a 2016 McInnes segment on women in the military accordingly: "If you're gonna start drafting women, what's next, letting them vote? . . . That's a joke, people."[22] Ah yes, explicitly clarifying your comment is a joke, that classic technique that every successful comic uses! Clearly, Fox News respects women—what with its many settlements with female employees filing harassment claims against the network—so Gutfeld's introduction is less a joke than a discursive frame to understand the subsequent segment as an elaborate troll. After Gutfeld opines on male athletes undergoing sexual reassignment and competing as women, McInnes scowls: "If we're going to do that, we're going to have to talk to President Hitler, because if women were soldiers for the past 100 years, we would've lost World War II." Two women co-panelists shout McInnes down, but he continues: "Equality sucks. By every metric, men have it worse off. We're more likely to get raped if you include prison." When his co-panelists again react with confusion and indignation, even Gutfeld has to butt in, smirking, "I will dispute the rape part." Throughout the segment, both McInnes and Gutfeld evoke Malice's idea of trolling, provoking the other panelists and laughing along with the viewers at home.

In another appearance on *Hannity* ostensibly about Hillary Clinton, McInnes commandeers the conversation and steers it straight into trolling territory. "Women do earn less in America because they choose to. . . . They're less ambitious; this is God's way, nature's way of saying women should be at home with the kids. They're happier there."[23] The segment's other panelist, lawyer Tamara Holder, indignantly responds "I hope that [*Hannity*] viewers do not take you, sir, seriously." Perfect, McInnes must be thinking, she's taken the bait. Holder runs down a list of McInnes's recent chauvinistic comments while he smirks, followed by this (lightly edited) exchange:

GAVIN MCINNES [TO HOLDER]: You would be much happier at home with a husband and children.

SEAN HANNITY [LAUGHING]: Oh boy, ohhhh boy.

TAMARA HOLDER: You know what, Gavin? You're not funny.

[Hannity cackles uncontrollably]

HOLDER: Sean, this isn't funny. . . . I think that your guest here is doing a disservice to all of your viewers, and a disservice to America.

Holder is right. McInnes isn't being funny in a conventional, setup-punch-line way. Instead, he's hunting Holder's vulnerabilities and exploiting them for comedic effect. The trolling humor arises in the first instance from McInnes misogynistically mansplaining to Holder her own areas of expertise. Considered in a broader context, he seeks out contradictions in popular post-feminist thought—that women can be both successful professionals and happy housewives. He trolls farther with a disingenuous retreat to biological determinism, stating that women are simply meant to be at home. This is what Holder means by McInnes doing a disservice even to the traditionally conservative Fox News audience—he's trolling viewers like her who do not recognize his ironic address. Of course, McInnes takes Holder's apoplectic reaction and simply uses it to raise the stakes of the bit again. Surely, when *Hannity* cuts to a break, Holder is irate, while one can imagine McInnes shrugging, "Why so serious?" As McInnes's appeal grew beyond the mainstream world of Fox News comedy, though, his jokes turned even uglier.

GAVIN MCINNES CARRIES A TORCH FOR THE ALT-RIGHT

By the dawn of the Trump era, the trolling comedy that McInnes helped mainstream had become a favored tactic of several high-profile right-wing performers fighting culture wars with liberals. Michael Malice calls these high-profile conservative figures "the new right," a group that uses levity to bridge mainstream conservatism and the racist, ethnonationalist alt-right ideology that burst into public consciousness at the 2017 Charlottesville Unite the Right Rally.

Milo Yiannopoulos, for instance, led an online harassment campaign of the Black comedian Leslie Jones before the release of the all-women remake of *Ghostbusters* in 2016. Of course, when he was suspended from

Twitter, Yiannopoulos claimed that his comments were just "provoca-tion," and that "trolls are the only people who tell the truth these days."[24] Another troll, Mike Cernovich, led a 2017 harassment campaign willfully misconstruing a years-old joke made by the liberal MSNBC pundit Sam Seder. An effective puppeteer, Cernovich made MSNBC look the fool as it first fired Seder, then rehired him after gaming out Cernovich's trolling act. And then there is the conspiracy theorist Alex Jones, whose entire trolling approach is designed to grift the paranoid and gullible into buy-ing supplements that counteract secret government plots to "to turn male bodies estrogenic."[25] A 2017 custody case outed Alex Jones as an elabo-rate troll, as his lawyer convinced a family court judge that his client was simply a performance artist playing an extremist, blowhard pundit.[26] So, Jones trolled not only thousands of followers out of their hard-earned cash, but also, apparently, his ex-wife and kids out of years of domestic stability. In the era of Trump, even the right-wing troll space that McInnes carved out was starting to get crowded.

McInnes staked a claim to new troll terrain by founding the Proud Boys. Initially, he sought to position the group as simply "a fraternal organiza-tion like the Elks Lodge" where guys could be dudes and make fun of lib-eral, PC culture.[27] As criminologists Shannon Reid and Matthew Valasik argue, the Proud Boys share "a hipster persona that uses irony and humor to facilitate far-right arguments that attack the political, social, and cul-tural status quo, generally opposing feminism, immigration, political cor-rectness, and establishment politics."[28] In other words, the Proud Boys are a collectivized embodiment of the persona McInnes had been building for the previous two decades on his march ever rightward. Their comedic public image is trollish—new members are beaten until they can name five breakfast cereals, lol—but their material practices take trolling to hateful, violent extremes. Members routinely engage in brutal campaigns of harassment and assault, both in online settings and in the streets. In one infamous incident from 2018, McInnes jokingly pretended to execute a Japanese socialist leader with a samurai sword. After the event, Proud Boys clashed outside with antifascist protestors, leading to the arrest of ten Proud Boys and the imprisonment of two. Again and again, the Proud Boys put McInnes's trollish provocations into violent practice, seeking cover for their crimes in the logic of "just kidding." If you get mad about all this, as a former Proud Boys figurehead said, it's just because the Proud Boys "make self-defense look like assault."[29]

For his part, McInnes continues to try to have it both ways. He left the group after the 2018 street brawl, but he continues to tacitly endorse their actions through trolling doublespeak. The morning after Trump's not-so-accidental "stand back and stand by" endorsement of the Proud Boys, for instance, news reports characterized the group as a "neo-fascist" "hate group," and as a "far-right fraternity with a violent reputation."[30] McInnes complained that the media just didn't get the Proud Boys' sense of humor, hiding behind Michael Malice's definition of trollish comedy—everything is permitted, so long as it's done in the service of turning your opponent into a performer. So, it's your fault if you are visibly alarmed by the fact that Proud Boys members rise in the ranks by "getting into a major fight for the cause."[31] And you're playing right into his troll hands when you act visibly disgusted by McInnes describing a woman as a "colostomy bag for various strangers' semen."[32] And if you tweet about how depraved McInnes is when he says Muslims are "mentally damaged in-breds," well, he got you good there.[33] According to him, these are just jokes based on pushing liberal buttons. So, definitely, don't read too much into the fact that 15 percent of respondents to a survey of regulars on the ultra-far-right neo-Nazi website *The Right Stuff* "mentioned McInnes as a step in their path to white nationalism or recommended using his videos and writing to convert others."[34] They must be in on the joke too!

The Southern Poverty Law Center, which tracks hate groups, describes McInnes as playing a "duplicitous rhetorical game."[35] Similarly, researcher Samantha Kutner calls him an "unreliable narrator" of his intentions and deeds.[36] In any case, to focus on the specifics of his words is to miss the broader issue: his "jokes" inspire horrifying actions among followers. McInnes serves as a sort of ideological lubricant for the right-wing-curious to slide from the seemingly innocuous world of online lulz to serious harassment to, occasionally, brutal street violence. He built his comedic persona using hipster-bro misogyny that could be read as enlightened irony, and he often excuses the Proud Boys as simply "western chauvinists."[37] But McInnes has welded his trolling humor to more avowedly racist and ethno-nationalist impulses. It's no accident, then, that neo-Nazis keep showing up at Proud Boys events and sharing his "comedy" videos like "10 Things I Hate about Jews."[38] As culture scholar Alexandra Minna Stern deftly outlines, the circuitry of white nationalism "does not operate at full capacity without the currents of gender and sexuality."[39] Proud Boys pledges may initially be intrigued by the group's joking toxic masculinity, but these jokes ease the way to more nefarious discourses about how white women must take up their natural roles as mothers in order to stave off white genocide at the hands of the Jews and immigrant hordes.

As we'll see in the following sections, (jokingly!) virulent misogyny, racism, and anti-Semitism provide guardrails on our descent deeper into the basement of the right-wing comedy complex. McInnes, disturbing though he is, at least does most of his damage in open, mainstream spaces that allow for public discussion and rebuke. As we step deeper into the basement, we find more enigmatic characters who, better hidden from the daylight, drink more deeply and depravedly from the trollish brew of comedy and hateful prejudice.

VITAL TROLLING: FROM BRONZE AGE PERVERT TO *MILLION DOLLAR EXTREME*

Trolls push liberals' buttons and few liberals have more buttons to push than academics. Alexandra Minna Stern's book-length study of the alt-right, for example, goes to great lengths to describe the abstract ideas of cultural theorists who best explain trolls such as McInnes and Yiannopoulos. Pointing to alt-right political agitator Steve Bannon's self-professed reading list, Stern cites esoteric thinkers such as René Guénon in describing what the contemporary troll world is up to. One gets a sinking feeling, however, that the joke might be on Stern—and us—as liberal theorists. Steve Bannon says he read Guénon, yes. And, who knows, maybe his advice to candidate Trump did rely on the notion of "hyper-acceleration" as "the conceptual scaffolding for a kind of palingenesis that will culminate with paroxysms" leading to a "golden age."[40] Not knowing what any of that actually means, it's difficult for us to say. Alternatively, we might consider if Bannon et al. are getting a hearty laugh at our expense, having sent us scurrying to the library in order to explain the fact that being a mean old jerk can be pretty effective sometimes. You don't need a PhD to know that a lot of people would rather associate with bullies than the bullied.

None of which is to say, however, that trolls don't have their own philosophers. They do. They are just, like our guide Michael Malice, trolls themselves. Traditional liberal academics like to separate comedy theorists from comedians themselves. Influential right-wing trolls like Malice, however, position themselves as part of the comedy. As they explain the ideas behind trolling, trolls like Malice also enact them, crafting confounding texts that are both very serious and, at the same time, meant to provoke anyone who takes them too seriously. The most influential troll thinkers/practitioners are those who merge the comic, if ugly, sensibility of trolling with ostensibly serious ideas that justify antisocial behavior. For troll-philosophers, there is nothing outside the troll. In other words, the people who provide the intellectual justification for trolling are not distant French thinkers from the nineteenth century. They are contemporary trolls like Malice with slightly better vocabularies than their 4chan-dwelling readers.

Michael Malice represents the most straightforward of thinkers who enact the praxis of trolling. He says he's going to troll, he trolls, and then he gets a book deal in order to explain what he did and why it's not bad. The true master of this genre, however, is Bronze Age Pervert (BAP), a pseudonymous right-wing author whose 2018 book, *Bronze Age Mindset* (*BAM*), has spent years in the upper echelons of the Amazon book sales rankings. BAP is a difficult figure to pin down. On the one hand, he represents himself as a classicist and a Nietzsche scholar, peppering his writing with roughly accurate references to Greek and German philosophy. On the other hand, his popular, if often suspended, Twitter account describes him as an "Aspiring Nudist Bodybuilder," and his prose seems manipulated by a sort of comic caveman filter that removes most of the articles from his sentences. For example, *Bronze Age Mindset* begins: "What if you've been misled about what is life? They do this by showing you two red marionette and shake them in front, then you stay mesmerized and clap like trained seal." This writing weird and, admittedly, kind of funny.

The average reader is forced to believe that BAP can't be serious. But he is. Maybe. *BAM* oscillates between the seemingly intellectual—"Darwin is meaningless without Malthus"—to the grandiose—"I will draw back the curtain on this Iron Prison and show you where it is you really live"—to the Jordan Peterson-esque practical, if questionable—"Something else I can recommend is coconut oil, and staying in the sun." It is a confusing text, one sure to be dismissed by readers accustomed to thinking of political theory in traditional terms. Nonetheless, *BAM*'s mode of thought and communication is extremely influential among contemporary right-wing political thinkers and joke makers. As Michael Anton, a Trump administration figure, writes, "In the spiritual war for the hearts and minds of the disaffected youth on the right, conservatism is losing" to *Bronze Age Mindset*.[41]

BAM's success is tied to its embrace of political vitalism, a vague, somewhat tongue-in-cheek philosophy focused on the deification of brute strength and a sense that people—liberals in particular—take moral precepts far too seriously. It is also outrageously misogynist, racist, and anti-Semitic. *BAM*'s vitalistic worldview is punctuated by trollish, over-the-top attacks on women and minorities aimed at stirring up the morally sensitive. "Nothing so ridiculous as the liberation of women has ever been attempted in the history of mankind," *BAM* writes. Also "the Jewish way of thinking . . . approaches mental deficiency and even retardation." Like Malice joking about Zionists controlling the world, these are exaggerated proclamations sure to provoke intense responses. They also, of course, echo abhorrent ideas no doubt harbored by many of *BAM*'s readers.

As even his staunchest defenders note, it is impossible to determine when *BAM* is making a serious point about man's will to thrive and when the book is trollishly trying to induce apoplexy in the reader. As the right-wing think tank Claremont Institute argues, "The fact that BAP is getting this much coverage . . . is the joke."[42] Happy for the youthful energy *BAM* brings to the right, many previously serious conservatives have been all too happy to embrace the book as a simultaneously political and comic treatise. *Bronze Age Mindset* is clearly supposed to be funny, supposed to be political, and supposed to feature vicious slanders aimed at women, racial minorities, Jews, and more. Any effort to sort out this ugly mélange is said to be evidence that you just don't get it. This formula, as we'll see on our next step down the basement stairs, finds its mirror in the vitalist comedy of Sam Hyde, creator of the trolling Adult Swim sketch comedy show *Million Dollar Extreme Presents: World Peace*.

MILLION DOLLAR EXTREME AND
VITAL TROLLING ON ADULT SWIM

If you've had a computer and a pulse at any point in the last decade, you've seen a TED talk. The short educational lectures prominently feature public intellectuals speaking in front of bold, block red letters to a conference room of paid attendees who want to know how to, like, disrupt conventional ideations and leverage innovative solutions, and stuff. This is almost certainly what the organizers of Drexel University's 2013 TEDx symposium had in mind when they booked Sam Hyde to give a keynote speech titled "Paradigm Shift 2070." What they got, instead, was a troll brimming with vitalist, Bronze Age Pervert–style rhetoric. Instead of a smart half-zip fleece, Hyde bursts onstage in a maroon sweatsuit and a Roman centurion costume straight out of a Halloween Express. He dives into a prank rant delivered in manic, rapid-fire Silicon Valley solutions to fictionalized social problems. He proposes "using cubes of trash as money" in order to solve environmental crises. He suggests sea farming as a key innovation space: "sea beets, sea yams, sea cabbage, have you ever had a sea salad? Have you ever had sea cheesy baked potatoes that blew your socks off? Cuz you're gonna be."[43] Instead of continuing the bit as a pure parody of TED talk pretensions, however, Hyde can't help but show his proclivity for violent, extremist rhetoric. In between several silly technological pitches, he suggests "race riots" as a solution to social unrest, as well as killing "the elderly and the disabled" and wiping Israel "off the map."[44] Press coverage at the time nonetheless portrayed Hyde's trolling generously.[45] Critics disregarded its disturbing elements and likened Hyde to Tim Heidecker, the celebrated absurdist comedian best known for Adult Swim's sketch comedy *Tim and Eric Awesome Show, Great Job!*.[46] However, when viewing Hyde's act through the lens of right-wing troll comedy, it is clear that the exciting energy identified by the critics and the ugly aspects ignored by them are inextricably linked. Full of vitalist energy, bravado, and moral recklessness, Hyde's 2013 TED talk was just a preview of the trolling sensibility that would soon become a force in American culture and politics.

In 2016, Hyde took his vitalist style to television in his own sketch comedy series on Adult Swim with *Million Dollar Extreme Presents: World Peace* (*MDE*). There, he used Adult Swim's hip, liberal comedy brand to create high-energy, absurdist humor that also traded in expressions of violent misogyny, racism, and anti-Semitism.[47] Just as *BAM* revels in over-the-top rhetoric demonizing women, Jews, and other minorities, *MDE* grew its fandom by throwing bloodied women through prop glass, casually invoking racial slurs, and flashing neo-Nazi symbols. Also like *BAM*, *MDE* found apologists ready to defend its ugliest excesses. The Claremont Institute happily framed *BAM* as provocative jocularity that gets young people excited to vote Republican. Adult Swim just as freely accepted Hyde's trolling, making space in its lineup both for experimental comedy fans and "members of a white-nationalist movement that generally supports Donald Trump."[48]

The *MDE* sketch "Nick Hosts a Wine Party," for example, demonstrates the show's trollish affinity for *BAM*-like, cartoonish misogyny. The sketch's upscale urban loft setting is initially evocative of left-friendly Adult Swim hits like *Tim and Eric* or *The Eric Andre Show*, ones that similarly set a festive tone before sharply puncturing it with an extreme act of verbal abuse, bodily excess, or physical violence. "Wine Party" however, hints at what's to come when a white character tells his Black girlfriend: "I got my best girl over by my side making me a complete man. . . . I found you under that bus, wherever I found you, in Australia, that shithouse. That place was gross, gross people there. I went there one time, I was puking." The exchange, like many throughout *MDE* and other Adult Swim shows, is improvised with a "public access" feel.[49] It lends the scene a surface sheen of "just kidding" that signals to viewers not to take anything, particularly shock-value racism, too seriously. At the same time, though, it clearly evokes Trumpian far-right ideologies that espouse the inferiority of Black women and encourages resentment for all things not American.

The sketch moves to an interaction in which *MDE* cast member Nick Rochefort insults the wife of his "brother," played by Sam Hyde. When she tries to exit the room, Nick trips her and smashes a wine glass in her face as she violently crashes through a glass coffee table. Guests react with shock while Nick looks on in satisfaction at the bloodied woman on the floor. The sketch again appears to tap into the Adult Swim heritage of comedies featuring absurd physical violence that is incongruous with its setting. In the case of "Wine Party," however, the violence reinforces *MDE*'s vitalist domination over women and others in lower positions of cultural power. Rather than retaliate angrily or in a comically exaggerated manner, Sam calmly asks Nick why he has tripped his wife. Nick indignantly denies his actions several times, eventually screaming "You're gonna sit here and point fingers at me . . . that I shoved her through a goddamned table?! You're f*cking crazy as she is!" Sam eventually concedes, denying the misogynistic violence that he, and the viewer, has witnessed.

On the one hand, "Wine Party" is a spectacle of pure misogynistic hate. On the other, it is an act of trolling much as Michael Malice describes it: saying foolish, often vile things in order to evoke a predictable, performative emotional response. *MDE's* trollish intent is to divide its Adult Swim audience into two groups. The first group is the trolled, those who react in horror to the brutal misogyny of the sketch. The second group is the trolls, amused as they envision the performance of indignation that the show has induced in the first group. After all, it's just kidding! The gag (if we can call it that) of "Wine Party" is built on this bifurcation: Nick is trolling Sam, with the bloodied and battered wife bandied between them as a comedic prop. In this violent exchange masked as hip irony, the sketch mirrors *Bronze Age Mindset's* world-historical narrative as a battle between alpha males' vitalistic will to power and beta males' concern for the welfare of women. In *MDE's* bizarre vitalist fantasy, the alpha males do the trolling, and the trolled liberal betas overreact because they don't get the joke.

MDE's vile, vitalist trolling doesn't stop at misogyny. Like Gavin McInnes, the show provides a prime example of how the right has appropriated tactics often used by left-wing ironists. For example, Sacha Baron Cohen, the liberal comedian behind the *Borat* films, often introduces anti-Semitism in order to expose and mock people who gleefully repeat it. He sings "Throw the Jew Down the Well" so as to record bigots singing along. *MDE* does the opposite. The show playfully, ironically obfuscates anti-Semitism, sliding it into unexpected places in order to troll those who worry about the persistence of Jew hatred. In the sketch "Jews Rock," for example, a sound stage filled with bright decor evoking *Teletubbies* or *Barney and Friends* is populated by a group of smiling children and costumed adults. A peppy, repetitive pop tune plays, as the stage performers bop around joyously and pretend to play musical instruments. Every so often, the lyrics "Jews Rock!" flash on screen, with one character dressed as a bird exclaiming "I love Jews!" As the sketch ends, it intersperses cutaways to "Adult Swim Executives" looking confused. The bit then fades into the next sketch without ceremony or further explanation.

Like all irony-laden Adult Swim texts, "Jews Rock" is polysemic and somewhat ambiguous. Bouncy, short, and built on non-sequiturs, it might be dismissed simply as weird anti-humor. After all, there is nothing Jewish whatsoever in the setting or music, with the visuals seemingly arbitrarily chosen and amusingly mismatched. Of course, with a little context, the sketch becomes much more alarming. The relentless, unexplained focus on Jews, alongside a reference to powerful media executives, reflects the show's popularity in online communities flush with anti-Semitic ideology. And then there is the presence of a curious symbol in the background of the video. It is, depending on one's perspective, either an upside-down peace sign or, alternatively, the logo of the National Alliance, a once powerful neo-Nazi group. The former, combined with the lyrics, might be taken as a reference to anti-Semitic conspiracies about Jews undermining world peace. The latter is plainly a Nazi symbol, which should be concerning to anyone who isn't a Nazi. The image is certainly ambiguous, but only in the most trollish of ways. Its humor is meant to derive from the anxiety it produces in those who, while unsure of the symbol's true meaning, are made ill at ease by the sketch's components. This fear is fanned by the numerous, supportive fans of the show who use online forums to praise Hyde for sneaking the hate symbolism into the program. Hyde, of course, can dismiss any concerns as overreactions to his silliness. However, he also knows full well that, alongside the slur-filled comedy bits that populate most *MDE* episodes, many will feel compelled to take the sketch as part of the recent resurgence of neo-Nazi ideology both online and in, for example, alt-right gatherings like the 2017 Unite the Right rally in Charlottesville, Virginia.

On various message boards *MDE*'s comedy is used to perpetuate a range of hateful jokes, including, but by no means limited to, the anti-Semitic. As one example among many, YouTube user "WeaponizedIrony," reposted the video with the description "In Memorial of the 6 Gorillion," using a bit of targeted nonsense to mock, or more likely deny, the six million Jews who died in the Holocaust. A plethora of online discussion spaces ranging from Reddit to the white nationalist message board Stormfront have seized upon the sketch as well, interpreting it as a comedic takedown of the purportedly Jewish executives who would eventually cancel the show.[50]

A hate symbol associated with the neo-Nazi National Alliance appears in *Million Dollar Extreme*'s "Jews Rock" music video sketch. (Adult Swim; author photo)

Since the show's cancellation, Hyde has embraced his role as a symbol of resistance to alleged Jewish dominance of the media industry. And, as always seems to be the case, our guide Michael Malice is there to explain and excuse a troll. In an interview with Malice in the *Observer*, Hyde begins by proclaiming that he got his Adult Swim show based on talent, as opposed to having a "Jewish uncle or something" to nepotistically work connections for him.[51] Discussing his show's cancellation, he draws a Star of David for the interviewer, blaming Jews for the demise of a modestly rated basic cable show that, it's worth reiterating, was replete with the most vile and violent of misogynist, racist images. Malice, like any good concierge, passes no judgment on Hyde, presenting him to a wide audience as just another quirky character from the funny world of the trolls. Hyde, for his part, has gone on to make it increasingly hard to believe his anti-Semitism is anything short of sincere by continuously railing against Jewish comedians whom he believes conspire to blackball him.[52]

In 2017, Hyde said the quiet part out loud, when he publicly donated to the defense fund of Andrew Anglin, the founder of the neo-Nazi website *The Daily Stormer*.[53] Anglin, among other things, is a frequent guest on *The Daily Shoah*, the Holocaust denying comedy podcast that, as we discuss in the next section, resides as deep in the right-wing comedy complex basement as we are willing to plumb. Importantly, though, the trip to this threshold of actual, literal Nazism started above ground in the relative sunshine of Fox News and *The Babylon Bee*. Each happily embraces Michael Malice's happy embrace of the trolling ethos and aesthetic. These outlets need Malice's edgy topicality to refresh their audience bases, and Malice needs the exposure that Fox News and its friends can provide to lend him long-term credibility. They all, ultimately, need to feed the trolls. Greg Gutfeld may not send people straight to Holocaust denial, but Gutfeld's affinity for Malice and McInnes makes the trip to the right-wing comedy complex basement a much shorter, steeper one than mainline Republicans would like you to think. In any case, we're at the bottom now. Looking down at our complex map, You Are Here has, finally, come to meet Here Be Nazis.

THE BASEMENT: RACISM, ANTI-SEMITISM, AND HOLOCAUST DENIAL AS COMEDIC TROLLING

Today's most successful Holocaust-deniers—figures such as the YouTube personality Nick Fuentes and the hosts of *The Daily Shoah* podcast—are comedic entertainers. This may seem counterintuitive. For right-minded people, what could be more serious than the Holocaust? What approach, other than the solemnly historical, could possibly be appropriate? But Holocaust denial is, by definition, history for people who don't care about history. Those attracted to knowing the truth of the world will not last long in a space that rejects the facticity of one of the most meticulously documented events in human history. But racists and anti-Semites, particularly Holocaust deniers, have long used irony and comic juxtaposition as a tool for disarming their audiences. They construct their appeal around the exotic, the taboo, and, yes, the comedic. The comedic basement of right-wing trolls that Fuentes and the neo-Nazi podcast *The Daily Shoah* occupy has been around a long time. Digital media convergence has allowed it to expand and, crucially, connect back up to the more respectable levels of the right-wing comedy complex. To understand what today's most deeply racist, anti-Semitic and Holocaust denying comics offer, however, it is necessary to understand just how far back the connection between neo-Nazism and comedy goes.

Ernst Zündel (1939–2017), a neo-Nazi German revisionist, provides a simple but powerful example. A publisher of Holocaust-denying literature,

Neo-Nazi and Holocaust denier Ernst Zündel tries comedy and
dresses foolishly as he espouses serious hate. (YouTube)

Zündel offered serious, if fallacious, rebuttals to academic research regarding Nazi atrocities. He would also nearly always appear in public wearing
a brightly colored construction helmet. Dressed otherwise formally for a
court date or a television interview, his garish headgear would clash with
his jacket and tie, a case study in trollish fashion faux pas. His visage was
clownish, but it was also perversely attractive in the manner of a circus
sideshow. Zündel would then use his screen time to describe Adolf Hitler
as a "decent man" and affably offer spurious science to deny the truth of
Nazi crimes against humanity.

   And he would tell jokes. "New York Jewry," according to one of his
zings, controls the United States despite being "as smart as a monkey
that saws off the branch on which it is perching."[54] He was roundly, accurately, described by the press as a "buffoon."[55] But he was a buffoon with
an audience, often finding himself surrounded by groups of young people
nodding and clapping along to his avant-garde performances of comically framed, insidious lies. His persona was one of carefully cultivated
inconsistency, combining the seriousness of a history lecture with the
incongruous charm of a dog wearing pants.

David Irving (1938–), made rightfully infamous as the villain of the Rachel Weisz film *Denial*, represents another ongoing strand in the disturbing world of Holocaust denial comedy. His is more of a patriarchal, Toastmasters brand of humor, aimed at communicating a command of history while he vomits waves of spurious facts and irresponsible historical conjectures. Real scholars are, of course, limited in how they introduce the Holocaust to their audiences. They must carefully prepare people for the serious information at hand. Irving, like the podcasters that populate the complex basement, feels no such limitation. His speeches begin like banquet addresses, following the old advice to always start 'em off with a joke. For example, in his lecture "The Manipulation of History," he begins with several anti-Semitic knee-slappers aimed at Holocaust survivor and Nazi-hunter Simon Wiesenthal. Stop him if you've already heard this one: "On the night after Halloween, Mrs. Wiesenthal says 'Simon, please put the mask back on!'" The crowd erupts in the exhilarating laughter of taboo. It is the same laughter that racists have engaged in during centuries of minstrel shows and that a teenager today might indulge by watching YouTubers like Nick Fuentes mock immigrants. Irving then puts a button on the bit by saying that the Nobel Peace Prize–winning Holocaust survivor Elie Wiesel deserves some sympathy because, hey, his name is "Weasel!"

Zündel and Irving pioneered the approach used today in the racist and anti-Semitic reeducation comedy of Fuentes and *The Daily Shoah*. When it comes to the Holocaust, these voices want you to think of your liberal teachers and professors droning on depressingly with facts about Nuremberg Laws and death camps, asking you to stare straight into the unbearable truth that humanity can be as bad as it has been. They do the same thing when they try to convince you that race science explains inequality. Regardless of the genre of hate they're projecting, they want you to have a good, guilt-allaying time learning about it. They want you to remember how they kept it weird and fun, and how much everyone freaked out—got trolled so hard!—when they did. They threw you some facts, most of which you've forgotten, but which added up to that relatively comforting idea that the Holocaust was overblown or that slavery was just a natural thing that used to happen. And boy do those professors overreact when you stay lighthearted and just ask a few questions. Sure, the approach forged by Zündel and Irving is going to fall on deaf ears when met by a crowd of serious, decent people. But there are sufficient people unserious and indecent enough to make quite a career out of mixing the right jokes with the right lies. The algorithms of digital media, combined with the cross-promotional nature of the right-wing comedy complex, make it all the easier to appeal to and collect such an audience.

America First with Nick Fuentes does just this. To be clear, Fuentes's depraved trolling reaches the lowest depths, regardless of the brand of hatred he is indulging. Vile slurs and stereotypes populate his frequent anti-immigrant rants. When it comes to Jews, however, Fuentes takes special relish, knowing that the seriousness of the Holocaust offers him a unique opportunity to brand himself as an edgy comedic voice. He is willing to go places beyond the racism and misogyny found in, for example, the *Legion of Skanks*. For Fuentes, like all occupants of the lowest depths of the complex, Holocaust denial is a yes-and, proposition. It is something he adds to the ubiquitous racism, misogyny, transphobia, and homophobia of right-wing comedy in order to stress his commitment to mixing comedy and hate. And, whereas Michael Malice displays his real right-wing troll chops merely by laughing along with anti-Semites, Fuentes proves his true bona fides by going straight to the source, channeling the cocktail of jokes and lies preferred by Zündel and Irving.

In a widely circulated and remixed bit from his podcast, for example, Fuentes reads a listener question and then responds:

> If I take one hour to cook a batch of cookies and Cookie Monster has fifteen ovens working twenty-four hours a day for five years, how long does it take Cookie Monster to make six million batches of cookies?
>
> I don't know, that's a good question! It doesn't really sound correct to me. Wait a second. It takes one hour to cook a batch of cookies and you have fifteen ovens, probably in four different kitchens right? . . . How long would it take you to make six million? It certainly wouldn't be five years, the math doesn't seem to add up there!

Fuentes goes on, laughing throughout, extending the ghoulish, depraved joke using Cookie Monster as a stand in for Hitler, the four kitchens as analogs for Auschwitz-Birkenau, Treblinka, Bełżec, and Chełmno,[56] and cookies as representations of the ravaged bodies of innocent Jews sent to their deaths for being who they were. He repeats discredited facts drawn straight from Zündel and Irving. He then guffaws, stretching out the darkly incongruous metaphor, claiming aerial photography shows that the ground around the "kitchens" is "not deep enough for mass cookie storage." He concludes: "That's all irony! I'm an irony bro, I love and respect everyone. Everything that the government says is true." Like Zündel and Irving, Fuentes lures you with a joke because he doesn't really want to argue. He merely wants to signal who he is, how far he'll go, and how good it would feel to be so transgressive. Malice might take you to the basement door, laughing at the Jewish Question, but Fuentes yanks you right in. The Cookie Question, how edgy!

Crucially, Fuentes also understands how the right-wing comedy complex works. Predictably, the bit caught the attention of the Jewish religiorational pundit Ben Shapiro, who possesses a right-wing audience a small fraction of which would make Fuentes the brightest light in the complex basement. Despite his flaws, Shapiro is, of course, about as far from a Holocaust denier as one can be. He denounced Fuentes in the sharpest terms, speaking on the subject with the appropriate levels of righteous indignation and careful consideration—which is exactly what Fuentes wanted. He turned Shapiro into the very sort of overserious lecturer that Holocaust deniers love to use as their foils. In a speech at Stanford University, Shapiro read the Cookie Question bit verbatim in his patented, deliberate cadence, trying to own Fuentes simply by exposing him. For most of the Stanford audience, it probably worked. But on his own show, Fuentes played Shapiro's speech back and laughed uproariously, proclaiming his success in "getting people riled up," and making the straitlaced Shapiro utter the ludicrous phrase "irony bro," in the context of a joke monologue about his own murdered ancestors. The trolling worked, insofar as Fuentes converted his rival into a performer, no doubt driving countless Shapiro listeners to look up his streaming show *America First with Nick Fuentes.*

Fuentes is, without question, a troll. His primary goal is to make others look ridiculous as they spend their energy defending positions that shouldn't need defending. The Cookie Question is a branding play, one that says little about Fuentes's actual beliefs about the Holocaust. By joking about an extremely unfunny thing, he denotes to listeners that he will not be falling prey to political correctness in his commentary on race, gender, immigration, or anything else. Fuentes jokes, says he's not joking, and then says once more that he is, taking the greatest joy in proclaiming Malice-style trolling victories whenever anyone takes him seriously. Certainly, this ambiguity does little to lessen the vile morality embedded in his hate jokes. It does, however, distinguish him from our final case study, one that unambiguously uses comedy, and the power of the right-wing comedy complex, to advocate for fully authentic white supremacist and Nazi perspectives.

THE DAILY SHOAH AND THE LOWEST DEPTHS OF THE RIGHT-WING COMEDY COMPLEX

On the internet, there's always something worse to find; we know this. It's just a matter of where you decide to stop looking. For us, in our consideration of the right-wing comedy complex, *The Daily Shoah* podcast is deep enough. To spell things out: *Shoah* is the Hebrew term for the Holocaust, the murder of six million Jews at the hands of the Nazis and their collaborators. *The Daily Show* is a groundbreaking liberal news satire show hosted for years by one of America's most popular Jewish entertainers, Jon Stewart. *The Daily Shoah* is a current events podcast peppered with comedy bits hosted by Nazis and featuring the vilest of far-right language and ideas.

Pretty clever.

You may not have laughed. But it is comedy, aimed at garnering an edge-hungry audience willing to pay a membership fee to hear what's funny in the world of Nazism today. To be clear, the vile hate comedy of *The Daily Shoah* is drenched in every conceivable element of homophobia, transphobia, sexism, Islamophobia, and racism. The show has featured hundreds of hours of racist jokes and parodies alongside the titular anti-Semitism that serves as the core marker of its branding. We focus here on the show's radical anti-Semitic humor not, of course, to suggest that such comedy is worse than that based in other forms of hatred, but instead as a case study to illustrate the extremes of which right-wing comedy is capable. *The Daily Shoah* itself, alongside numerous parallel productions, creates perversely hateful comedy aimed at any group targeted by far-right white supremacy.

And, crucially, *The Daily Shoah* is, through a series of corridors and stairwells, connected all the way back to the top of the right-wing comedy complex. There is the most direct path: Greg Gutfeld celebrates Gavin McInnes for his alt-right hipster cool. McInnes and the Proud Boys, according to the Southern Poverty Law Center, drive significant traffic to therightstuff.biz, the homepage of *The Daily Shoah*. Then there is a more circuitous path, the 4chan bypass. Michael Malice spends a full book and dozens of media appearances explaining why the provocative, offensive jokes targeting women and minorities on the 4chan message board are morally palatable and politically effective. More than a few of those 4chan memes, it turns out, originate on *The Daily Shoah*.[57] And, then, there is the more leisurely, philosophical pathway. Joe Rogan and the *Skanks* turn anti-Black slurs and Jews-in-ovens jokes into the exercise of personal rights and acts of political self-actualization. Then, Bronze Age Pervert goes a step farther, telling you to be a real, vital (white) man by "de-Judaizing" yourself and escaping feminine weakness. Next, Sam Hyde makes abstract comic art about how everyone takes racism, misogyny, and anti-Semitism way too seriously. Nick Fuentes devotes hours to winking, anti-immigrant punditry and then adds some made-up Holocaust facts and muppets to the hate equation. Don't worry, though, he's just riling you up with the mass grave jokes. Finally, *The Daily Shoah* is the last step: the one that says yes, we're joking about all these hatreds, but we are not *just* joking.

We are loath to give too much air time to the people who host the show. But this podcast has recorded hundreds of episodes, each multiple-hours long, and it has revealed that its humor—as demented as it is—is a viable form of right-wing comedy in America today. Moreover, by tapping into the larger contemporary ecosystem of right-wing comedy more generally, its brand embodies obvious dilemmas for American culture and needs to be exposed and understood. Generally speaking, *The Daily Shoah* uses its anti-Semitism, racism, and other forms of hate speech both to incite and to inspire. Like Nick Fuentes, who dips in and out of his trolling character and balances provocation with plausible deniability, the hosts of *TDS* take a troll's pleasure in imagining the decent listener retch at their bile. But they also envision an ideal listener, who comes for the jokes and stays for the ideology. This *Daily Shoah* quote is particularly instructive:

> Even people that are, like, sympathetic and right wing and even think the idea of the white state is good, they still get all fucked up and weird talking about the Holocaust. But when you talk to people that are under 20 years old, they don't give a fuck about the Holocaust. They think it's hilarious. They think Hitler is funny and cool, and the idea of gassing Jews is just a fucking joke. Like they don't give a shit. They don't care. It's hilarious.

Here *The Daily Shoah* describes the road clearing that has been done by years of edgy, "just trolling" comedy, as well as a general lack of historical literacy among young Americans. *The Daily Shoah* audience, which is estimated in the tens of thousands, has been primed by the myriad Holocaust jokes that have found their way into the world of contemporary comedy.[58] Many are likely to have spent time in the darker corners of the right-wing comedy complex, hearing the normalization of slurring and Holocaust denying prevalent in the examples cited above. Lacking interest in or knowledge of historical reality, these listeners look to obliterate sacred spaces and defy what they understand as political correctness in the most egregious ways possible. Laughing with *The Daily Shoah* is, for some, the logical apotheosis of the trolling mindset, allowing them to turn their very selves into that which sends the rest of us into apoplectic fits. For others, it is merely the casual expression of hateful beliefs to which they are truly committed. For *The Daily Shoah*, however, they are all current customers and potential soldiers for the cause of white supremacy.

Even in its depravity, *The Daily Shoah* displays a skill for entertainment, embracing and exploiting the podcast medium to cultivate community through informality, familiarity, and comedy. Structured very much like the *Legion of Skanks* podcast, the program features winding, semi-focused topical discussions that intertwine friendly (hate-)banter, jovial political (hate-)rhetoric, and scripted (hate-)comedy sketches. Embracing the "intimate" nature of podcasting, the show allows listeners to feel at home with a group of regular-sounding middle-aged Americans who, it just happens, are despicable Nazis.[59] Bringing listeners into this unusual space, the show's hosts engage in a push-pull strategy of mixing vaguely plausible political perspectives with troll-style shock humor. Many discussions begin with serious renditions of hard-right political arguments. For example, the very first *Daily Shoah* episode starts with the hosts outlining an anti-immigration platform that is difficult to distinguish from that offered by Donald Trump during his 2016 presidential run. Such argumentation is then peppered with escalating mockery of opponents, shock-inducing racial slurs, and, nearly always, jokes about Jews in ovens or gas chambers. It is, in style, tone, and proclivity toward offensive language, rather similar to what one finds up the complex stairs on the *Skanks*. But whereas the *Skanks* slur to get laughs and enact an ill-conceived praxis of free speech, *The Daily Shoah* uses laughing hate-speech toward bigger, uglier, and more explicit political ends.

As the show has developed, it has found astonishingly influential ways of layering trollish online humor into its vile advocacy for white supremacy, racial segregation, and even genocide. As an example, it has created an audio version of a Nazi yellow "Jude" star that the hosts affix to ostensibly Jewish names as they mention them on the podcast. It is an exaggerated, silly echo effect, perhaps parallel to the "awooga!" noise Bugs Bunny makes when he sees a sexy lady rabbit, except wildly anti-Semitic. The intent is to jokingly, but nonetheless fully seriously, draw attention to the supposed cabal of Jewish people the hosts believe are acting against the "white race." And though the gag should strike the reader as utterly distasteful and obscenely sophomoric, it has also been wildly successful. A popular feature of *The Daily Shoah* itself, it has leaped into the broader online world of right-wing message boards in its visualized "triple parentheses" adaptation. For the coauthor of this book, it would look like this: (((Matt Sienkiewicz))). Most users of it will, of course, say they're just trolling when they invoke it and wait for the oversensitive to overreact to a little punctuation.[60]

More than any other example cited in this book, most readers will be unable to face the humor in *The Daily Shoah*. It is nonetheless crucial to understand, and accept, that humor is a big part of what its listeners are tuning in for. They may have a perverse, morally indefensible sense of the funny, but funny is nonetheless core to the show's appeal. As *The Daily Shoah* has developed over the years, it has embraced sketch comedy and parodic news commentary alongside its panel talk format. These segments, labeled "The Merchant Minute" after the anti-Semitic merchant stereotype, are scripted and preproduced, addressing a variety of current events while mimicking *The Daily Show*'s news features and *Saturday Night Live*'s "Weekend Update." They are also the most vile thing we have ever forced ourselves to listen to.

A representative, painful, example comes from episode 300 of *The Daily Shoah* in 2018. It begins with an opening song parody, set to Oasis's hit "Wonderwall": "Today, is gonna be the day that we're gonna fucking gas the Jews." The hosts laugh, as the song goes on, getting worse for multiple verses, all of which we'll spare you so as to not ruin your local '80s, '90s, and Today! radio station forever. The narrator then praises a homophobic political candidate for blaming World War II on gay men, before laughingly castigating said cretin because "he did not even deny the six trillion"—a mocking reference to the six million Jewish Holocaust victims. Bouncing around, he recounts a story in which a woman he presumes to be Jewish resists arrest and refuses to say her name because the "echo" would shatter the local neighborhood windows—an evocation of their own sound effect/triple parentheses in-joke. Going on, he proclaims that while in a chokehold, the woman says she cannot breathe which is, he jokes, "just like what her ancestors suffered in the chambers." The host then, in a comic southern accent, praises an Alabama politician for posting a Valentine reading, "My love burns for you like six thousand Jews." There is more, and there is worse, as "Jew York lawyers" and the "kike government" conspire to admit immigrants of color, described in terms so vile we cannot bring ourselves to type them. The segment ends with a bit of media commentary, bemoaning the demise of ABC's *Roseanne* reboot, which we discussed in chapter 2. Describing the entertainment industry in the most anti-Semitic of terms and joking that television is really "talmudvision," he declares that *Roseanne* had to be destroyed for its rebuttal of Jewish liberal values. Before returning to the Oasis parody, the narrator demands that his listeners "fuck TV and the kikes that run it," exhorting them to watch online entertainers PewDiePie and the animated web series *Murdoch Murdoch* instead.

You, we hope, did not laugh. But the show's other hosts did and, one imagines, so did many listeners. As philosopher Scott Woodcock notes, people, and perhaps particularly racists, often take "amusement in the fact that they are part of an inside joke that celebrates membership in a group with attitudes that are resented by non-members."[61] The references to vocal echoes alongside the toggling numbers of Holocaust victims and sundry other racial slurs do just this. The jokes may be extremely limited in their wit, but they play off of community knowledge and create a sense of in-group status for those who have become intimate with the show. They also, however, do something more, as indicated by the segment's final call to action. This community of hate-comedy is also a potential audience segment, growing to the point where, plausibly, it may be able to rent space above ground in the right-wing comedy complex someday soon.

OUT OF THE BASEMENT AND BACK UP THROUGH THE RIGHT-WING COMEDY COMPLEX

The right-wing comedy complex basement is a subterranean space in part because its contents are less directly connected to mainstream media platforms. Whereas the above-ground portion of the complex utilizes the slick, moving walkways of TV listings, podcast cross-promotion, and You-Tube algorithms, trolling basement businesses have to rely on creakier, more shadowy connection points. *Million Dollar Extreme* was once on cable TV, but has now been exiled to Hyde's paywalled, independent website. Nick Fuentes clips still pop up on YouTube, but the podcaster himself has been permanently banned for hate speech.[62] *The Daily Shoah* is relegated to its own, hate-filled website. As we have argued, denizens of the above-ground complex can, and do, find their way downstairs. To do so, however, they must be willing to traverse a danker, dustier path, dirtying both their sense of morality and their web browser's history in the process.

At the beginning of this chapter, we began our descent into this hate-filled basement at an alt-right dinner party. There, we followed Michael Malice's lead down into the depths of the complex after being lured in with a simple anti-Semitic joke about "ZOG," the Zionist-Occupied Government of the United States. For Malice, it was a funny, innocuous, self-deprecating means of making alt-right friends laugh and infuriating those of us who take such anti-Semitic language and the other forms of racism and hate speech seriously. Malice and his fellow party goers were, he assures, just joking. Just trolling. But they were also pointing out to newcomers who might have ventured into this above-ground party that there are also some corridors to the complex basement that are not explicitly noted on the public directory, and that don't show up on a regular Google search. But as we followed Malice deeper down those stairs, and the distance from the realm of mainstream media increased, the jokes got worse.

In this chapter, we highlighted a sampling of what lurks down in that basement of the right-wing comedy complex. There are others, just as bad, that we only alluded to. But there is one more program that provides a final illustration of the perversity—and consequent dangers to the rest of us—that this virulent form of right-wing comedy entails: the web series *Murdoch Murdoch*. Littered with actual Nazi flags and swastikas, the show follows a group of well-spoken white supremacists as they discuss current events, debate Nietzschean philosophy, vilify immigrants, beat women bloody, and blame it all, of course, on ZOG. It is as terrible as it sounds, but it is also stylish in its production and, at a distance, aesthetically similar to much mainstream animated comedy. Its cutout, mixed-media style of animation instantly recalls *South Park* and much of the Adult Swim lineup, as does the show's brisk engagement with current events and popular online trends. Its ideology may be indistinguishable from that of *The Daily Shoah*, but its feel is that of a zeitgeisty Instagram reel. Appropriating a style associated with trendy lefty artists, *Murdoch Murdoch* is only one step—if a big Nazi goosestep—away from state-of-the-art comedy.

There are other hate-driven shows and podcasts looking to connect with people who will follow Malice into the dank cellar of the right-wing comedy complex. But *Murdoch Murdoch* happens to be a good example of the way such basement-dwelling comedy is also knocking at the door of the main floor, eager to come out. For example, anyone with an internet connection can easily find this show. You won't even have to get your hands too dirty, as each episode is advertised on a little website you have probably stumbled across, www.youtube.com. As of 2021, the show's YouTube channel had fifty thousand followers who could watch short, edited versions of its full-length videos. YouTube viewers could also click on a link to a merchandise page, where they could find playful, colorful gifts for the fashionable Nazi who has everything. YouTube didn't include the link to the full-length videos, but a simple Google search provided them.

The characters of the far-right internet series *Murdoch Murdoch* enact a Superman parody with a Nazi twist. (YouTube)

Although *Murdoch Murdoch*'s YouTube page is prone to frequent removals and reappearances, it is clear that the creators strive to bring their basement-dwelling comedy above ground.

A show like *Murdoch Murdoch* reminds us that staircases, no matter how dusty or disgusting, go both up and down. The show collects the core aspects of all of the trolling—and worse—comedy efforts we have described in this chapter and drags them above ground. It leans heavily on the justifications dreamed up by Michael Malice, who in order to excuse an aesthetic and political mode he likes—trolling—downplays the moral depravity embedded within it. *Murdoch Murdoch* also plays off of liberal biases. For years, liberals were happy to associate provocative art, and particularly experimental comedy, with progressive ideology. The rise of Trumpism eventually exposed *Million Dollar Extreme*'s exploitation of this myopia, but not before *MDE* established an audience and a template for future alt-right comedy efforts. *Murdoch* cites serious philosophy, just like *Bronze Age Mindset*, offering simultaneously literate and ridiculous accounts of what you may remember from your college seminar on romanticism. *Murdoch* also follows Nick Fuentes's joking-not-joking rhetoric both to heighten its anti-PC edge and to attract full-blown Nazi idealogues to the show.

Like any good complex property, *Murdoch Murdoch* offers different things to different shoppers. For those who see racial slurs, anti-Semitic conspiracies, and Nazi ideology as trollish provocation, it is a show with strong production values and online-savvy, topical jokes sure to drive the libs mad. For those referred to it by *The Daily Shoah*, it's Nazism, but fun— an alternative to the broadcast television offered by those scheming Jews who forced *Roseanne* off air. And while *Murdoch* remains a niche property in the right-wing comedy complex, it hides in plain sight, a simple RSS-feed straight into the YouTube accounts of tens of thousands. It is an example of a new, small-scale construction just offsite from the right-wing comedy complex, A/B-tested in the basement and now installed next door to the real thing on a trial basis. No, Greg Gutfeld will not be recommending Nazi cartoons any time soon. But, soon enough, he's going to need a whole lot of new customers, particularly given the Fox News demographic's tilt toward the nearly dead. It is hard to believe he will be turning away those *Murdoch Murdoch* fans who stroll back over to his big box store, perhaps following in reverse the Michael Malice–forged trail we have outlined. In the United States, media, like a mall, is a business far before it is an ideology. If trolling and its penchant for depravity sells, it will, eventually, as we discuss in this book's concluding chapter, be on all the shelves.

Conclusion

PERFORMING RIGHT AND LEFT:
THE FUTURE OF POLITICAL COMEDY

It is late February of 2020, and Mike Pence is going on and on. We're just outside of Washington, D.C., at CPAC, the Conservative Political Action Conference and, to be honest, things are getting a little slow. We've seen our share of Fox News personalities, over-the-top Uncle Sam costumes, and dogs wearing MAGA paraphernalia. And things are also a little tense. In addition to the constant background radiation stress of the Trump presidency, there's also something called COVID-19 creeping into our consciousness. And, it turns out, spreading unbeknownst throughout the conference. But, no worry. Pence is on it, he says; it's totally under control. Phew. He drones on about supporting the troops, border security, and the evils of abortion. There's a brief moment of excitement, clamor. A Trump impersonator barrels through the room, right past us, holding a young woman over his shoulder. This was, it turns out, Sacha Baron Cohen, clandestinely filming *Borat Subsequent Moviefilm*. But as fast as he came, he's escorted out, and Pence is back to taxes or something. We're bored. We have come to see how comedy fits into the world of contemporary right-wing activism and, so far, the best we've got is Pence comparing President Trump to a monster truck, but in the good way.

Right-wing comedians Diamond and Silk thrill attendees of the Conservative Political Action Conference before performing a roast of liberal politicians. (author photo)

So we head out of Pence's overstuffed ballroom, only to find ourselves caught in another mosh pit of red baseball hats. They all stare up at an empty escalator, a vague sense of anticipation filling the already full space. Perhaps Trump's about to come down it, as he's famously wont to do. We strike up a conversation with a nice Arizonan couple attending their tenth consecutive CPAC. They're kind and friendly, full of smiles and in love with the president. But they do have their grievances. Obama ruined their small business. An army of leftist "alien professors" has "abducted" their poor son at Northern Arizona University. We tell them that we teach at universities ourselves, although perhaps not ones as extreme as the infamous Bolshevik bastion of NAU. They smile at us; we're cute. It's a nice chat. And just as we think to ask them why we're all out here breathing on top of each other, a wave of excitement rolls through the crowd. "Diamond and Silk!" our new friends exclaim. They point to the two fabulously sequined women riding up the moving stairs. "Do you like them?" we ask. Yes, they *love* them, they say, incredulous at the question. And before we can get out "Why?" they cut us off: "They're funny!"

Well, funny to them. Like most of the figures we discuss in this book, Diamond (née Lynnette Hardaway) and Silk (née Rochelle Richardson) are anathema both to liberals and to comedy critics, the latter being more or less a subgroup of the former. The cultural commentator Lawrence Ross goes so far as to describe the Black comedians' act as a "political minstrel show," one that traffics in racist stereotypes for the enjoyment of white viewers.[1] For our Arizonan friends and their fellow conservatives, however, Diamond and Silk represent something else entirely. Rising to internet fame with viral videos in support of the 2016 Trump campaign, Diamond and Silk's notoriety denoted a tonal shift on the American right. Their appearances on Fox News programs such as *Watters' World* and *The Five*, which coincided with increased visibility for Greg Gutfeld and Jesse Watters, merged the outrage element of conservative talk media with a lighter tone evocative of liberal satire. Popping into shows in a manner reminiscent of *The Daily Show* correspondents, Diamond and Silk performed a double act in which Diamond offered incredulous caricatures of liberal positions while Silk nodded along, adding an occasional "that's right!" or "uh-huh" as punctuation. They are a right-wing Lewis Black with a Penn and Teller twist and a healthy drizzle of racial tokenism. A strange brew, certainly, but one lapped up by conservatives tired of the over-serious postures taken up by right-wing politicians and personalities in the preceding decades.

On screen, it is difficult for a nonpartisan to fully grasp Diamond and Silk's appeal. Their schtick is predictable and repetitive; their lack of substance emphasized by the televisual monotony of news talking-head framing. Under the live, bright stage lights of CPAC, however, they shine. We follow our newfound friends from Arizona back into the main ballroom, where Trump advisor Kellyanne Conway is asking Secretary of Education Betsy DeVos something about charter schools. The crowd is quiet, disinterested. Kellyanne and Betsy, perhaps the whitest women on earth, exit. Diamond and Silk enter. The atmosphere is electric, as they dive into a performance that is equal parts standup routine, comedy roast, and political rally. Diamond rails against the evils of one-size-fits-all socialism as

Silk sways her hips: "One size does not fit all. I can't fit into a size six if I wear a size sixteen." The crowd erupts. The country needs "More free thinkers instead of free loaders," Diamond continues, sending another wave of laughter through the audience of white exurbanites.

Then, the real fun begins, as they turn their attention to the then-robust field of Democratic hopefuls for president. Joe Biden is "at the pool table . . . but there's no balls on the table," Diamond says emphatically as Silk clumsily mimes a bad billiards game. Bernie Sanders "keeps talking about a revolution, and he's the one who looks like he's still stuck in the Revolutionary War," while Elizabeth Warren "don't know if she's black, white, pinstripe, polka dot, or plaid." With the crowd worked into a lather from these more overtly comic bits, Diamond and Silk bring it home with rapid-fire one-liners straight out of a vaudeville routine: "Black people don't need reparations, Black people need liberation from the Democrat plantation. . . . The last four letters in 'Democrats' spell 'rats.' The last four letters in 'Republican' are 'I can.'" Clearly, it's not the type of knowing, ironic satire that liberal pundits and researchers celebrate. But Diamond and Silk do have their talents and comedic advantages. They possess a commanding stage presence, selling their jokes in the manner of an arena comic like Dane Cook or Kevin Hart. And, they simply don't have to try very hard. Their audience, long starved for comedy specific to its taste and always ready to take a jab at the libs, is sold before they step on the stage. Diamond and Silk create a laughter of community and anti-community, and it works. It is right-wing, overtly partisan, standup comedy.

As we took it all in, we knew: it would have been both impossible and intellectually dishonest for us to try to "that's not funny" away the feeling of collective comic euphoria all around us. We could craft convenient definitions of humor or deconstruct the Joe Biden pool table joke to show how it doesn't quite reach the formal properties of incongruity described by the best philosophers. And we know enough postmodern theory to look at the painting, say "This is not a pipe!" and feel very smart about it, as the Arizonans shake their heads. But there were people on stage, famous from TV, telling jokes and receiving a room full of laughter in return. They were being mean, yes, so maybe it's better to call it cruelty, not comedy? Perhaps, but they weren't any crueler to Joe Biden than we wanted Jon Stewart to be to George W. Bush on an average mid-2000s week night. The CPAC crowd had a different taste in political comedy than we did, but they nonetheless loved and, more importantly, were galvanized by the collective laughter. CPAC attendees identified their approach to politics as one compatible with, and increasingly defined by, being funny. Diamond and Silk's modest talents only emphasized this reality. If such rudimentary material had this much power, imagine what might be once the performers developing in the right-wing comedy complex start gaining broader recognition. Liberals certainly do not need to laugh at Diamond and Silk. They should, however, understand that such comedy is a growing part of right-wing self-definition and political organization.

RYAN LONG STEALS OUR WORST IDEA

Diamond and Silk prove that comedy and right-wing politics can cohabitate. A more aggressive school of right-wing thought argues the relationship is an exclusive one, with liberals having divorced themselves from comedy in the post-Trump era. Yes, this argument fails, but it does so in a way that should feel very familiar. For years, liberal discourse has asserted that the right's penchant for outrage and its affection for authority made right-wing comedy impossible. Today, right-wing voices proclaim that the left's puritanical fear of causing offense and obsession with pluralism leaves it with nothing funny to say. Although this role reversal may be inconceivable to most liberals, young conservatives nonetheless find great pride and hope in the idea that they will soon dominate the comedic sphere.

Comedian Ryan Long, famous in right-wing social media circles for his viral comedy sketches and provocative standup routines, leads this movement of right-wing comedy optimism. The emerging head of marketing at the right-wing comedy complex, Long uses his jokes and his punditry to advance the idea that the liberal comedy industry is a house built on shifting sands. According to Long: liberal comedians spend too much of their time canceling each other on Twitter and not enough on honing material; liberal media executives devote so much energy to filling identity quotas that they've forgotten what makes people laugh; and liberal comedy, stunted by years of politically correct critique and finally broken by anger in the Age of Trump, has simply lost the ability to be funny. The comedy business as liberals know it, he argues, will eventually collapse, making room for a grand expansion of the right-wing comedy complex.

There is little reason to believe fully in Long's assessment. It is, however, valuable to understand his logic and to consider how he uses comedy, and the right-wing comedy complex, to make his case. Long's narrative begins with his roots in Canadian music and comedy. He describes his time working within Canada's government-funded entertainment industry as both creatively stifling and marked by excessive concern for diversity and representation. His ironic punk band was forced to change its lyrics to appease a wide range of sensitivities when applying for grants. His sketch videos on the Canadian Broadcasting Corporation's website were more popular than their competitors but were nonetheless never developed into broadcast shows. The CBC, he maintains, had no interest in promoting the funniest material, only that which checked the right progressive boxes. In this part of Long's story, the CBC stands in for government intervention and the concept of comedic oversight writ large. Liberals, the argument goes, use the power of established institutions and the algorithms of social media in order to force-feed people what they *should* find funny, ignoring what they actually do. Such efforts, Long contends, are doomed to failure.

Long's own comedy, then, serves to critique what he sees as the affected, counterintuitive opinions expressed by taste-making liberal comedy elites. Liberals, he argues, prefer a good scolding over a hearty laugh. For example, his 2018 standup special, *Nanette 2*, derives much of its comedy from the negative space created by the discourse surrounding Hannah Gadsby's 2018 Netflix standup special *Nanette*. Gadsby's *Nanette* is a layered and complicated text, one that starts out as a conventional identity-based standup routine and ends as a searing tale of abuse and personal trauma. Along the way, Gadsby offers intriguing, if controversial, ideas about the role that self-deprecating humor plays in the psychological development of oppressed minority groups. Long, however, has no interest in these intimate, serious details. His joke-title of *Nanette 2* is less about *Nanette* itself than it is an evocation of the liberal media celebration of Gadsby's groundbreaking routine. Yes, Long's *Nanette 2* mocks Gadsby's nuanced approach to gender construction. "There are seventy-two genders now," he jokes, "which means men are now better than seventy-one genders!" More importantly, however, Long uses the reference to mock liberals who admonish comedy for being funny. His true targets are those who, like *Vulture* magazine, praise *Nanette* for exposing "the shortcomings of comedy as a medium for expressing pain."[2] In reality, this form of comedy criticism is a niche element of liberal comedy discourse, attending to an important but relatively small bit of innovative standup. It makes a great headline, however, reinforcing a growing right-wing consensus around the stereotype of the humorless liberal.

After moving to New York City in 2019, Long grew his audience via a series of online sketches playing with the polarized politics of the Trump era. Though marking himself as apolitical whenever possible, Long's online presence focuses largely on the failings of liberal comedy and finds corresponding praise on the right for doing so. For example, his sketch "Comedians against Comedy" mocks #metoo advocacy videos. "Time's up" for comedy, the sketch announces, conflating the exposing of sexual misconduct with the practice of calling out offensive humor. "A lot of people think being a comedian is about getting laughs, writing jokes, or creating content," Long offers as a setup. "But being a real comedian," the bit continues, "is about preventing other people from getting laughs." Parodying the online outrage proffered by humorless humorists, Long ironically argues that in today's liberal world, "being a comedian is about challenging the idea that being a comedian is about challenging ideas." Just as liberal humor theorists have long aimed to define real comedy as something inaccessible to the right, Long contends that the left has cut itself off from the pleasures of real comedy.

Long's critique of liberal comedy intermixes naturally with broader, similarly cartoonish portrayals of progressive culture. This dynamic is most clearly at play in his 2020 star-making viral sketch, "When Wokes and Racists Actually Agree on Everything," which has garnered over seven million views across various online platforms. In the video, Long dons a T-shirt labeled "RACIST" while his friend puts one on reading "WOKE." As jaunty music fills the soundtrack, the duo revels in the alleged similarities between their respective ideologies. Both insist "everything should be looked at through the lens of race." Both believe that "white people should be making white food." Both advocate hiring practices "based on race." When WOKE proclaims that white men fetishize "ethnic women," RACIST giddily exclaims "He's against interracial dating!" The sketch

Paleocomedian Bill Burr promotes a viral video from up-and-coming right-wing comedian Ryan Long on Twitter. (Twitter)

became an online sensation, particularly on the right. Bill Burr, paleo-comedic superstar, described the video as "Perfect," bringing Long to the attention of the right-wing media world and comedy complex.

The logic of the bit, of course, is far from perfect. The "woke" perspectives put forth are partial at best, bearing little relation to actual liberal political positions. They exaggerate and elide, cobbling together talking points uttered by some progressive voices in order to construct a cartoon version of an ideological opponent. Or, as Long would put it, they are jokes, inspired by reality but taken with the sorts of liberties that being funny and provocative requires. Either way, the sketch is an exercise in comic incongruity, succeeding in using exaggeration and juxtaposition to amuse conservatives while amplifying their preconceived notions.

This powerful combination gained the attention of numerous right-wing intellectual spaces. The bit's success, combined with Long's professional history, became the building block for a new ideological edifice in the right-wing comedy complex. Long quickly established himself as a representative of the comedic non-left, making media appearances on purely political right-wing podcasts. On the self-described "heterodox" *Quillette Podcast*, he detailed the inability of liberal comics to speak truth in comedy due to their political commitments. According to Long, audiences, if they hadn't already, would soon discover that the right offers greater honesty in its comedy. On the farther right *Federalist Radio Hour*, he explained how Comedy Central could no longer tell a good joke from a progressive one. The only solution, he suggested, was to "fire everyone" and start over with a group of comedy elites who are no longer hampered by years of ideological indoctrination. This, predictably, brought him fully into the right-wing comedy complex, including an invitation to the *Legion of Skanks* podcast, where he promoted his own podcast and took up his place in the libertarian bar district. His point, always, was that the comedy industry has been captured by the fundamentally unfunny progressive left.

Liberals should not worry about the literal truth of Long's argument, which is, itself, a comedy bit best characterized as conservative clapter, "message-driven comedy that inadvertently prioritizes political pandering above comedic merit."[3] There are, however, lessons to be learned. First, consider the commitment many liberals have to the principle that conservatives are constitutionally averse to humor and that humor is ontologically allergic to conservatism. This book has, we hope, shown that while the truly funny is in the eye of the beholder, the comedy business knows no ideological bounds. An intellectually honest look at Long dissolves his paper-thin case but is similarly destructive to chauvinistic left-wing comedy theories. Second, Long represents the political power embedded in younger right-wing comedians. Diamond and Silk stirred their audience with little more than schoolyard taunts wrapped in mediocre puns.

Long's satire, while not persuasive to an ideological opponent, has the evident power to excite and mobilize a range of conservative fans. If comedians like Long and fellow rising conservative comic JP Sears are taking the CPAC stage in a few years, they will be doing so with comedic skill and years of online training. Lastly, in a limited sense, Long probably has a point. Obviously, there are many great liberal comedians doing searing, hilarious bits on politics, culture, and life. Nothing about liberalism or progressivism stands in opposition to the funny. That said, recent years have seen at least some self-seriousness and risk-aversion creeping into traditionally liberal comedy, ceding metaphorical real estate to the right and lowering its political value.

"THAT'S (STILL) NOT FUNNY": CONSERVATIVES, LIBERALS, AND THE TWENTY-FIRST-CENTURY POLITICAL COMEDY LANDSCAPE

So, you've taken the full tour. You've seen Greg Gutfeld's surprisingly successful mashup of Jon Stewart and Sean Hannity. You've rehashed the Good Old, or least Old Old, Days with Tim Allen. You've been owned by Steven Crowder. You've gotten high on your own toxicity with the *Legion of Skanks*. You've put on your boots and let Michael Malice guide you through a dirty basement full of trolls, Nazis, and trolling Nazis. You've sat in the front row at CPAC and you've listened to Ryan Long explain what it all means. And, after all that, you're probably saying, "You know what? Still not funny."

We hear you.

Yet, as we've detailed throughout the preceding chapters, the rightwing comedy complex has become a booming, interconnected media ecosystem that pulls in significant audiences and, crucially, encourages them to move around from product to product. The stakes of recognizing this reality are quite high. The core of the complex, represented by corporate entities such as Joe Rogan and Fox News, reflect a dynamism on the right that allows regressive aspects of American culture to adapt, smooth over ideological contradictions, and accommodate new adherents. And it's only downhill from there. No, *Murdoch Murdoch* and the Proud Boys are not very likely to become the central pillars of conservative comedy. But, through their interconnected presence to the larger right-wing comedy complex structure, they have found a secure place from which to influence the conservative political world for years to come. The complex itself thus plays a crucial role in maintaining the full breadth of right-wing, Republican fusionism, using overlapping, cross-referencing modes of comedy to suture together a movement that unites populists with radical individualists, libertines with religious fundamentalists, traditionalists with trolls, and white supremacists with all of the above.

And, because liberals (quite sensibly) don't find most of this content funny, this right-wing comedy world and its implications go largely unremarked upon by mainstream comedians, pundits, and academics. This is a big mistake, both in conceptual and strategic terms. At the level of intellectual engagement, the waving dismissal of right-wing comedy is essentially an act of attempted sorcery, whereby carefully chosen words are supposed to make real-life problems dissolve in a puff of smoke. Sure, it is fun and satisfying to define words like *comedy*, *satire*, and *irony* in a fashion that excludes their ugliest embodiments and those who craft them. In reality, however, this liberal psychological complex only serves to confuse things and obfuscates the diverse ways in which laughter shapes our politics. You may believe pineapple doesn't belong anywhere near a pizza, but it does not help to look at your friend's extra-large Hawaiian slice and pretend you literally don't know what it is. Being gross can be regarded as an aesthetic or ethical failure, but it does not turn a pineapple pizza into a hat or a conservative comedy routine into a reactionary political speech. When liberals define comedy too narrowly, it becomes just an odd, marginal branch of left-wing politics—a situation that is neither desirable nor true.

From a liberal perspective, the strategic implications of liberals' self-serving definition of comedy are very real. Of course, for many readers of this book, the problem of Republican fusionism described above is no mystery at all. It's simple: the seemingly contradictory Republican coalition holds together because everyone involved hates progressive ideas. Also, some might add, many conservative subgroups are supportive, or at least tolerant, of racist institutions steeped in white supremacy. While the truth of such claims is beyond our purview, they, in any case, only provide an answer as to *what* binds together American conservatism, leaving aside the more important question of *how* the binding takes place. In a previous era, mainstream religion, media, schooling, or any number of other sources would have been the obvious sites at which to smooth over conservative ideological tensions. To some extent this remains true today. However, the current moment, a time in which even a major cultural force like Fox News only reaches a fragment of the American populace, requires a more nuanced answer as to who wields the blowtorch that welds together contemporary right-wing politics. We argue that the right-wing comedy complex plays just such a role. It sorts right-wing audiences into distinct groups, allowing them to maintain their specific cultural practices while connecting them to the broader conservative plan of political action. Disrupting or countering this reality requires understanding it.

The lesson for liberals—ourselves included—to take from all of this is not quite the same as Ryan Long's overblown critique of left-wing comedy. However, there is something we can learn from our comedy antagonists. Ultimately, comedy scholars, critics, and gatekeepers must nurture comedy and allow it to develop as freely as possible. The pleasures of comedy should raise up political ideas and implications, with plenty of room for good-faith missteps, unintentional offenses, and just plain silliness. If liberals abandon these ideals, ideologically ambivalent comedy fans may well be attracted to a right-wing complex that, if nothing else, celebrates pleasure and dismisses guilt.

Ryan Long isn't correct in saying that only the right offers truthful, true comedy today. Sometimes, however, it *feels* like he could be, particularly if you're particularly online. At the very least, he's right about the "now's not the time for jokes" tendency in many of today's most talented and celebrated liberal comedy figures. For example, days after the 2020 election, as Trump denied Biden's win with spurious lies, *The Late Show*'s Stephen Colbert couldn't get through his monologue without tearing up. "We all knew he would do this. What I didn't know is that it would hurt so much." Certainly, Colbert was commenting on a serious moment in American history. There are, however, thousands of broadcasts, podcasts, tweets, and maybe even a surviving newspaper or two around to take such seriousness fully seriously. *The Late Show*, by contrast, has a choice whether or not to make sadness and anxiety a major part of the show's variety. After seeing

Colbert's bizarre, self-satisfied performance of pitiable outrage, it's hard not to see some measure of truth in conservatives' (otherwise bad faith) criticisms of liberal celebrities as humorless elites. At the very least, liberal comedians like Colbert seem to be adding a pain tax for anyone wishing to enjoy their comedic pleasures. And as with any tax, certain liberals will pay with pride, while many from across the political spectrum will do whatever they can to avoid the bill.

We began this book by bemoaning liberals' inability and unwillingness to fully grapple with the rise of comedy on the right. At the same time, liberals also spent much of the Trump era complaining that America's most cartoonish president ruined political comedy. The theory, often advanced, is that by being so brazenly ridiculous, Trump made it impossible for the Trevor Noahs of the world to one-up him. Indeed, in a *New York Times* piece entitled "How President Trump Ruined Political Comedy" from October 2020, the writer asks two *Daily Show* executives if they avoided certain types of comedy under Trump. "Sarcasm," they reply. Flummoxed that the landmark political satire show of the twenty-first century would disavow its trademark style, the *Times* writer opines that "Consumers of this brand of comedy are so horrified by Trump that irreverence can feel like betrayal. . . . Liberal infotainment has turned away from sarcasm in favor of straightforward indignation at a news cycle that often feels absurd already."[4] But Trump did not make comedy impossible. He did, however, put an easier, cheaper option on the menu. Comedy, and especially topical comedy produced on a tight deadline, is really hard to write. There's a reason why even the pros at *Saturday Night Live* flop at least once an episode—and often in the politically themed cold opens. In a time of media industry turmoil, a turn away from comedy toward the lesser artforms of righteous anger offered a clear, material advantage: consistency. Desperate to find a foothold in radically changing times, many comedy outlets aimed at anti-Trump audiences forwent laughter for a liberal version of clapter. Instead of waiting for the comedy muses to strike, it was more efficient to simply wait for Trump to tweet and incredulously repeat it. True, Trumpism and its aftermath is not funny. That's why we need liberal comedians to keep making biting, pleasurable jokes about it. If they don't, the right-wing comedy complex is ready to pull in anyone seeking comedic pleasure.

The left is full of diverse, engaging, and emerging forms of comedy. If there is a positive lesson that the disparate strands of left-leaning comedy can learn from the right-wing comedy complex, it is that cross-promotion and fusionism, even among people with ideological differences, is a powerful organizing tool. From the outside, it seems unlikely, perhaps impossible, that the fervent Evangelicals from *The Babylon Bee* are able to host and joke with an anarcho-libertarian atheist such as Michael Malice. But they do and, in doing so, have turned a relatively small group of very different right-wing comedians into a viable, self-sustaining structure of money-making properties. The left, despite its far greater wealth of comedic talent, is often hesitant to do the same, dividing more sharply along lines of intra-ideological orientation. If we liberals focus our energy on fusing our disparate comedic practices, guiding them back toward mainstream cultural discourse, and downplaying intramural disagreements the way the right does, what power might we wield then? Once we acknowledge the right-wing complex, as well as understand how and why it was built, we can brace against its future expansion and fortify our own, more durable comedy edifice. Failing this, the gorgeous architecture of liberal comedy risks following the creeping decline of so many Searses and Blockbuster Video stores. A possibility that, we say with confident honesty, is not funny.

Notes

INTRODUCTION

1. Yes, we know, it didn't really work out that way, but bear with us.
2. Koblin, "Peak TV Hits a New Peak."
3. Adler, "Frank Meyer: The Fusionist as Federalist."
4. Hobbes, *Leviathan*, 125.
5. To be sure, other cultural theorists, particularly those who've considered older forms of satire, have acknowledged the form's conservative potential. See, for instance, Rosenblum, "Smollett as Conservative Satirist."
6. Zupančič, *The Odd One In: On Comedy*, 30.
7. Eco, "The Frames of Comic Freedom.", 33.
8. See Critchley, *On Humour*.
9. Mercer, "Carnivalesque and Grotesque," 9.
10. Pérez, "Racism without Hatred," 957.
11. See, among others, Gray, Jones, and Thompson, *Satire TV*; Baym, *From Cronkite to Colbert*; Day, *Satire and Dissent*.
12. See, among others, LaMarre, Landreville, and Beam, "The Irony of Satire"; Hmielowski, Holbert, and Lee, "Predicting the Consumption of Political TV Satire"; McClennen and Maisel, *Is Satire Saving Our Nation?*
13. Dagnes, *A Conservative Walks into a Bar*, 5.
14. Day, *Satire and Dissent*, 3.

15. Green, "Why Aren't Conservatives Funny?"; Jacobs, "Liberals Love to Laugh; Conservatives, Not So Much"; Rich, "Can Conservatives Be Funny?"

16. Young et al., "Psychology, Political Ideology, and Humor Appreciation," 137.

17. Young, *Irony and Outrage*, 196.

CHAPTER 1. FOX NEWS AND MAINSTREAM RIGHT-WING COMEDY

1. Fox News, "Do You Wake Up in a Sweat Overcome with Regret?"

2 Littleton, "Fox News Draws Late-Night Comedy Crowd with 'Gutfeld!'"

3. Kaseko, "We Asked *The Daily Show*'s Correspondents: Could a Conservative *Daily Show* Succeed?"

4. In early 2021, the weekly *The Greg Gutfeld Show* rebranded as the nightly *Gutfeld!* Many of the examples we draw on from this chapter are from *The Greg Gutfeld Show*.

5. Hesse, "Why Does Every 'Conservative '*Daily Show*' Fail?"

6. Learmonth, "The Lure of Latenight."

7. Baumgartner and Morris, "*The Daily Show* Effect," 362; Rottinghaus et al., "'It's Better Than Being Informed,'" 292.

8. Pérez and Greene, "Debating Rape Jokes," 277.

9. Holmes, "What Happens When Conservatives Learn the Word 'Skit.'"

10. Author interview, August 8, 2019.

11. Author interview, August 13, 2019.

12. McElwee, "The Plight of Conservative Comedy."

13. LeftOfCenter, "Michael Loftus Proves Right Wing Comedy Is an Oxymoron."

14. Rich, "Can Conservatives Be Funny?"

15. Loftus, "Will the Right-Wing Satire Show Shake up the Scene?"

16. Baym, "Rush Limbaugh with a Laugh-Track," 176.

17. Borchers, "Almost Every Asian Stereotype."

18. BBC, "'Party Bros' Troll LA Council Meeting."

19. St. John, "A Publishing Pest Moves On."

20. Sanneh, "In Praise of Fox News's Greg Gutfeld."

21. Ellefson, "Fox News' 'Gutfeld!' Finally Overtook Colbert's 'Late Show' in Viewers Tuesday."

22. Steinberg, "Fox News Makes Pitch for Late-Night Crowds."

23. Bergson, *Laughter.*

24. Hutcheon, *Irony's Edge.*

25. Young, *Irony and Outrage*, 124–132.

26. Shephard, "Is *Gutfeld!* the Worst Show on Television?"

27. Greene, "'Deplorable' Satire," 34.

CHAPTER 2. MAKING COMEDY GREAT AGAIN

1. Drolet and Williams, "Radical Conservatism," 25.

2. Francis, "The Buchanan Revolution, Part I."

3. We use this term to evoke the nativist, anti-immigrant Know Nothing Party of the 1850s, as well as to denote the fact that paleocomedians such as Huckabee don't seem to know things.

4. Weinraub, "The Joke Is on Liberals."

5. Marx, Sienkiewicz, and Becker, *Saturday Night Live and American TV*.

6. Justin Gray, "Dennis Miller."

7. Cluchey, "Daily Ror-Shocked."

8. Van Buren, "Critical Analysis of Racist Post-9/11 Web Animations."

9. Cluchey, "Daily Ror-Shocked."

10. "The Top Talk Radio Audiences—February 2014."

11. Miller, "Dennis Miller Facebook Post."

12. Huang, "Understanding Bourdieu," 48.

13. See, among others, Hilmes, *Only Connect*; Murray, *Hitch Your Antenna to the Stars*.

14. See, among others, Spigel, *Make Room for TV*; Marc, *Comic Visions*.

15. Cook, "Introduction," 2.

16. Feuer, "Situation Comedy, Part 2," 69.

17. Bodroghkozy, Groove Tube, 229–230.

18. See Marx, "Expanding the Brand."

19. Martin, *The Generic Closet*, 102–142.

20. Mills, "Comedy Verite: Contemporary Sitcom Form," 65.

21. Thompson, "Comedy Verité?"

22. Daly, "New Arch Rival."

23. Andreeva, "Full 2011–2012 TV Season Series Rankings."

24. Futon Critic, "ABC's *'Last Man Standing'* Posts Huge Time-Slot Gains in Its First Season."

25. Daly, "New Arch Rival."

26. Selk, "For Tim Allen."

27. Maglio and Gajewski. "Did Tim Allen's Nazi Germany Joke Help Kill *'Last Man Standing'*?"

28. Futon Critic, "*'Last Man Standing,' 'The Cool Kids'* and *'Hell's Kitchen'* Drive FOX to Its Most-Watched Friday in a Decade."

29. Quoted in Hibberd, "Tim Allen Gets Candid."

30. Apparently, The Malt Shop and the Ol' Swimmin' Hole were closed for renovation.

31. See Rowe, *The Unruly Woman*.

32. Weiss, "How Trump Inspired the *'Roseanne'* Reboot."

33. Lipsitz, *Time Passages*, 42.

CHAPTER 3. RELIGIO-RATIONAL SATIRE

1. *The Daily Wire*, "Ben Shapiro's Best Moments—OWNING SJWs and Liberals."
2. *The Daily Wire*.
3. Nieland, "Politainment."
4. Shepherd, "Ben Shapiro, Conservative Columnist, Apologizes."
5. Shapiro, *No One's Laughing*.
6. Greenwood, "Ben Shapiro Apologizes for Columbus Day Video."
7. Shapiro, *The Right Side of History*, 74.
8. Strauss, "Jerusalem and Athens."
9. Machan, "Leo Strauss: Neoconservative?"
10. Friedsdorf, "How Breitbart News Destroyed Andrew Breitbart's Legacy."
11. *The Babylon Bee*, "Dems Recommend Drinking Bleach."
12. Crowder, "Why NOT Having Sex Might Be God For You."
13. Murphy, "CPAC: Where Ashley Judd Rape Jokes Happen."
14. Dickson, "The Unmaking of a Conservative Pundit."
15. Stallybrass and White, *The Politics and Poetics of Transgression*, 53.
16. Serwer, "The Cruelty Is the Point."
17. And we have to admit that as college professors ourselves, it is kind of adorable to watch them try.
18. Hobbes, *Leviathan*, 125.
19. Maza, Twitter Post.
20. Vaidhyanathan, *Anti-Social Media*, 6.
21. Nicholson, "Top Publishers on Facebook in July 2020."
22. Roose, "What If Facebook Is the Real 'Silent Majority'?"
23. Roose.
24. Smietana, "Fake News That's Good for the Soul."
25. *The Babylon Bee*, "Local Family Attending Church on Easter"
26. Ford, "I Sold the *Babylon Bee* and am No Longer Running It."
27. Hofstadter, "The Paranoid Style in American Politics."
28. Hodstadter.
29. Wilson, "What Is Shadow Banning."
30. Subramanian, "The Macedonian Teens Who Mastered Fake News."
31. Evon, "Did a Georgia Lawmaker Claim."
32. French, "Hands off the *Babylon Bee*."
33. French.
34. Kerstcher, "No, America Wasn't Sold to 5 Billionaires."
35. Evon, "Did a Judge Order That a White Woman Be Tried as an African-American?"
36. Mikkelson, "Were WWE Staff Forced to Shoot Aggressive Wrestler?"

37. Wemple, "Opinion: Facebook Admits Mistake in Flagging Satire about CNN."

38. Yahoo! News, "Fake Onion Story Causes Confusion for California Town."

39. Jacobs, "Why Conservatives Just Aren't into Comedy."

40. Pigliucci, "Conservatives Lack Sense of Humor."

41. Rosteck, "Irony, Argument and Reportage in Television Documentary."

42. Rosteck, 286.

43. Sheldon, "*The Babylon Bee*: Countersymbols and Christian Satire," 33–45.

44. Sheldon.

45. Sheldon.

46. Mohler, "Would you Trade Eternal Life for a Ferrari?"

47. *The Babylon Bee*, "Joel Osteen Warns It Is Far Too Soon to Reopen the Bible"; "Joel Osteen Encourages Congregation to Continue Scriptural Distancing"; "Joel Osteen Tests Negative for Christianity"; "AOC Is a Strong, Intelligent Woman."

48. As of the spring of 2021, there is not a single mention of Osteen on onion .com.

49. *The Babylon Bee*, "Joel Osteen Warns It Is Far Too Soon to Reopen The Bible."

50. Pew Research Center, "Americans' Views on Trump, Religion and Politics."

51. Sullivan, "Trump's Good Friday Tweet."

52. Sullivan, "Trump's Good Friday Tweet."

53. Jones, "White Evangelicals Made a Deal with the Devil."

54. "Trump: 'I Have Done More for Christianity Than Jesus.'"

55. Galli, "Trump Should Be Removed from Office."

56. Fisher, "Trump Attacked the Evangelical Magazine *Christianity Today.*"

57. By "fake Trump" we mean the one referred to in the *Bee*'s fake news story. This qualifier is necessary only because the real Trump calling *Christianity Today* "radical left" is no less ridiculous, or humorous, than the fake quotes that the *Bee* comes up with.

58. *The Babylon Bee*, "Motorcyclist Who Identifies as Bicyclist Sets Cycling World Record."

59. Hillson, "What's so Funny about That?," 2.

60. *The Babylon Bee*, "CDC: People With Dirt On Clintons Have 843% Greater Risk of Suicide."

61. Siemaszko, "Info Wars' Alex Jones Is a 'Performance Artist.'"

62. Bump, "Don't Blame the Seth Rich Conspiracy on Russians."

63. Higgins, "Alex Jones' 5 Most Disturbing and Ridiculous Conspiracy Theories."

64. Young, *Irony and Outrage*, 73.

65. Young, 81.

66. Young, 119.

67. Crowder, Twitter post.

CHAPTER 4. THE LEGIONS OF LIBERTARIAN PODCASTERS

1. Sienkiewicz and Jaramillo, "Podcasting, the Intimate Self, and the Public Sphere."

2. Kiley, "In Search of Libertarians."

3. Kiley.

4. Block, "Natural Rights, Human Rights, and Libertarianism," 30.

5. Block, 32.

6. Berry and Sobieraj, "Understanding the Rise of Talk Radio," 763.

7. Berry and Sobieraj, *The Outrage Industry*, 7.

8. Thompson, "Podcasts Are Becoming the Left's Right-Wing Talk Radio."

9. Faris, "How a New Generation of Left-Wing Podcasters."

10. Holmes, "Joe Rogan's Podcast Is Moving Exclusively to Spotify."

11. Rogan, "I've Been Liberal My Whole Life."

12. Rogan, "Joe Rogan Experience #1454."

13. Mahbubani, "Bernie Sanders Is Embracing an Endorsement from Joe Rogan."

14. Haskins, "YouTube Gives a New Home to Racist Views on IQ."

15. Rogan, "Joe Rogan Experience #820."

16. Bronner and Bacon, "What Defines the Sanders Coalition?"

17. Lutz, "Joe Rogan Would 'Rather Vote for Trump Than Biden' after Endorsing Sanders."

18. Cohn, "Is Biden Gaining Older Voters, and Losing Young Ones?"

19. *Huffington Post*, "Larry Flynt, *Hustler Magazine* Publisher, On Gay Rights, Politics and Porn."

20. Schindler, "Expanded Safeguards for Advertisers."

21. Faife, "YouTube's 'Controversial' Video Creators Are Planning an Exit."

22. Faife.

23. Sullivan, "The Platforms of Podcasting: Past and Present," 8.

24. Carman, "The Podcasting World Is Now Spotify versus Everybody Else."

25. Florini, "The Podcast 'Chitlin' Circuit,'" 210.

26. Keiles, "Even Nobodies Have Fans Now."

27. Curtin, "On Edge."

28. Gomez quoted in Taylor, "Luis J. Gomez Is Changing the Future of Digital Comedy."

29. Gomez quoted in Taylor.

30. Gomez quoted in Taylor.

31. Cusack, "Nonconsensual Insemination: Battery."

32. Simons, "The Seething Stand-Up Underground."

33. Author interview, May 30 2020. See Heaton, "Apple Podcast Reviews."

34. Green Peace, "The Reason Foundation."

35. Ames, "As Reason's Editor Defends Its Racist History."

36. Beck, "Glenn Beck: Don't Move to Canada. Talk to the Other Side."

37. Author interview, May 30, 2020.

38. Slobodian, "Anti-'68ers and the Racist-Libertarian Alliance."

39. Slobodian, 380.

40. Slobodian, 381.

41. Lewis, "The Insidious Libertarian-to-Alt-Right Pipeline."

42. Malice, *The New Right*, 12.

CHAPTER 5. TROLLING THE DEPTHS OF THE RIGHT-WING COMEDY COMPLEX

1. Phillips, *This Is Why*, 153.

2. Greene, "'Deplorable' Satire"; Nagle, *Kill All Normies*. See: Roose, "Trump Rolls Out"; Chen, "The Internet Trolls Have Won"; Ohlheiser, "Pepe the Frog Became a Hate Symbol"; Weigel, "An Image Linking Trump."

3. Malice, *The New Right*, 71.

4. Malice, Twitter post.

5. Malice, Twitter post.

6. Tea Partiest, "Greg Gutfeld and Michael Malice Break Down Trump's Expert 'Troll Game.'"

7. Greene, "'Deplorable' Satire," 42.

8. Nagle, *Kill All Normies*, 18.

9. Malice, *The New Right*, 102.

10. Malice, 23.

11. Malice, 24.

12. *Get Off My Lawn* podcast, Oct. 5 2020.

13. Grigoriadis, "The Edge of Hip."

14. Grigoriadis.

15. "*Vice* Rising: Corporate Media Magazine Woos World's Punks."

16. McInnes, "Letter to Gawker from Gavin McInnes"

17. Malice, *The New Right*, 139.

18. See Marx, "Expanding the Brand" for an overview of how television networks like Comedy Central used liberal-courting, edgy comedy to expand their brand appeal in the 2010s.

19. McInnes, "Feminist Witch Hunts Are Rape"; McInnes, "Taking Back Our Country from the PC Police."

20. McInnes, "Transphobia Is Perfectly Natural."

21. Molloy, "How Fox News Helped."

22. Edwards, "Fox News Guest."

23. 7 Figure Squad, "Fox News Guest Says Women Are 'Less Ambitious, Happier at Home, God's Way.'"

24. ABC News, "Milo Yiannopoulos Interview."

25. Henderson, "The 'Soy Boy' Conspiracy Theory."

26. Siemaszko, "Info Wars' Alex Jones Is a 'Performance Artist.'"

27. McInnes, "We Are Not Alt-Right."

28. Reid and Valasik, *Alt-Right Gangs*, 24.

29. Quoted in Callaghan, *All Gas No Brakes*, "Proud Boys Rally."

30. Belam and Gabbatt, "Proud Boys"; Reid, "Proud Boys, Told by Trump to Stand Back and Stand By"; Hawkins, Wootson and Timberg, "Trump's 'Stand By' Remarks."

31. The Canadian Press, "Proud Boys."

32. Media Matters Staff, "Proud Boys Founder Gavin McInnes."

33. *Get Off My Lawn* podcast, April 24, 2018.

34. Miller, "McInnes, Molyneux and 4chan."

35. Southern Poverty Law Center, "Proud Boys."

36. *I Don't Speak German* podcast, April 3 2019.

37. McInnes, "We Are Not Alt-Right."

38. TOI Staff, "Ex-Vice Founder."

39. Stern, *Proud Boys*, 75.

40. Stern, 93.

41. Anton, "Are the Kids, Al(t)Right?"

42. Burton, "Mycenaean Rhapsody."

43. Hyde, "2070 Paradigm Shift Transcript."

44. Hyde.

45. Petri, "The Most Glorious TED Talk Takedown You Will Witness before 2070."

46. Thompson, "TEDx Drexel Got Pranked This Weekend."

47. Evan Elkins details Adult Swim's subcultural appeal in "Cultural Identity and Subcultural Forums."

48. Sims, "The Battle Raging over Adult Swim's Alt-Right TV Show."

49. Sconce, "*Tim and Eric's Awesome Show*," 77.

50. Stormfront, "Jews Get *Million Dollar Extreme* Taken off Cartoon Network."

51. Malice, "Trump Supporter Sam Hyde."

52. Mariani, "*Million Dollar Extreme*'s Adult Swim Show."

53. Pearce, "Neo-Nazi Website Raises."

54. The Fifth Estate, "Ernst Zundel."

55. Cosh, "Revisionism in a Hard Hat."

56. We feel compelled to add the death camps of Sobibór and Majdanek, at which tens of thousands of Jews also died, but here we go again, offering depressing facts in the face jocular Holocaust irony.

57. Harper and Graham, "The Red Pill and YouTube."

58. Marantz, "Birth of a White Supremacist."

59. Sienkiewicz and Jaramillo, "Podcasting, the Intimate Self, and the Public Sphere."

60. Importantly, if you see it today in mainstream social media, it is very possibly coming from a Jewish user trying to reclaim the symbol away from anti-Semites. This is an understandable response to dealing with the mix of seriousness and frivolity found on the far-right these days, but one that also acknowledges the power invested in the fringe. In any case, it serves as an ongoing advertisement for and reminder of the ways in which the comic can naturally intertwine with the depraved.

61. Woodcock, "Comic Immoralism," 211.

62. Thalen, "YouTube Deplatforms White Nationalist Nick Fuentes."

CONCLUSION

1. Ross, "Donald Trump's Factory of Ignorant Black Surrogates."

2. Fox, "How Funny Does Comedy Need to Be?"

3. Pandya, "The Rise of Clapter Comedy."

4. Brooks, "How President Trump Ruined Political Comedy."

Bibliography

ABC News. "Milo Yiannopoulos Interview: No Regrets on Leslie Jones Attack: Part 1." YouTube Video, 4:09, September 2, 2016, https://www.youtube.com/watch?v=jkrY6Ny7pMg&t=318.

Adler, Jonathan H. "Frank Meyer: The Fusionist as Federalist." *Publius* 34, no. 4, Conservative Perspectives on American Federalism (Autumn, 2004): 51–67.

Ames, Mark. "As *Reason*'s Editor Defends Its Racist History, Here's a Copy of Its Holocaust Denial 'Special Issue,'" July 24, 2014. https://pando.com/2014/07/24/as-reasons-editor-defends-its-racist-history-heres-a-copy-of-its-holocaust-denial-special-issue/.

Andreeva, Nellie. "Full 2011–2012 TV Season Series Rankings." *Deadline*, May 24, 2012. https://deadline.com/2012/05/full-2011-2012-tv-season-series-rankings-277941/.

Anton, Michael. "Are the Kids Al(t)Right?" *Claremont Review of Books*, 2019. https://claremontreviewofbooks.com/are-the-kids-altright/.

The Babylon Bee. "AOC Is a Strong, Intelligent Woman, Snopes Is an Excellent Fact-Checker, and Joel Osteen Is a Biblically Faithful Preacher." April 1, 2020. https://babylonbee.com/news/aoc-is-a-strong-intelligent-woman-snopes-is-an-excellent-fact-checker-and-joel-osteen-is-a-biblically-faithful-preacher.

———. "CDC: People With Dirt On Clintons Have 843% Greater Risk of Suicide." November 9, 2017. https://babylonbee.com/news/cdc-people-dirt-clintons-843-greater-risk-suicide.

——. "Dems Recommend Drinking Bleach after Learning It Could Cause an Abortion." April 25, 2020. https://babylonbee.com/news/dems-support -drinking-bleach-after-learning-it-could-cause-an-abortion.

——. "Joel Osteen Encourages Congregation to Continue Scriptural Distancing." April 20, 2020. https://babylonbee.com/news/joel-osteen-encourages -congregation-to-continue-scriptural-distancing.

——. "Joel Osteen Tests Negative for Christianity." March 25, 2020. https:// babylonbee.com/news/joel-osteen-tests-positive-for-heresy.

——. "Joel Osteen Warns It Is Far Too Soon to Reopen the Bible." May 18, 2020. https://babylonbee.com/news/joel-osteen-it-is-far-too-soon-to-reopen -the-bible

——. "Local Family Attending Church on Easter Just in Case God Is Real." March 26, 2016. https://babylonbee.com/news/family-attending-church -easter-just-case-god-real/.

——. "Motorcyclist Who Identifies as Bicyclist Sets Cycling World Record." October 25, 2029. https://babylonbee.com/news/motorcycle-that-identifies -as-bicycle-sets-world-cycling-record.

——. "Trump: 'I Have Done More For Christianity Than Jesus.'" December 23, 2019. https://babylonbee.com/news/trump-i-have-done-more-for -christianity-than-jesus.

Baumgartner, Jody, and Jonathan S Morris. "The *Daily Show* Effect: Candidate Evaluations, Efficacy, and American Youth." *American Politics Research* 34, no. 3 (2006): 341–67.

Baym, Geoffrey. *From Cronkite to Colbert: The Evolution of Broadcast News.* New York: Oxford University Press, 2009.

——. "Rush Limbaugh with a Laugh-Track: The (Thankfully) Short Life of the '½ Hour News Hour.'" *Cinema Journal* 51, no. 4 (2012): 172–78.

BBC. "'Party Bros' Troll LA Council Meeting." December 8, 2017, sec. US & Canada. https://www.bbc.com/news/av/world-us-canada-42283221/party -bros-troll-la-council-meeting.

Beck, Glenn. "Glenn Beck: Don't Move to Canada. Talk to the Other Side." *New York Times*, November 11, 2016, sec. Opinion. nytimes.com/2016/11/11/ opinion/glenn-beck-dont-move-to-canada-talk-to-the-other-side.html.

Becker, Amy B., Michael A. Xenos, and Don J. Waisanen. "Sizing Up *The Daily Show*: Audience Perceptions of Political Comedy Programming." *Atlantic Journal of Communication* 18, no. 3 (2010): 144–57.

Belam, Martin, and Adam Gabbatt. "Proud Boys: Who Are the Far-Right Group That Backs Donald Trump?" *Guardian*, September 30, 2020. https://www .theguardian.com/world/2020/sep/30/proud-boys-who-are-far-right-group -that-backs-donald-trump.

Bergson, Henri. *Laughter: An Essay on the Meaning of the Comic.* Translated by Cloudesley Brereton and Fred Rothwell. New York: Macmillan, 1911.

Berry, Jeffrey M., and Sarah Sobieraj. *The Outrage Industry: Political Opinion Media and the New Incivility.* Studies in Postwar American Political Development. Oxford: Oxford University Press, 2016.

———. "Understanding the Rise of Talk Radio." *PS: Political Science & Politics* 44, no. 4 (2011): 762–67. https://doi.org/10.1017/S1049096511001223.

Block, Walter E. "Natural Rights, Human Rights, and Libertarianism." *American Journal of Economics and Sociology* 74, no. 1 (2015): 29–62.

Bodroghkozy, Aniko, and Lynn Spigel. *Groove Tube: Sixties Television and the Youth Rebellion.* Durham, NC: Duke University Press, 2001.

Borchers, Callum. "Almost Every Asian Stereotype You Can Think of, in One Fox News Segment." *Washington Post,* October 5, 2016, sec. The Fix. https://www.washingtonpost.com/news/the-fix/wp/2016/10/05/almost-every-asian-stereotype-you-can-think-of-in-one-fox-news-segment/.

Bronner, Laura, and Perry Bacon Jr. "What Defines the Sanders Coalition?" FiveThirtyEight, February 26, 2020. https://fivethirtyeight.com/features/what-defines-the-sanders-coalition/.

Brooks, Dan. "How President Trump Ruined Political Comedy." *New York Times,* October 7, 2020. https://www.nytimes.com/2020/10/07/magazine/trump-liberal-comedy-tv.html.

Bump, Philip. "Don't Blame the Seth Rich Conspiracy on Russians. Blame Americans." *Washington Post,* July 9, 2019. https://www.washingtonpost.com/politics/2019/07/09/dont-blame-seth-rich-conspiracy-russians-blame-americans/.

Burton, Tara Isabella. "Mycenaean Rhapsody." *American Mind,* October 23, 2019. https://americanmind.org/features/conservatism-in-the-bronze-age/mycenaean-rhapsody/.

Business Wire. "FOX News Channel Reclaims Lead Sweeping Total Day and Primetime Viewers and Demo for the Month of March." March 30, 2021. https://www.businesswire.com/news/home/20210330005946/en/FOX-News-Channel-Reclaims-Lead-Sweeping-Total-Day-and-Primetime-Viewers-and-Demo-for-the-Month-of-March.

Callaghan, Andrew. *All Gas No Brakes.* "Proud Boys Rally," October 3, 2020, https://www.youtube.com/watch?v=8DyTXpnFpZU.

The Canadian Press. "Proud Boys: 'Willing to Go Places and Disrupt Things.'" *Toronto Sun,* July 6, 2017. https://torontosun.com/2017/07/06/proud-boys-willing-to-go-places-and-disrupt-things.

Carman, Ashley. "The Podcasting World Is Now Spotify versus Everybody Else." *The Verge,* May 21, 2020. https://www.theverge.com/21265005/spotify-joe-rogan-experience-podcast-deal-apple-gimlet-media-ringer.

Chen, Brian X. "The Internet Trolls Have Won. Sorry, There's Not Much You Can Do." *New York Times,* August 8, 2018. https://www.nytimes.com/2018/08/08/technology/personaltech/internet-trolls-comments.html.

Cluchey, Jeremy. "Daily Ror-Shocked: Is CNBC's Dennis Miller Funny?" *Media Matters for America* (blog), July 7, 2004. https://www.mediamatters.org /cnbc/daily-ror-shocked-cnbcs-dennis-miller-funny.

Cohn, Nate. "Is Biden Gaining Older Voters, and Losing Young Ones?" *New York Times*, April 22, 2020, sec. TheUpshot. https://www.nytimes.com/2020/04 /22/upshot/polls-biden-trump-election.html.

Concha, Joe. "Fox News's '*Greg Gutfeld Show*' Draws More Viewers Than Weeknight Hosts Seth Meyers, James Corden." *The Hill*, May 29, 2019. https://thehill.com/homenews/media/445898-fox-newss-greg-gutfeld-show -draws-more-viewers-than-weeknight-hosts-seth.

Cook, Jim. "Introduction." In *BFI Dossier 17: Television Sitcom*, edited by Jim Cook. London: British Film Institute, 1982.

Cosh, Colby. "Revisionism in a Hard Hat: How Ernst Zündel Charmed the Gullible." *National Post*, August 8, 2017.

Critchley, Simon. *On Humour*. London: Routledge, 2002.

Crowder, Steven. Twitter post, August 17, 2016, 6:30 p.m. https://twitter.com /scrowder/status/766039451495723012.

———. "Why NOT Having Sex Might Be Good for You." Fox News, November 12, 2014. https://www.foxnews.com/opinion/why-not-having-sex-might-be-good -for-you.

Curtin, Michael. "On Edge: Culture Industries in the Neo-Network Era." In *Making and Selling Culture*, edited by Richard Ohmann, Gage Averill, Michael Curtin, David Shumway, and Elizabeth Traube. Hanover, NH: Wesleyan University Press, 1996.

Cusack, Carmen. "Nonconsensual Insemination: Battery." *Journal of Law and Social Deviance* 3 (April 3, 2012).

Dagnes, Alison. *A Conservative Walks into a Bar: The Politics of Political Humor*. New York: Palgrave Macmillan, 2012.

The Daily Wire. "Ben Shapiro's Best Moments—OWNING SJWs and Liberals." October 26, 2019. https://www.youtube.com/watch?v=5_6B6W-_ANI&amp ;t=9s.

Daly, Sean. "New Arch Rival." *New York Post*, November 1, 2012. https://nypost .com/2012/11/01/new-arch-rival/.

Day, Amber. *Satire and Dissent: Interventions in Contemporary Political Debate*. Bloomington: Indiana University Press, 2011.

Day, Amber, and Ethan Thompson. "Live from New York, It's the Fake News! *Saturday Night Live* and the (Non)Politics of Parody." *Popular Communication* 10, nos. 1–2 (2012): 170–82.

Dickson, Caitlin. "The Unmaking of a Conservative Pundit." *Daily Beast*, November 3, 2013. https://www.thedailybeast.com/the-unmaking-of-a -conservative-pundit?ref=scroll.

Drolet, Jean-François, and Michael C Williams. "Radical Conservatism and Global Order: International Theory and the New Right." *International Theory* 10, no. 3 (2018): 285–313.

Eco, Umberto. "The Frames of Comic Freedom." In *Comedy Studies Reader*, edited by Nick Marx and Matt Sienkiewicz, 25–33. Austin: University of Texas Press, 2018.

Ellefson, Linsdsey. "Fox News' *Gutfeld!* Finally Overtook Colbert's *Late Show* in Viewers Tuesday." *The Wrap*, August 19, 2021. https://www.thewrap.com /gutfeld-ratings-win-colbert/.

Edwards, David. "Fox News Guest: 'By every metric men have it worse—we're more likely to get raped.'" *Raw Story*, February 7, 2016. https://www .rawstory.com/2016/02/fox-news-guest-by-every-metric-men-have-it-worse -were-more-likely-to-get-raped/.

Elkins, Evan. "Cultural Identity and Subcultural Forums: The Post-network Politics of Adult Swim." *Television & New Media* 15, no. 7 (2014): 595–610.

Evon, Dan. "Did a Georgia Lawmaker Claim a Chick-Fil-A Employee Told Her to Go Back to Her Country?" Snopes.com, July 24, 2019. https://www.snopes .com/fact-check/georgia-lawmaker-go-back-claim/.

———. "Did a Judge Order That a White Woman Be Tried as an African-American?" Snopes.com, August 23, 2018. https://www.snopes.com/fact -check/judge-white-woman-tried-african-american/.

Extra. "Fox News Channels *Gutfeld!* Debuts with Strong Ratings." April 15, 2021. https://extratv.com/2021/04/14/fox-news-channel-s-gutfeld-debuts -with-strong-ratings/.

Faife, Corin. "YouTube's 'Controversial' Video Creators Are Planning an Exit." *Vice News*, April 27, 2017. https://www.vice.com/en_us/article/nzpke8 /youtubes-controversial-video-creators-are-planning-an-exit.

Faris, David. "How a New Generation of Left-Wing Podcasters Are Dethroning Rush Limbaugh and Right-Wing Talk Radio." *The Week*, September 13, 2017. https://theweek.com/articles/723980/how-new-generation-leftwing -podcasters-are-dethroning-rush-limbaugh-rightwing-talk-radio.

Feuer, Jane. "Situation Comedy, Part 2." In *The Television Genre Book*, edited by Glen Creeber, Toby Miller, and John Tulloch. London: British Film Institute, 2001.

The Fifth Estate. "Ernst Zundel: 'Gift to the World' (1993)—The Fifth Estate." YouTube Video, 23:11, July 28, 2017. https://www.youtube.com/watch?v= sN92noK1E6w&list=PLzmYFMaOPfpkXOMZyPOlcqnFq2zoDtcKy&index= 17&t=0s.

Fisher, Anthony L. "Trump Attacked the Evangelical Magazine *Christianity Today* by Calling It 'Radical Left,' and It Shows Just How Meaningless the Phrase Has Become for Him." Business Insider, December 20, 2019. https://

www.businessinsider.com/trump-attack-christianity-today-evangelical-all
-critics-radical-far-left-2019-12.

Florini, Sarah. "The Podcast 'Chitlin' Circuit': Black Podcasters, Alternative
Media, and Audio Enclaves." *Journal of Radio & Audio Media* 22, no. 2
(July 3, 2015): 209–19. https://doi.org/10.1080/19376529.2015.1083373.

Ford, Adam. "I Sold the *Babylon Bee* and Am No Longer Running It." Adam4d
.com. Accessed January 2, 2021. https://adam4d.com/i-sold-the-babylon-bee
-and-am-no-longer-running-it/.

Fox, Jesse David. "How Funny Does Comedy Need to Be?" *Vulture*, September 4, 2018. https://www.vulture.com/2018/09/post-comedy-how-funny-does
-comedy-need-to-be.html.

Fox News. "Do You Wake Up in a Sweat Overcome with Regret?" July 28, 2019.
https://www.foxnews.com/transcript/do-you-wake-up-in-a-sweat-overcome
-with-regret.

Francis, Samuel T. "The Buchanan Chronicles, Part I." *Chronicles*, July 1992.
https://www.chroniclesmagazine.org/the-buchanan-revolution-part-i/.

French, David. "Hands Off the Babylon Bee." *National Review*, July 30, 2019.
https://www.nationalreview.com/2019/07/hands-off-the-babylon-bee/.

Friedersdorf, Conor. "How Breitbart News Destroyed Andrew Breitbart's Legacy."
The Atlantic, November 15, 2017. https://www.theatlantic.com/politics/archive
/2017/11/how-breitbart-destroyed-andrew-breitbarts-legacy/545807/.

Futon Critic. "ABC's '*Last Man Standing*' Posts Huge Time-Slot Gains in Its
First Season." May 9, 2012. http://www.thefutoncritic.com/ratings/2012/05
/09/abcs-last-man-standing-posts-huge-time-slot-gains-in-its-first-season
-692101/20120509abc01/.

———. "'*Last Man Standing*,' '*The Cool Kids*' and '*Hell's Kitchen*' Drive FOX to
Its Most-Watched Friday in a Decade.", October 3, 2018. http://www
.thefutoncritic.com/ratings/2018/10/03/last-man-standing-the-cool-kids-and
-hells-kitchen-drive-fox-to-its-most-watched-friday-in-a-decade-746015
/20181003fox01/.

Galli, Mark. "Trump Should Be Removed from Office." *Christianity Today*,
December 19, 2019. https://www.christianitytoday.com/ct/2019/december
-web-only/trump-should-be-removed-from-office.html.

Gray, Jonathan, Jeffrey P. Jones, and Ethan Thompson, eds. *Satire TV: Politics
and Comedy in the Post-network Era*. New York: New York University Press,
2009.

Gray, Justin. "Dennis Miller: Not So Black and White." *Vulture*, July 3, 2013.
https://www.vulture.com/2013/07/dennis-miller-not-so-black-and-white
.html.

Green, Joshua. "Why Aren't Conservatives Funny?" *Washington Monthly*,
September/October 2012. https://washingtonmonthly.com/magazine/septoct
-2012/why-arent-conservatives-funny/.

Green Peace. "The Reason Foundation: Koch Industries Climate Denial Front Group," n.d. https://www.greenpeace.org/usa/global-warming/climate -deniers/front-groups/the-reason-foundation/.

Greene, Viveca S. "'Deplorable' Satire: Alt-Right Memes, White Genocide Tweets, and Redpilling Normies." *Studies in American Humor* 5, no. 1 (2019): 31–69. Accessed January 4, 2021. doi:10.5325/studamerhumor.5.1.0031.

Greenwood, Max. "Ben Shapiro Apologizes for Columbus Day Video Slammed as Racist." *The Hill*, October 10, 2017. https://thehill.com/homenews/media /354781-ben-shapiro-apologizes-for-racist-columbus-day-video.

Grigoriadis, Vanessa. "The Edge of Hip: *Vice*, the Brand." *New York Times*, September 28, 2003. https://www.nytimes.com/2003/09/28/style/the-edge -of-hip-vice-the-brand.html.

Harper, Daniel, and Jack Graham, hosts. "The Red Pill and YouTube." I Don't Speak German (podcast), April 9, 2019, https://idontspeakgerman.libsyn .com/i-dont-speak-german-episode-14-the-red-pill-and-youtube.

Haskins, Caroline. "YouTube Gives a New Home to Racist Views on IQ." *Vice News*, April 12, 2019. https://www.vice.com/en_us/article/43jgkb/youtube -gives-a-new-home-to-racist-views-on-iq.

Hawkins, Derek, Cleve R. Wootson, and Craig Timberg. "Trump's 'Stand by' Remark Puts the Proud Boys in the Spotlight." *Washington Post*, October 1, 2020. https://www.washingtonpost.com/nation/2020/09/30/proudboys1001/.

Heaton, Andrew. "Apple Podcast Reviews." Alienating the Audience, n.d. https://podcasts.apple.com/us/podcast/alienating-the-audience/id14881 71922#see-all/reviews.

Henderson, Alex. "The 'Soy Boy' Conspiracy Theory: Why the Alt-Right Believes Soybeans Are Part of a Vast Left-Wing Plot against Manhood." Schwartzre-port, November 12, 2018. https://www.schwartzreport.net/the-soy-boy -conspiracy-theory-why-the-alt-right-believes-soybeans-are-part-of-a-vast -left-wing-plot-against-manhood/.

Hesse, Josiah. "Why Does Every Conservative *Daily Show* Fail?" *Vulture*, December 2, 2013. https://www.vulture.com/2013/12/why-does-every -conservative-daily-show-fail.html.

Hibberd, James. "Tim Allen Gets Candid about Politics and Trump: 'I'm Kind of an Anarchist.'" *Entertainment Weekly*, September 13, 2018. https://ew.com /tv/2018/09/13/tim-allen-interview/.

Higgins, Tucker. "Alex Jones' 5 Most Disturbing and Ridiculous Conspiracy Theories." CNBC, September 15, 2018. https://www.cnbc.com/2018/09/14 /alex-jones-5-most-disturbing-ridiculous-conspiracy-theories.html.

Hillson, Tim R., and Rod A. Martin. "What's So Funny about That? The Domains-Interaction Approach as a Model of Incongruity and Resolution in Humor." *Motivation and Emotion* 18, no. 1 (1994): 1–29. https://doi.org/10 .1007/bf02252473.

Hilmes, Michele. *Only Connect : A Cultural History of Broadcasting in the United States*. Fourth edition. Boston: Wadsworth/Cengage Learning, 2014.

Hmielowski, Jay D., R. Lance Holbert, and Jayeon Lee. "Predicting the Consumption of Political TV Satire: Affinity for Political Humor, *The Daily Show*, and *The Colbert Report*." *Communication Monographs* 78, no. 1 (2011): 96–114.

Hobbes, Thomas. *Leviathan*. Edited by C. MacPherson. New York: Penguin Classics, 1981.

Hofstadter, Richard. "The Paranoid Style in American Politics." *Harper's*, November 1964. https://harpers.org/archive/1964/11/the-paranoid-style-in -american-politics/.

Holmes, Aaron. "Joe Rogan's Podcast Is Moving Exclusively to Spotify—and It's the Platform's Latest Addition to the Podcast Empire It's Building to Compete with Apple and Google." *Business Insider*, May 19, 2020. https://www.business insider.com/joe-rogan-experience-podcast-spotify-exclusive-2020-5.

Holmes, Dave. "*'Headlines Tonight with Drew Berquist'* Is What Happens When Conservatives Learn the Word 'Skit.'" *Esquire*, April 26, 2019. https://www .esquire.com/entertainment/a27275357/headlines-tonight-with-drew -berquist.

Huang, Xiaowei. "Understanding Bourdieu: Cultural Capital and Habitus." *Review of European Studies* 11, no. 3 (2019): 45.

Huffington Post. "Larry Flynt, *Hustler Magazine* Publisher, On Gay Rights, Politics and Porn." October 11, 2011, sec. Queer Voices. https://www.huffpost .com/entry/larry-flynt-gay-rights-hustler-magazine_n_1086970.

Hutcheon, Linda. *Irony's Edge: The Theory and Politics of Irony*. London: Routledge, 1995.

Hyde, Sam. "2070 Paradigm Shift Transcript." GitHub, 2016. https://gist.github .com/edwinfinch/6c6f74541097d1c45672ffo69bf236a2.

Jacobs, Tom. "Liberals Love to Laugh—Conservatives Not so Much." *Pacific Standard Magazine*, November 27, 2017. https://psmag.com/social-justice /why-arent-conservatives-funny.

———. "Why Conservatives Just Aren't Into Comedy." *The Week*, December 27, 2017. https://theweek.com/articles/744515/why-conservatives-just-arent-into -comedy.

Jones, Jeffrey P. *Entertaining Politics: New Political Television and Civic Culture*. Lanham, MD: Rowman & Littlefield, n.d.

Jones, Sarah. "White Evangelicals Made a Deal with the Devil. Now What?" *Intelligencer*, December 6, 2020. https://nymag.com/intelligencer/2020/12 /white-evangelicals-made-a-deal-with-trump-now-what.html.

Kaseko, Baraka, and Marah Eakin. "We Asked *The Daily Show*'s Correspondents: Could a Conservative *Daily Show* Succeed?" October 19, 2017. https:// www.avclub.com/we-asked-the-daily-show-s-correspondents-could-a-conse -1819675251?rev=1508431443450.

Keiles, Jamie Lauren. "Even Nobodies Have Fans Now." *New York Times Magazine*, November 13, 2019. https://www.nytimes.com/interactive/2019/11/13/magazine/internet-fandom-podcast.htm.

Kertscher, Tom. "No, America Wasn't Sold to 5 Billionaires. That's a Headline from *The Onion*." Politifact, February 11, 2020. https://www.politifact.com/factchecks/2020/feb/11/viral-image/no-america-wasnt-sold-5-billionaires-s-headline-on/.

Kiley, Jocelyn. "In Search of Libertarians." Pew Research Center, August 25, 2014. https://www.pewresearch.org/fact-tank/2014/08/25/in-search-of-libertarians/.

Koblin, John. "Peak TV Hits a New Peak, With 532 Scripted Shows." *New York Times*, January 9, 2020. https://www.nytimes.com/2020/01/09/business/media/tv-shows-2020.html.

Kutner, Samantha. *I Don't Speak German*, episode 13. April 3, 2019. https://idontspeakgerman.libsyn.com/i-dont-speak-german-episode-13-gavin-mcinnes-and-the-proud-boys.

LaMarre, Heather L., Kristen D. Landreville, and Michael A. Beam. "The Irony of Satire: Political Ideology and the Motivation to See What You Want to See in *The Colbert Report*." *International Journal of Press/Politics* 14, no. 2 (2009): 212–31.

Learmonth, Michael. "The Lure of Latenight." *Variety*, September 3, 2006. https://variety.com/2006/tv/news/the-lure-of-latenight-1117949420/.

LeftofCenter. "Michael Loftus Proves Right Wing Comedy Is an Oxymoron." Crooks and Liars. *Media Bites* (blog), September 18, 2014. https://crooksandliars.com/2014/09/michael-loftus-proves-right-wing-comedy.

Lewis, Matt. "The Insidious Libertarian-to-Alt-Right Pipeline." *Daily Beast*, August 23, 2017. https://www.thedailybeast.com/the-insidious-libertarian-to-alt-right-pipeline.

Lipsitz, George. *Time Passages: Collective Memory and American Popular Culture*. Minneapolis: University of Minnesota Press, 1990.

Littleton, Cynthia. "Fox News Draws Late-Night Comedy Crowd with '*Gutfeld!*'" *Variety*, October 20, 2021. https://variety.com/2021/tv/news/fox-news-gutfeld-greg-late-night-comedy-1235093369/

Loftus, Michael. "Will the Right-Wing Satire Show Shake up the Scene?" *The Flipside*. CBC, September 17, 2014. https://www.cbc.ca/player/play/2521258636.

Lotz, Amanda D. *Cable Guys: Television and Masculinities in the 21st Century*. New York: New York University Press, 2014.

Lutz, Tom. "Joe Rogan Would 'Rather Vote for Trump Than Biden' after Endorsing Sanders." *Guardian*, April 4, 2020..

Machan, Tibor R. "Leo Strauss: Neoconservative?" *Philosophy Now*, January–February, 2007. https://philosophynow.org/issues/59/Leo_Strauss_Neoconservative.

Maglio, Tony, and Ryan Gajewski. "Did Tim Allen's Nazi Germany Joke Help Kill '*Last Man Standing*'?" *TheWrap*, May 10, 2017. https://www.thewrap .com/last-man-standing-canceled-tim-allen-nazi-germany-joke/.

Mahbubani, Rhea. "Bernie Sanders Is Embracing an Endorsement from Joe Rogan, Who's Getting Blasted for His Past Sexist and Racist Comments." Business Insider, January 24, 2020. https://www.businessinsider.com/bernie -sanders-joe-rogan-endorsement-offensive-comments-2020-1.

Malice, Michael. *The New Right: A Journey to the Fringe of American Politics*. New York: All Points Books, 2019.

———. "Trump Supporter Sam Hyde on Why Political Correctness Canceled His Adult Swim Show." *Observer*, December 12, 2016. https://observer.com/2016 /12/million-dollar-extremes-sam-hyde-speaks-out-on-adult-swim -cancellation/.

———. Twitter post, September 23, 2020, 8:29 a.m. https://twitter.com/michael malice/status/1308775462580219904?s=20

Marantz, Andrew. "Birth of a White Supremacist." *The New Yorker*, October 9, 2017. https://www.newyorker.com/magazine/2017/10/16/birth-of-a-white -supremacist.

Marc, David. *Comic Visions: Television Comedy and American Culture*. Second edition. Malden, MA: Blackwell, 1997.

Mariani, Robert. "Million Dollar Extreme's Adult Swim Show Becomes Collateral Damage Of Trump's Victory." *The Federalist*, December 12, 2016. https://thefederalist.com/2016/12/12/million-dollar-extremes-adult-swim -show-becomes-collateral-damage-trumps-victory/

Martin, Alfred J. Jr. *The Generic Closet: Black Gayness and the Black-Cast Sitcom*. Bloomington: Indiana University Press, 2021.

Marx, Nick. "Expanding the Brand: Race, Gender, and the Post-politics of Representation on Comedy Central." *Television & New Media* 17, no. 3 (2016): 272–87.

Marx, Nick, Matt Sienkiewicz, and Ron Becker, eds. *Saturday Night Live and American TV*. Bloomington: Indiana University Press, 2013.

Maza, Carlos. Twitter post, August 12, 2020, 5:21 p.m. https://twitter.com /gaywonk/status/1293658774935396357.

McClennen, Sophia, and Remy Maisel. *Is Satire Saving Our Nation? Mockery and American Politics*. New York: Springer, 2016.

McElwee, Sean. "The Plight of Conservative Comedy: Where's the Right's *Daily Show*?" *The Atlantic*, March 12, 2014.

McInnes, Gavin. "Feminist Witch Hunts Are Rape." *Taki's Magazine*, August 23, 2016. https://www.takimag.com/article/feminist_witch_hunts _are_rape_gavin_mcinnes/.

———. *Get Off My Lawn* podcast, April 24, 2018.

———. *Get Off My Lawn* podcast, Oct 5 2020.

———. "Letter to Gawker from Gavin McInnes." Gawker, September 29, 2003. http://gawker.com/013468/letter-to-gawker-from-gavin-mcinnes.

———. "Transphobia Is Perfectly Natural." Thought Catalog, August 18, 2014. https://thoughtcatalog.com/gavin-mcinnes/2014/08/transphobia-is-perfectly-natural/.

———. "Taking Back Our Country from the PC Police." *Taki's Magazine*, May 28, 2016. https://www.takimag.com/article/taking_back_our_country_from_the_pc_police_gavin_mcinnes/.

———. "We Are Not Alt-Right." *Proud Boy Magazine*, September 24, 2017. https://web.archive.org/web/20190323171829/https://officialproudboys.com/proud-boys/we-are-not-alt-right/.

Media Matters Staff. "Ben Shapiro: The Movie *'Get Out'* Is Racist against White People." Media Matters for America, July 1, 2020. https://www.mediamatters.org/ben-shapiro/ben-shapiro-movie-get-out-racist-against-white-people.

———. "Ben Shapiro: 'The Sound Was off on His Computer' Is the Most Likely Explanation for Trump Retweeting 'White Power' Chant." Media Matters for America, June 29, 2020. https://www.mediamatters.org/ben-shapiro/ben-shapiro-sound-was-his-computer-most-likely-explanation-trump-retweeting-white-power.

———. "Proud Boys Founder Gavin McInnes Calls Female Journalists 'Colostomy Bags for Various Strangers' Semen.'" Media Matters for America, May 22, 2018. https://www.mediamatters.org/maga-trolls/proud-boys-founder-gavin-mcinnes-calls-female-journalists-colostomy-bags-various.

Mercer, Kobena. "Carnivalesque and Grotesque: What Bakhtin's Laughter Tells Us about Art and Culture." In *No Laughing Matter: Visual Humor in Ideas of Race, Nationality, and Ethnicity*, ed. Angela Rosenthal, David Bindman, and Adrian W. B. Randolph. Hanover, NH: Dartmouth College Press, 2015.

Mikkelson, David. "Were WWE Staff Forced to Shoot Aggressive Wrestler after Child Climbed into Steel Cage?" Snopes.com, June 17, 2017. https://www.snopes.com/fact-check/wwe-shoot-aggressive-wrestler/.

Miller, Cassie. "McInnes, Molyneux, and 4chan: Investigating Pathways to the Alt-Right." Southern Poverty Law Center, April 19, 2018. https://www.splcenter.org/20180419/mcinnes-molyneux-and-4chan-investigating-pathways-alt-right.

Miller, Dennis. "Dennis Miller Facebook Post." Facebook. *Real Dennis Miller* (blog), May 18, 2020. https://www.facebook.com/RealDennisMiller/posts/10157985223571391.

Mills, Brett. "Comedy Verite: Contemporary Sitcom Form." *Screen (London)* 45, no. 1 (2004): 63–78.

Mohler, Albert. "Would You Trade Eternal Life for a Ferrari? The False Gospel of Prosperity Theology." The Southern Baptist Theological Seminary, May 3,

2019. https://albertmohler.com/2019/05/03/would-you-trade-eternal-life-for
-a-ferrari-the-false-gospel-of-prosperity-theology.

Molloy, Parker. "How Fox News Helped Turn Proud Boys Founder Gavin McInnes
into a Right-Wing Media Star." Media Matters for America, October 1, 2020.
https://www.mediamatters.org/gavin-mcinnes/how-fox-news-helped-turn
-proud-boys-founder-gavin-mcinnes-right-wing-media-star.

Murphy, Tim. "CPAC: Where Ashley Judd Rape Jokes Happen." *Mother Jones*,
March 18, 2013. https://www.motherjones.com/politics/2013/03/cpac-where
-ashley-judd-rape-jokes-happen/.

Murray, Susan. *Hitch Your Antenna to the Stars: Early Television and Broadcast Stardom*. New York: Routledge, 2005.

Nagle, Angela. *Kill All Normies: Online Culture Wars from 4Chan and Tumblr
to Trump and the Alt-Right*. Alresford, UK: Zero Books, 2017.

Nicholson, Benedict. "These Were the Top Publishers on Facebook in July
2020." NewsWhip, August 20, 2020. https://www.newswhip.com/2020/08
/top-publishers-facebook-july-2020/.

Nieland, Jörg-Uwe. "Politainment." In *The International Encyclopedia of
Communication*, edited by Wolfgang Donsbach. Malden, MA: Wiley
Blackwell. 2008. https://onlinelibrary.wiley.com/doi/full/10.1002/978140
5186407.wbiecp047.

Ohlheiser, Abby. "Analysis: Pepe the Frog Became a Hate Symbol. Now He's
Just a Dead Hate Symbol." *Washington Post*, April 28, 2019. https://www
.washingtonpost.com/news/the-intersect/wp/2017/05/08/pepe-the-frog
-became-a-hate-symbol-now-hes-just-a-dead-hate-symbol/.

Pandya, Herschel. "The Rise of 'Clapter' Comedy." *Vulture*, January 10, 2018,
https://www.vulture.com/2018/01/the-rise-of-clapter-comedy.html.

Pearce, Matt. "Neo-Nazi Website Raises $150,000 to Fight Southern Poverty
Law Center Lawsuit." *Los Angeles Times*, June 6, 2017. https://www.latimes
.com/nation/la-na-daily-stormer-20170602-story.html.

Pérez, Raúl. "Racism without Hatred? Racist Humor and the Myth of 'Color-
blindness.'" *Sociological Perspectives* 60, no. 5 (2017): 956–974.

Pérez, Raúl, and Viveca S. Greene. "Debating Rape Jokes vs. Rape Culture:
Framing and Counter-Framing Misogynistic Comedy." *Social Semiotics* 26,
no. 3 (2016): 265–282. https://doi.org/10.1080/10350330.2015.1134823.

Petri, Alexandra. "The Most Glorious TED Talk Takedown You Will Witness
before 2070." *Washington Post*, October 14, 2013. https://www.washington
post.com/blogs/compost/wp/2013/10/14/the-most-glorious-ted-talk
-takedown-you-will-witness-before-2070/.

Pew Research Center. "Americans' Views on Trump, Religion and Politics."
Religion and Public Life, March 12, 2020. https://www.pewforum.org/2020
/03/12/white-evangelicals-see-trump-as-fighting-for-their-beliefs-though
-many-have-mixed-feelings-about-his-personal-conduct/.

Phillips, Whitney. *This Is Why We Can't Have Nice Things: Mapping the Relationship between Online Trolling and Mainstream Culture.* Cambridge, MA: MIT Press, 2016.

Pigliucci, Massimo. "Conservatives Lack Sense of Humor, Study Finds." *Psychology Today,* May 5, 2009. https://www.psychologytoday.com/us/blog /rationally-speaking/200905/conservatives-lack-sense-humor-study-finds.

Quinones, Peter R. "Bonus: Dave Smith and Pete on Why Rothard Matters." The Libertarian Institute, July 13, 2019. https://libertarianinstitute.org /mance/bonus-2/.

Reid, Richard. "Proud Boys, Told by Trump to Stand Back and Stand By, 'All but Guarantees Violence.'" *Los Angeles Times,* September 30, 2020. https:// www.latimes.com/world-nation/story/2020-09-30/proud-boys-joe-biggs -portland.

Reid, Shannon, and Matthew Valasik. *Alt-Right Gangs.* Oakland: University of California Press, 2020.

Rich, Frank. "Can Conservatives Be Funny?" *New York Magazine,* May 15, 2014. https://nymag.com/news/frank-rich/conservative-comedians-2014-5/index3 .html.

Rogan, Joe. "I've Been Liberal My Whole Life." From Joe Rogan Experience #1412—Jimmy Dore. https://www.youtube.com/watch?v=9ctTmQn8w7A& feature=youtu.be.

———. "Joe Rogan Experience #820—Milo Yiannopoulos." Joe Rogan Experience. https://www.youtube.com/watch?v=LnH67G7vAu4.

———. "Joe Rogan Experience #1454—Dan Crenshaw." Joe Rogan Experience. https://www.youtube.com/watch?v=B-DiuM5KsPM.

Roose, Kevin. "What If Facebook Is the Real 'Silent Majority'?" *New York Times,* August 27, 2020. https://www.nytimes.com/2020/08/27/technology /what-if-facebook-is-the-real-silent-majority.html.

———. "Trump Rolls Out the Red Carpet for Right-Wing Social Media Trolls." *New York Times,* July 10, 2019. https://www.nytimes.com/2019/07/10/ business/trump-social-media-summit.html.

Rosenblum, Michael. "Smollett as Conservative Satirist." *ELH* 42, no. 4 (1975): 556–579.

Ross, Lawrence. "Donald Trump's Factory of Ignorant Black Surrogates." *The Root,* August 31, 2016. https://www.theroot.com/donald-trump-s-factory-of -ignorant-black-surrogates-1790856566.

Rosteck, Thomas. "Irony, Argument, and Reportage in Television Documentary: See It Now versus Senator McCarthy." *Quarterly Journal of Speech* 75, no. 3 (1989): 285–285. https://doi.org/10.1080/00335638909383878.

Rottinghaus, Brandon, Kenton Bird, Travis Ridout, and Rebecca Self. "'It's Better Than Being Informed': College-Aged Viewers of *The Daily Show.*" In *Laughing Matters: Humor and American Politics in the Media Age,* edited by Jody Baumgartner and Jonathan Morris, 303–318. New York: Routledge, 2007.

Rowe, Kathleen. *The Unruly Woman: Gender and the Genres of Laughter.* Austin: University of Texas Press, 1995.

Sanneh, Kelefa. "In Praise of Fox News's Greg Gutfeld." *The New Yorker,* March 3, 2015. https://www.newyorker.com/culture/cultural-comment/greg -gutfeld-red-eye-conservative-comedy.

Sconce, Jeffery. "'*Tim and Eric's Awesome Show, Great Job!*': Metacomedy." In *How to Watch Television,* edited by Jeffery Jason Mittell and Ethan Thompson, 74–82. New York: New York University Press, 2013.

Schindler, Philipp. "Expanded Safeguards for Advertisers." Google. *Ads* (blog), March 21, 2017. https://blog.google/topics/ads/expanded-safeguards-for -advertisers/.

Selk, Avi. "For Tim Allen, Being a Non-Liberal in Hollywood Is like Being in 1930s Germany." *Washington Post,* March 18, 2017, sec. Arts and Entertainment. https://www.washingtonpost.com/news/arts-and-entertainment/wp /2017/03/18/for-tim-allen-being-a-non-liberal-in-hollywood-is-like-being-in -1930s-germany/.

Serwer, Adam. "The Cruelty Is the Point." *The Atlantic,* November 25, 2019. https://www.theatlantic.com/ideas/archive/2018/10/the-cruelty-is-the-point /572104/.

7 Figure Squad. "Fox News Guest Says Women Are 'Less Ambitious, Happier at Home, God's Way.'" YouTube Video, 6:42, May 19, 2015. https://www.youtube .com/watch?v=vtRVyb_08qM.

Shapiro, Ben. *No One's Laughing: Cancel Culture Is Killing Comedy. The Daily Wire,* August 9, 2020. https://www.youtube.com/watch?v=PYyMFTMlinA.

———. *The Right Side of History: How Reason and Moral Purpose Made the West Great.* New York: HarperCollins, 2019.

Sheldon, Zachary. "*The Babylon Bee*: Countersymbols and Christian Satire." *Journal of Communication & Religion,* January 2019, 33–45. https://www .researchgate.net/profile/Zachary-Sheldon-2/publication/333951619_The _Babylon_Bee_Countersymbols_and_Christian_Satire/links/5d0e89dc299 bf1547c772ae8/The-Babylon-Bee-Countersymbols-and-Christian-Satire.pdf.

Shephard, Alex. "Is *Gutfeld!* the Worst Show on Television?" *The New Republic,* April 8, 2021. https://newrepublic.com/article/161985/gutfeld-worst-show -television.

Shepherd, Ken. "Ben Shapiro, Conservative Columnist, Apologizes for Offensive 'Columbus Day' Video," *Washington Times,* October 10, 2017. https://www .washingtontimes.com/news/2017/oct/10/ben-shapiro-conservative -columnist-apologizes-offe/.

Siemaszko, Corky. "InfoWars' Alex Jones Is a 'Performance Artist,' His Lawyer Says in Divorce Hearing." NBC News, April 17, 2017. https://www.nbcnews

.com/news/us-news/not-fake-news-infowars-alex-jones-performance-artist
-n747491.

Sienkiewicz, Matt, and Deborah L. Jaramillo. "Podcasting, the Intimate Self, and the Public Sphere." *Popular Communication* 17, no. 4 (2019): 268–72. https://doi.org/10.1080/15405702.2019.1667997.

Simons, Seth. "The Seething Stand-Up Underground That Gave Rise to Shane Gillis." *Slate*, September 26, 2019. https://slate.com/culture/2019/09/shane -gillis-snl-conservative-comedy-legion-of-skanks.html.

Sims, David. "The Battle Raging over Adult Swim's Alt-Right TV Show." *The Atlantic*, January 26, 2017. https://www.theatlantic.com/entertainment/ archive/2016/11/the-raging-battle-over-adult-swims-alt-right-tv-show/508016/.

Slobodian, Quinn. "Anti-'68ers and the Racist-Libertarian Alliance: How a Schism among Austrian School Neoliberals Helped Spawn the Alt Right." *Public Culture* 15, no. 3 (2019): 372–86.

Smietana, Bob. "Fake News That's Good for the Soul." *Washington Post*, April 29, 2019. https://www.washingtonpost.com/news/acts-of-faith/wp/2016/04 /04/fake-news-thats-good-for-the-soul/.

Southern Poverty Law Center. "Proud Boys." Accessed January 4, 2021. https:// www.splcenter.org/fighting-hate/extremist-files/group/proud-boys.

Spigel, Lynn. *Make Room for TV: Television and the Family Ideal in Postwar America*. Chicago: University of Chicago Press, 1992.

Stallybrass, Peter, and Allan White. *The Politics and Poetics of Transgression*. Ithaca, NY: Cornell University Press, 1986.

St. John, Warren. "A Publishing Pest Moves On." *New York Times*, May 4, 2003, sec. Style. https://www.nytimes.com/2003/05/04/style/a-publishing-pest -moves-on.html.

Steinberg, Brian. "Fox News Makes Pitch for Late-Night Crowds." *Variety*, May 31, 2019. https://variety.com/2019/tv/news/fox-news-greg-gutfeld-late -night-ratings-1203229106/.

Stern, Alexandra Minna. *Proud Boys and the White Ethnostate: How the Alt-Right Is Warping the American Imagination*. Boston: Beacon Press, 2020.

Stormfront. "Jews Get *Million Dollar Extreme* Taken off Cartoon Network." December 8, 2016. https://www.stormfront.org/forum/t1190243/.

Strauss, Leo. "Jerusalem and Athens: Some Introductory Reflections." *Commentary*, September 3, 2015. https://www.commentarymagazine.com/articles /leo-strauss/jerusalem-and-athens-some-introductory-reflections/.

Subramanian, Samanth. "The Macedonian Teens Who Mastered Fake News." *Wired*, October 14, 2020. https://www.wired.com/2017/02/veles-macedonia -fake-news/.

Sullivan, Amy. " Trump's Good Friday Tweet Shows His Ignorance about Christianity." *Washington Post*, April 12, 2020. https://www.washingtonpost .com/outlook/2020/04/12/trump-good-friday-christianity/.

Sullivan, John L. "The Platforms of Podcasting: Past and Present." *Social Media + Society* 5, no. 4 (October 1, 2019): 2056305119880002. https://doi.org/10.1177/2056305119880002.

Taylor, Mick. "Luis J. Gomez Is Changing the Future of Digital Comedy." *The Interro Bang !? Comedy News* (blog), March 15, 2018. https://theinterrobang.com/luis-j-gomez-changing-future-digital-comedy/.

Talkers Magazine. "The Top Talk Radio Audiences—February 2014," https://web.archive.org/web/20140209101821/http:/www.talkers.com/top-talk-radio-audiences/.

Tea Partiest. "Greg Gutfeld and Michael Malice Break Down Trump's Expert 'Troll Game'" YouTube video, 2:29, January 24, 2019, https://www.youtube.com/watch?v=JZO2wrxITQ8.

Thalen, Mikael. "YouTube Deplatforms White Nationalist Nick Fuentes." *The Daily Dot*, February 14, 2020. https://www.dailydot.com/layer8/nick-fuentes-youtube-channel-terminated/.

Thompson, Alex. "Podcasts Are Becoming the Left's Right-Wing Talk Radio." *Vice News*, August 31, 2017. https://www.vice.com/en_us/article/a3jadk/podcasts-are-becoming-the-lefts-right-wing-talk-radio.

Thompson, Andrew. "Watch: TEDx Drexel Got Pranked This Weekend." *Philadelphia Magazine*, October 6, 2013. https://www.phillymag.com/news/2013/10/06/tedx-prank-philadelphia-drexel-sam-hyde/.

Thompson, Ethan. "Comedy Verité? The Observational Documentary Meets the Televisual Sitcom." *Velvet Light Trap*, no. 60 (2007): 63–72.

TOI Staff. "Ex-Vice Founder: Israelis Have 'Whiny Paranoid Fear of Nazis.'" *Times of Israel*, March 16, 2017. https://www.timesofisrael.com/alt-right-star-says-israelis-have-whiny-paranoid-fear-of-nazis/.

Trump, Donald J. Twitter post, April 10, 2020, 10:32 a.m. https://twitter.com/realDonaldTrump/status/1248619884688199682.

Vaidhyanathan, Siva. *Anti-Social Media: How Facebook Disconnects Us and Undermines Democracy*. Oxford: Oxford University Press, 2018.

Van Buren, Cassandra. "Critical Analysis of Racist Post-9/11 Web Animations." *Journal of Broadcasting & Electronic Media* 50, no. 3 (September 1, 2006): 537–54. https://doi.org/10.1207/s15506878jobem5003_11.

"Vice Rising: Corporate Media Woos Magazine World's Punks." Strausmedia, February 16, 2015. http://www.nypress.com/news/vice-rising-corporate-media-woos-magazine-worlds-punks-DVNP1020021008310089998.

Weigel, David. "An Image Linking Trump to the Alt-Right Is Shared by the Candidate's Son." *Washington Post*, April 28, 2019. https://www.washingtonpost.com/news/post-politics/wp/2016/09/11/an-image-linking-trump-to-the-alt-right-is-shared-by-the-candidates-son/.

Weinraub, Bernard. "The Joke Is on Liberals, Says Dennis Miller, Host of His Own Show Again." *New York Times*, January 15, 2004, sec. Arts. https://www

.nytimes.com/2004/01/15/arts/the-joke-is-on-liberals-says-dennis-miller
-host-of-his-own-show-again.html.

Weiss, Joanna. "How Trump Inspired the 'Roseanne' Reboot." Politico, March
26, 2018. https://www.politico.com/magazine/story/2018/03/26/roseanne
-reboot-trump-voters-217711.

Wemple, Erik. "Opinion: Facebook Admits Mistake in Flagging Satire about
CNN Spinning the News with a Washing Machine." *Washington Post*,
March 2, 2018. https://www.washingtonpost.com/blogs/erik-wemple/wp
/2018/03/02/facebook-admits-mistake-in-flagging-satire-about-cnn
-spinning-the-news-with-a-washing-machine/.

Wilson, Jason. "What Is 'Shadow Banning,' and Why Did Trump Tweet about
It?" *Guardian*, July 26, 2018. https://www.theguardian.com/media/2018/jul
/26/what-is-shadow-banning-conservatives-twitter-trump.

Woodcock, Scott. "Comic Immoralism and Relatively Funny Jokes." *Journal of
Applied Philosophy* 32, no 2, May 2015, 203–16.

Yahoo! News. "Fake *Onion* Story Causes Real Confusion for California Town."
October 31, 2011. https://www.yahoo.com/news/blogs/cutline/fake-onion
-story-causes-real-confusion-california-town-145806545.html

Young, Dannagal G. *Irony and Outrage: The Polarized Landscape of Rage, Fear,
and Laughter in the United States*. Oxford: Oxford University Press, 2020.

Young, Dannagal G., Benjamin E. Bagozzi, Abigail Goldring, Shannon Poulsen,
and Erin Drouin. "Psychology, Political Ideology, and Humor Appreciation:
Why Is Satire So Liberal?" *Psychology of Popular Media Culture* 8, no. 2
(2019): 134–47.

Zupančič, Alenka. *The Odd One In: On Comedy*. Cambridge, MA: MIT Press,
2008.

Index

Founded in 1893,
UNIVERSITY OF CALIFORNIA PRESS
publishes bold, progressive books and journals
on topics in the arts, humanities, social sciences,
and natural sciences—with a focus on social
justice issues—that inspire thought and action
among readers worldwide.

The UC PRESS FOUNDATION
raises funds to uphold the press's vital role
as an independent, nonprofit publisher, and
receives philanthropic support from a wide
range of individuals and institutions—and from
committed readers like you. To learn more, visit
ucpress.edu/supportus.